1 SHADE GARDENING

Executive Producer: Richard M. Ray
Contributing Authors: Alvin Horton,
Randy Peterson
Photography: Michael Landis
Art Director: Richard Baker
Book Design and Production: Lingke Moeis
Research Editor: Randy Peterson
Copy Editor: Miriam Boucher
Production Editor: Kathleen Parker
Illustrations: Charles Hoeppner
Typography: Linda Encinas
Additional Photography: William Aplin,
Susan A. Roth
Cover Photo: Michael Landis
Acknowledgements: Buchart Gardens,
Victoria, B.C., CAN; Tom Courtright,
Orchard Nursery, Lafayette, CA;
Jimmy Grimes, Smyrna, GA; Jim Gibbs,
Smyrna, GA; Dana Jones, Atlanta, GA;
Japanese Garden Society of Oregon, Portland,
OR; Robert Rodler, Huntington, NY.
Notice: This publication is designed to provide
accurate and authoritative information in
regard to the subject matter covered. Any
recommendations or suggestions are made
without guarantee. The authors and publisher
disclaim all liability.

2 AZALEAS & RHODODENDRONS

Follows Page 64 of Book 1

Shade Gardening

On a sweltering summer day when even the roses are drooping, a shady garden spot can offer a delightfully cool retreat. It may be 90°F on the lawn, but beneath the spreading branches of an oak tree, the temperature is likely to be a welcome 75°F. That same oak, casting its cooling shade on the house, will keep the indoor temperatures down also.

Shade means comfort—comfort to people and comfort to plants. Though shady spots in many a yard are unsightly barren patches of ground, it doesn't have to be so. The comfort you find in the shade is an equal comfort to countless beautiful garden plants. If you have considered the shady areas of your yard impossible to garden in, it's time to explore some possibilities. Shade offers special gardening opportunities that are diverse and exciting. This book is designed to help you discover and make the most of them.

Masses of sherbet-colored tuberous begonias *(Begonia x tuberhybrida)* or white impatiens *(Impatiens wallerana)* could brighten beds beneath trees or around a shaded patio. You can decorate a dimly lit wall with the heavy flower clusters of Chinese jasmine *(Jasminum polyanthum)* and enjoy their spicy fragrance on a sultry summer evening. Under a grove of trees, instead of an expanse of fallen leaves, you can plant groups of azaleas *(Rhododendron* species), daffodils *(Narcissus* species), and crocus *(Crocus* species) to put on an unmatched display in spring.

Gardening in the shade does require some know-how. Knowing

At left: A meandering path leads to a cool, rustic retreat created by a vine-covered arbor.

Periwinkle (*Vinca minor*)

Clematis (*Clematis* sp.)

Viburnum (*Viburnum* sp.)

Kurume azalea (*Rhododendron* hybrid)

3

Many choices are open to the gardener when grouping plants in dappled shade.

Small spaces can achieve grand effects when plants are grown under the light shade cast by an overhead lath screen.

Cool beds of maidenhair fern (*Adiantum pedatum*) add greenery along a brick walkway in the bright open shade on the north side of a house.

what kind of shade you are dealing with—not all shade is the same—knowing which plants will do well there, and knowing how to plant and care for them properly are the only secrets. This book will give you all that know-how. And it presents more than 300 kinds of shade-loving plants for you to choose among.

WHAT KIND OF SHADE DO YOU HAVE?

Not all shade is alike. Shade may be cast by the branches of a tall tree or be caused by the shadow of a building. Some shady spots change dramatically with the seasons and others do not. The plants you choose and the gardening techniques that make gardening in the shade a success depend upon understanding the kind of shade you have.

The sources and qualities of shade are many, but it's possible to describe shade as four general types: light shade, open shade, half-shade, and deep shade. Each type represents, of course, a range rather than a single degree of shade. These key terms are used throughout this book to guide you in evaluating the quality of shade in your garden and in selecting suitable shade-loving plants.

Light shade: Frequently described as dappled shade, light shade is encountered beneath the branches of high-branched, open trees. Trees with finely divided foliage, such as thornless honey locust (*Gleditsia triacanthos inermis*) or silk tree (*Albizia julibrissin*), cast dappled shade. Other trees can be pruned and the branches thinned so they cast light shade. Weak direct sunlight may shine fully on this area early in the morning and late in the afternoon, but during the rest of the day the ground is dappled with the constantly changing pattern of shadow and light that filters through the gaps in the foliage overhead.

Lightly shaded areas are usually cool and they are often moister than

deeply shaded areas because rainfall can reach the ground. If tree roots are surface ones, then soil improvement, watering, and fertilizing will increase the vigor of any plants you grow there.

A wide range of both green and flowering plants can be grown in dappled shade. Enchanting woodland gardens with paths and perhaps even a babbling brook are naturals in large areas of dappled shade. On the more formal side, you can choose an Oriental style setting or a traditional one with beds of flowering plants.

Open shade: North sides of houses, tall evergreen windbreaks, or walls and narrow side yards are usually in shadow year round, however they may receive considerable reflected light because the area is open to the sky. The area beneath a roof overhang may also be similarly shaded. This kind of bright shade is called open shade since the area is open to the sky. If nearby walls or pavement are light colored, considerable additional brightness is caught by these areas.

Air circulation and rainfall are often excellent in these areas, offering wonderful possibilities for successful gardening. Almost all shade plants thrive in bright open shade, except those that require some direct sun for a few hours of the day.

Deep shade: This is the darkest shade for gardening. No direct sunlight falls on the ground, except perhaps briefly very early or late in the day. Indirect or reflected light is also limited. Deep shade is found year round beneath dense evergreen trees such as Southern magnolias (*Magnolia grandiflora*), hemlocks (*Tsuga* species), and some pines (*Pinus* species). The thickly foliaged and low branching trees such as beech (*Fagus* species) and Norway maple (*Acer platanoides*) cast deep shade, but only in summer. Because they drop their leaves for the winter, full sun shines in these areas part of the year.

Though shady spots are often thought of as cool, moist spots, deeply shaded areas beneath trees are often dry because the dense canopy of foliage acts as an umbrella, preventing rain from reaching the ground. The greedy surface roots of many kinds of trees also rob the topsoil of moisture and nutrients.

Deeply shaded areas are most frequently areas that are bare of ground-covering plants. Though there isn't enough light to grow flowering plants in deep shade, many ferns and ground covers will flourish there, if the ground is kept watered and fertilized. It also helps if the soil is improved. The plants that do best in deep shade are often shallowed-rooted creeping kinds that are native woodland plants—these are naturals for competing successfully with tree roots.

Early-spring-flowering bulbs can be a beautiful addition to areas beneath deciduous trees, which are deeply shaded only in summer. Bulbs will do well there especially if the trees are late-leafing kinds. The bulbs bloom and their foliage has time to bask in full sunlight before the trees' leaves emerge to shade the already withering foliage.

Half-shade: This is a combination of full sun for part of the day and open or deep shade during the rest of the day. Half-shade is often found on the east or west sides of a house that are fairly open to the sky. Full morning sun may fall on the east side of the house, however, as the sun moves across the sky, the house's shadow will transform the sunny spot into a shaded spot. And on the west side of a house, just the opposite happens, with the area being in shadow in the morning and brightly lit in the afternoon.

Some people don't even think of these half-shade spots as problem spots, because so many plants do well there. Which plants flourish in half-shade depends upon the degree of direct sun and the deepness of the shade. If the area is brightly lit

for at least four hours, even some sun-loving plants will do fairly well there, though they may not flower as much as they would if grown in all-day sun.

In actuality, these simple definitions of shade aren't so clear cut. The amount of light that falls on any part of your garden is modified by your climate. One climate factor is latitude: sun—and shade—is brighter in Atlanta than in Montreal. Another factor is altitude: shade is brighter in mile-high Denver than in Kansas City. Relative humidity even affects the strength of the sunshine: summer shade is brighter in dry El Paso than in muggy, hazy New Orleans.

Still another important factor is the percentage of sunny days during the growing season in your area. Regional variations are dramatic. For example, in June, Seattle has 49 percent sunshine but Fresno has 95 percent. In such places as Seattle, shade is more of a challenge than it is an asset because even open and light-shade areas are gloomy when the sky is cloudy.

Within your garden, mini-variations in the environment can affect the way shade treats your plants. White or light-colored surfaces reflect more light and make the surrounding area brighter. In dry, windy spots a given amount of sunlight may burn shade-loving plants that might benefit from the same amount of sunlight in cooler, more humid spots.

To understand the shade in your garden, observe the different shaded areas carefully through the seasons. The way climate affects shade gardening is discussed in more detail beginning on page 20.

Don't overlook the fact that as a garden grows and young trees mature into stately giants—or even when a fence is put up by the next-door neighbor—shade changes. As it does, you will most likely have to make adjustments—either remove or prune trees or replant with more suitable plant material.

Deciduous trees provide a sheltering canopy of cooling shade in spring and summer, encouraging healthy growth of azaleas and other shade-loving plants.

Different levels of shade intensity are found in every garden, making it possible to create distinctive settings within the landscape.

A shaded path and flowering plants turn this dim spot into a cool retreat.

Flowering dogwood (*Cornus* sp.) is an effective understory tree, putting on a brilliant floral show in spring.

SHADE-LOVING PLANTS

There are few obvious differences between shade-loving plants and sun-loving plants. Each shade plant has evolved in some degree of shade and is at home there, just as a sun plant is at home in the sun. Some shade plants have broad leaves, to gather as much light as possible. Others simply have leaves that are very light-sensitive—these are usually thin and are susceptible to drying out.

Placed in more shade than it prefers, a flowering plant produces fewer blossoms or fails to bloom at all. At best, it becomes a foliage plant that merely tolerates that degree of shade. Placed in too much shade, any plant—even a shade-loving plant—will weaken as it stretches toward light. Its stems elongate and become spindly. Vigor declines. Eventually the plant dies.

Shade-loving plants prefer coolness. The lower temperature that is part of shade is as important to them as is the lower light intensity. Shade from a tree canopy is particularly cooling—often 15°F or more cooler than nearby sunny spots—because as moisture evaporates from tree leaves it takes heat with it. The air is cool and fresh beneath the canopy of a tree. Shade plants love it. They also love the cooling effect of grass and ground covers growing in the sun surrounding the shaded areas. These may be 10° to 14°F cooler than bare soil would be in the same location, and are even cooler than dark paved surfaces.

Shade-loving plants are quick to suffer from overheating. Good air circulation without dryness helps to counteract the ill effects of high temperatures, but hot, dry air is particularly damaging. Lightly shaded areas in dappled light beneath trees are often more cool and humid than open-shade areas, especially if shade is cast by a building and there is pavement nearby. These differences can mean a different choice of plants for the two areas.

Even if your garden is shady, you don't have to surrender it to solid greenery, unless that is what you really want. Shade gives you the opportunity to enjoy special flowers such as tuberous begonia *(Begonia x tuberhybrida)*, monkshood *(Aconitum carmichaelii)*, and foxglove *(Digitalis purpurea)*, which don't tolerate full sun. There is a wide choice of shade-loving varieties of flowering and evergreen shrubs, small flowering trees, flowering annuals, perennials, bulbs, ferns, and ground covers that flourish in lightly shaded and half-shaded garden sites. Open shade caters to a wide selection of plants too, but those that do well in deep shade are fewer.

ANNUALS

Annuals are plants that grow from seed, produce flowers, set seed and then die in a single growing season. In general, because they require so much energy to complete their life cycle in such a short time, annuals need lots of sun. Some annuals however are adapted to shade and will brighten lightly shaded or half-shaded spots with colorful flowers throughout the growing season.

The most popular annuals for planting in shady beds are impatiens *(Impatiens wallerana)*, coleus *(Coleus x hybridus)*, and begonias *(Begonia* species). So popular are these plants that they are nicknamed "the big three." There are many varieties of the big three to choose from; you'll find them listed in the charts on pages 30 to 34.

PERENNIALS

Flowering perennials are plants that live for many years in the garden and usually flower during a particular season—early spring or late summer for instance. They are herbaceous plants, meaning that the aboveground parts die to the ground during the winter, but the cold-hardy roots sprout new top growth each spring.

Flowering perennials don't require much care. They spread and the clumps increase in size, requiring dividing every several years.

You can replant the divisions and thus increase the number of plants you have.

Often the best perennials for shade gardens are hybrids of woodland plants such as columbine (*Aquilegia x hybrida*), bellflowers (*Campanula* species), or foxglove (*Digitalis purpurea*). These do well in both light shade and half shade and are most at home when planted in groups in a garden border. Wildflower species, such as trillium (*Trillium* species), bluebells (*Mertensia virginica*), and violets (*Viola* species) look beautiful year after year planted in the shade of a grove of trees.

BULBS

Gardeners call plants that have fleshy underground storage parts "bulbs," though botanists distinguish bulbs further into "true bulbs," corms, rhizomes, and tubers. Bulbs usually bloom during or after a very active period of growth, then flowers and foliage die to the ground. The plant lies dormant for the rest of the year. In warm areas, some bulbs, such as Kaffir lily (*Clivia miniata*), are evergreen.

Some bulbs grow and bloom in shade and others grow and bloom in sunny spots that become shaded later in the growing season. Early-blooming bulbs require sun from spring into early summer; their foliage naturally dies about the time late-leafing trees begin to cast heavy shade. Later-blooming bulbs will grow happily in light or half shade, where there is enough brightness for healthy growth and enough shade to prevent foliage from burning.

In mild climates, subtropical evergreen bulbs can be grown in light shade. They need protection from strong sun and from cold in winter.

To grow spring bulbs best, plant them in areas shaded by late-leafing deciduous trees such as sour gum (*Nyssa sylvatica*) or Amur cork tree (*Phellodendron amurense*), or plant them beneath high-branching deciduous trees, such as some oaks

Hybrid tuberous begonias (*Begonia x tuberhybrida*) produce masses of blossoms in clear colors to brighten shady nooks from early spring through summer.

Bellflowers (*Campanula* sp.) create a delightful display when mass planted in a naturalistic setting in light shade.

Daffodils (*Narcissus* hybrids) bring the charm of their sunny blooms to shady garden sites during their spring flowering time.

A ferny dell tucked into a shady garden corner forms a cool retreat when the temperature is uncomfortable elsewhere in the yard.

Camellias (*Camellia* sp.) are attractive year round and are prized for their lavish flowers (shown below) that add garden color in winter months in mild climates.

(*Quercus* species), that form thick, broken canopies.

Crocus (*Crocus* species and hybrids) and daffodils (*Narcissus* hybrids) are very successful planted with evergreen ground-cover plants such as English ivy (*Hedera helix*), pachysandra (*Pachysandra terminalis*), or periwinkle (*Vinca minor*) in the shade beneath deciduous trees. They will add color to these ground covers during the spring season and the ground cover camouflages the withering foliage.

Later-blooming woodland bulbs such as the many species of *Scilla* will spread and naturalize in shady spots. When planted in masses, their display is truly breathtaking and they will persist and increase for many years.

FERNS

Most ferns are native to cool, moist, shaded forests or woodlands and are ideal plants for shady gardens. A special, indefinable beauty sets them apart from all other plants. They have delicate-looking foliage and a clumping habit that combines well with perennials and wildflowers.

Plant them in scattered groups in a woodland for a natural appearance or use them in a perennial border or in a shady side yard. A garden stream—even a tiny bird-bath-sized pool—bordered with mossy rocks and a few ferns creates a charming focal point that makes a sanctuary of any shade garden. You can use tall ferns in clumps for bold effects, small ferns under shrubs, in planters, or in the crevices of shaded rock walls. Many ferns make excellent ground covers.

Ferns, in their amazing diversity, are widely used in shade gardens in every part of the continent. Ranging from 1 foot to 30 feet tall, ferns offer a broad choice. In form and texture, foliage is quite diverse—including the delicate tracery of rounded leaflets set on black wire-like stems of the maidenhair ferns (*Adiantum* species); the frilly fronds of mother fern (*Asplenium bulbiferum*), the massive finely-divided fronds of the palm-treelike tree

ferns (several species); and the curiously downy, handlike fronds of staghorn fern (*Platycerium bifurcatum*).

Some ferns, like lady (*Athyrium filix-femina*), cinnamon (*Osmunda cinnamomea*), and giant chain ferns (*Woodwardia fimbriata*), adapt to boggy soils. At the other extreme, such ferns as bear's foot (*Humata tyermannii*), lace (*Microlepia strigosa*), and sword ferns (*Nephrolepis exaltata*) tolerate some dryness.

Most of the top-rated ferns are native North American plants. They are available at nurseries as container-grown plants and as bare-root plants from mail-order nurseries. It's best not to transplant ferns from the wild since some species are becoming endangered.

SHRUBS

Shrubs are the solid citizens of the garden. Bulbs, annuals, ferns, and perennials fill low spaces with color and greenery, but many of them come and go seasonally. Shrubs are the year-round mainstays of your shade garden, providing a backdrop for seasonal plants and often putting on a colorful show of flowers or fall foliage of their own. For shaded gardens, there is a wide and diverse choice of shrubs.

You may select deciduous shrubs, which drop their leaves for the winter, or evergreen ones, which retain their leaves year round. Semi-evergreen shrubs lose most of their leaves in cold climates and retain more of them where winters are milder.

The "big three" of flowering shrubs for shade are azaleas, rhododendrons, and camellias. They flower profusely in light or half shade and are handsome plants when not in bloom. Where they are adapted, these three groups of shrubs are unparalleled for their dependable performances.

Various types of azaleas are adapted to climates from Ontario to Florida, however the prime growing areas are mainly the states along the Atlantic Seaboard, coastal British Columbia, and the Northwest, where the climate is moist and the soil is acid. Evergreen azaleas are best adapted to the Southeast and the coastal areas of the West from central California to British Columbia, but hardier strains for colder areas have been developed. Deciduous azaleas thrive from Canada to the southern Appalachians and in the Northwest. Rhododendrons reach their pinnacle of perfection in the Northwest, but also thrive on the Atlantic Seaboard except in the hottest-summer areas of the South. All are worth the special care needed to grow them well outside their prime areas.

Camellias bloom in southern gardens (Zones 8 to 10) in fall and winter, when most other colors have been erased from the garden. Their waxy-petaled flowers and glossy leaves can be cut and enjoyed in vases and as corsages. Camellias combine well in lightly shaded gardens with azaleas and rhododendrons and in cold climates can be used as container plants on an enclosed, unheated porch or in a cool greenhouse.

VINES

Vines are problem solvers in many landscape situations and are invaluable in shady gardens. Taking up little ground space, a climbing vine is an ornamental asset in narrow gardens and side yards, which are usually shady most of the day. They can fill in the side of a narrow passageway without blocking it, covering the wall with year-round greenery or brilliant autumn color and winter tracery.

Climbing by clinging tendrils, twining stems, or adhesive discs, vines can quickly cover a blank wall or fence with softening foliage and flowers. Use them on a trellis or arbor to create privacy or act as a garden divider. Some shade-loving vines flower extravagantly and sometimes fragrantly; most make quick, solid ground covers even on steep banks and can cover open fences and arbors to provide shade and privacy.

Vines may be deciduous or evergreen, so choose the right kind according to the needs of your landscape. Perhaps year-round greenery is important, or maybe foliage in summer and openness in winter is desirable, if the vine is to cover a garden structure.

Vines, even more than other plants, grow vigorously and cover rapidly. Choose a fast grower, but remember that some fast growers don't stop where you want them to, or they mat heavily and require frequent thinning. Learn as much as you can about how a vine behaves before you buy and plant it.'

Many of the vines included in the chart on pages 50-52 are useful for growing on an overhead structure for the purpose of *creating* shade. Far faster-growing than trees, vines such as evergreen clematis (*Clematis armandii*), the jasmines (*Jasminum* species) and wisteria (*Wisteria* species) can cover pergolas, arbors, and open fences. But like other plants discussed in this book, these and other vines also grow in some degree of shade.

GROUND COVERS

Low plants that spread quickly by underground or trailing stems are called ground covers. They are admired for their ability to blanket the ground with foliage, and sometimes flowers, without needing much care. Ground covers can really dress up a garden, filling in spaces between other plants, creating an edging or border for a walkway, and growing in difficult shady or sunny sites. They are also useful for erosion control.

There are many beautiful ground covers suitable for creating low-maintenance plantings in shade gardens. The "big three" ground covers for shade are English ivy (*Hedera helix*), periwinkle (*Vinca minor*), and pachysandra (*Pachysandra terminalis*). These popular and easy-to-grow evergreen plants adapt to any kind of shade and are real problem solvers in deep shade, such as beneath the spreading branches of a beech tree (*Fagus* species), where it's difficult to grow anything.

Wisteria vines (*Wisteria* sp.) bear graceful trusses of flowers and create shade by clambering over trellises, pergolas, and arbors.

Pachysandra (*Pachysandra terminalis*) forms a dense ground cover in any kind of shade.

Japanese maple (*Acer palmatum*) casts light shade and is an excellent patio tree.

Maidenhair tree (*Ginkgo biloba*) is a well-behaved tree that is easy to garden under.

LAWNS

Most lawn grasses love sun, and the areas of the lawn shaded by trees or in narrow side yards are often thin and meager at best. This problem is usually due to planting the wrong kind of grass in the shady site. Several kinds of grass do well in light or half shade and can be planted either straight or as mixtures to create that desirable emerald-green sweep of lawn.

A mix for a shady lawn contains grasses adapted to various degrees of shade, so that coverage is complete. Usually the best-adapted grass will take over and crowd out the less successful varieties in each area. The chart on page 58 lists the best shade-tolerant grass varieties. Where shade is too deep even for these grasses, choose a ground cover such as English ivy (*Hedera helix*) or pachysandra (*Pachysandra terminalis*).

TREES

Trees are the visually dominant and most permanent plants in your yard and garden. *Canopy trees* are the tall trees that form a lofty ceiling, casting shade that determines what can—and can't—grow beneath them. Lower-growing, small trees that thrive in the shade of taller trees are called *understory trees.* Shade gardens often consist of tall canopy trees that are pruned high to accommodate a scattering of flowering understory trees beneath. Unless understory trees are planted too densely, they are usually open enough to plant shade-loving perennials, ferns, and ground covers beneath them.

The best trees for gardening beneath are high-branching, open ones that filter rather than block sunlight. They should have deep roots rather than surface-matting ones, so they don't compete with garden plants for moisture and nutrients. (Top-rated canopy trees are listed on page 11, understory trees are on pages 59-62.). Most of the recommended understory trees are North American woodland natives.

Because deciduous trees admit winter and early spring sunlight and, therefore, create more gardening possibilities, deciduous trees are preferred to evergreen ones in shade gardens. In addition to providing shade, many small trees bear beautiful flowers. Shadbush (*Amelanchier canadensis*), Eastern redbud (*Cercis canadensis*), flowering dogwood (*Cornus florida*), Cornelian cherry (*Cornus mas*), Japanese snowbell (*Styrax japonicus*), and hawthorns (*Crataegus* species) are among the early spring bloomers. Later bloomers are fringe tree (*Chionanthus virginicus*), sweet bay magnolia (*Magnolia virginiana*), and sourwood (*Oxydendrum arboreum*). For fall and winter color strawberry tree (*Arbutus unedo*) provides a spectacular flower show.

Many of these trees have colorful berries or interesting pods. Dogwoods (*Cornus* species), hollies (*Ilex* species), strawberry tree (*Arbutus unedo*), sourwood (*Oxydendrum arboreum*), hawthorns (*Crataegus* species), New Zealand laurel (*Corynocarpus laevigata*), Cornelian cherry (*Cornus mas*), and shadbush (*Amelanchier canadensis*) all offer visual excitement over extended periods of time. Japanese maples (*Acer palmatum*) and vine maples (*Acer circinatum*) bear winged seed capsules into autumn.

Colored foliage is another asset of many of these small trees. Some Japanese maple varieties are red throughout the season, and all are brilliant in fall. Leaves of Allegheny serviceberry (*Amelanchier laevis*) start and end the season colorfully.

The following trees are too shallow-rooted or cast too heavy a shade to garden under successfully: Norway maple (*Acer platanoides*), silver maple (*Acer saccharinum*), tree-of-heaven (*Ailanthus altissima*), modesto ash (*Fraxinus velutina*), walnut trees (*Juglans* species), southern magnolia (*Magnolia grandiflora*), poplar trees (*Populus* species).

Deciduous Trees for Casting Shade

Botanical/ Common Name	Zones and Regions	Height/Spread	Comments
TREES THAT CAST LIGHT SHADE			
Albizia julibrissin Silk Tree	7-10 A,B,C,D E,H,I,J	To 25-35 ft. high wider than tall.	Large leaves are divided into feathery leaflets. Pink, powder-pufflike blossoms held high above foliage in summer, followed by large seed pods. Heat and drought tolerant. Fast growing.
Acer palmatum Japanese Maple	6-8 A,B,C, F,G,H,I	To 20-25 ft. high equally as wide.	A handsome small tree with lobed leaves that turn bright colors in fall. Well-behaved, excellent around patios. Many varieties available differing in size, leaf shape, and fall color. Some grow best in sun, others in partial shade.
Cladrastis lutea Yellowwood	4-9 A,B,F, G,H,I	To 30 ft. high, 15 ft. wide.	One-foot-long compound leaves are divided into 7 to 11 leaflets. Foliage turns yellow in fall. Fragrant white flowers in long clusters bloom in spring. Good lawn tree. Tolerates wet soil.

Gleditsia triacanthos inermis
  'Moraine'
  Moraine Thornless Honey Locust
	4-10
	A-I
		To 50 ft. high,
		30 ft. wide.
			Twice compound leaves divided into 7 to 15 leaflets. A good lawn tree. Tolerates wet soils.

Koelreuteria paniculata Golden-Rain Tree	5-9 All regions.	To 30 ft. high, equally as wide.	1-1/2-foot-long compound leaves divided into 8 to 18 leaflets. Yellow flowers bloom in summer and are followed by interesting seedpods.
Phellodendron amurense Amur Cork Tree	4-8 A,B,E, F,G,H,I	To 40 ft. high, equally as wide.	Leaves are 12 to 16 inches long and divided into 5 to 13 leaflets. A good lawn tree for cities and open areas.
TREES THAT CAST HALF SHADE			
Celtis occidentalis Common Hackberry	4-8 A-I	To 40 ft. high, equally as wide.	Bright green leaves with toothed edges. Leafs-out late in spring. Good street tree. Tolerates drought and harsh conditions.
Cercidiphyllum japonicum Katsura Tree	4-9 A,B,F, G,H,I,J	To 40 ft. high 20-30 ft. wide.	Leaves heart-shaped, 4 in. long, reddish when expanding in spring, gold and scarlet in fall. Protect from hot, drying wind.
Fraxinus species Ash	2-10 All regions.	To 35-70 ft. high, and nearly as wide.	A large family of tough, fast-growing trees with leaves divided into as many as 12 to 13 leaflets. Tree size varies by species. Many have brightly colored fall foliage.
Ginkgo biloba Maidenhair Tree	4-9 A,B,C, F,G,H,I	To 60 ft. high, equally as wide.	Leaves are fan-shaped, 4 inches wide, turn gold in autumn, drop all at once. A good lawn or street tree. Tolerates air pollution.
Nyssa sylvatica Sour Gum	5-9 A,B,C,E, G,H,I,J	To 40 ft. high, 20 ft. wide.	Leaves are 2 to 6 inches long, turn brilliant orange-red in fall. Good lawn tree. Tolerates wet soil.
Pistacia chinensis Chinese Pistache	7-10 B,C,D, E,I,J	To 60 ft. high, equally as wide.	Leaves are up to 12 inches long, divided into 10 to 16 leaflets, and turn bright yellow to fiery red in fall. Needs careful pruning when young.
TREES THAT CAST FULL SHADE			
Alnus species Alders	3-10 A,B,C,E, F,G,H,I	To 35-90 ft. high, about half as wide.	Several species of fast-growing trees that thrive in wet soils. Useful where shade is needed quickly, but must be deep watered or will produce surface roots.
Morus alba White Mulberry	5-9 All regions.	To 40 ft. high, 40-60 ft. wide.	An extremely fast growing tree valuable where shade is needed immediately. Tolerates extreme conditions, including heat and drought. Large lobed leaves turn yellow in fall. Choose fruitless varieties.
Platanus x acerifolia London Plane Tree	5-10 A,B,C,D, E,G,H,I,J	To 50 ft. high, 30-40 ft. wide.	Leaves have 3 to 5 lobes and are 4 to 8 inches across. Good street or lawn tree. Fast growing. Tolerates drought, pollution, and wet soils.
Quercus coccinea Scarlet Oak	4-9 All regions.	To 70 ft. high, 40-50 ft. wide.	Leaves have 7 to 9 deep lobes, 5 to 6 inches long, and turn scarlet in fall. Good street or lawn tree.
Quercus robur English Oak	5-9 A,B,C, E,G,H,I	To 40-80 ft. high, equally as wide.	Leaves are 5 inches long with 3 to 7 rounded lobes. No fall color.
Quercus rubra Northern Red Oak	4-10 A,B,C,E, F,G,H,I	To 60-80 ft. high, nearly as wide.	Leaves are 7 inches long with 7 to 11 lobes, turn red in fall. Native to the Eastern United States. Many other native American oaks make excellent shade trees.
Tilia cordata Littleleaf Linden	4-8 A,B,E, F,G,H,I	To 40 ft. high, 20 ft. wide.	Heart-shaped leaves are 2-1/2 in. long, dark green with silvery undersides. Other species of linden also make good shade trees.

Designing Shade Gardens

A shade garden is not an entity unto itself. It can be a garden in just about any style you want it to be and differs from "sun gardens" only because the plants that grow there and the care techniques needed are different. Depending upon the type of shade you have, you can plant a traditional perennial flower border, a wildflower garden, a shrubbery border, or a landscaped garden retreat. Shade gardens can be as diverse in style and design as the gardeners planting them.

Perhaps the only common thread through all shade gardens is the lack of direct sunlight—this means that the garden site is naturally dim and must rely more heavily on the design of the garden to bring it out of obscurity. Understanding how to combine foliage and flowers to play up their interesting textures and how to use color to brighten a shaded area is basic to creating a shade garden that is as pleasing to look at as it is for the plants to grow in. Incorporating accents and focal points will help create a harmonious setting.

TEXTURE

Small finely divided leaves and dainty flowers have a *fine texture*, which is restful to look at and can be used effectively in large-scale plantings. On the other hand, plants with large, undivided leaves and big flowers have a *bold texture*. Bold textures are busier and more visually exciting than fine textures and should be used more sparingly than fine textures.

At left: By selecting plants carefully, your shade garden can include colorful flowers all during the year.

Aaron's beard (*Hypericum calycinum*)

Boston ivy (*Parthenocissus* sp.)

Camellia (*Camellia* sp.)

Peony (*Paeonia* hybrid)

13

A ground cover planting of fine-textured periwinkle (*Vinca minor*) is a beautiful foil for the picturesque drama of a rugged tree trunk.

To keep a shade garden filled with visual excitement, arrange blooming plants, such as these tulips (*Tulipa* sp.) in a mass.

Siberian scilla (*Scilla siberica*) naturalizes freely in shady sites, offering its rich blue, bell-shaped flowers in early summer.

In a shade garden, where the light is already somewhat dim, the shadows cast by bold-leaved plants are larger and darker than those of small-leaved plants. This is something to consider when you are trying to brighten up an area. Overusing tall large-leaved plants will further cast the area into darkness. Fine-textured plants that filter but do not stop the light will keep it brighter.

You will notice too that fine-textured plants seem smaller and farther away than they really are. And just the opposite seems true of bold-textured plants. A rule of thumb followed by many gardeners is that in small enclosed gardens fine-textured plants should predominate and the bold-textured ones are best planted in small clumps as accents; in larger, more open gardens, bold-textured plants can be used in larger sweeps in the distant areas, with the closer plants becoming increasingly more fine-textured. This gradation in texture creates a visually harmonious arrangement of plants.

To create interesting textural patterns, contrast bold- and fine-textured foliage plants. It is usually best to plant the finer-textured ones in a large group and contrast this with a smaller clump of bold-textured foliage. For instance, in a ground cover planting of the small-leaved periwinkle (*Vinca minor*), you might plant several clumps of plantain lily (*Hosta* species)—its clusters of broad upright leaves are effectively set off by the small ovals of the periwinkle, creating an accent that draws your eye. Without the contrasting bold-textured foliage, the periwinkle would look pretty but have no focus. If the same area were planted with a mass of plantain lily, the many big leaves would become a busy clutter of overpowering foliage.

Plan too for interesting winter textures, visualizing how your shade garden will appear when deciduous plants are bare. Bare stems of even bold-leaved plants often take on a fine-texture, especially if the shrubs are very twiggy.

COLOR

Yellows, reds, and oranges are warm colors that suggest sunlight and heat. Blues, greens, and purples are cool colors that seem to make the temperature drop a few degrees. In a shade garden, you may choose to use warm colors in a perennial border, for instance, if you wish to down play the shade. But in a woodland setting where you wish to reinforce the image of cooling shade, planting flowers of blue and lavender work to your advantage.

The most important aspect of choosing flower and foliage colors for shady spots is to consider whether the colors reflect light or absorb it. Shadows tend to absorb color, but bright color or massed color shines through. For instance, white and pale pastels are bright colors and will bounce light back into the garden. But deep purple and red are dark colors that absorb light and will recede further into the shadows. A large sweep of white-flowered impatiens planted beneath a tree will make the area glow, however, if the same area were planted instead with red-flowered impatiens, the area would seem dimmer still.

You can use combinations of colors to create effective displays. A favorite for shade gardens is a combination of blue and white flowers, which are very cooling together with green foliage. Other themes might be pink and lavender, or yellow, blue, and white. When dark colors are used, use them sparingly in contrast to the brighter, lighter shades.

Green gardens: Many shade gardens are predominately foliage gardens. There's nothing wrong with that, but their beauty depends even more upon the contrast of textures, arrangement of plants, and incorporation of pleasing accents. It is important that you plan carefully to achieve the effect you are striving for. Calm green gardens can play up the contrast of the many shades of green. Use the steel-blue green of bold-textured blue-leafed plantain lily *(Hosta sieboldiana)* to set off the delicate emerald-green foliage of maidenhair fern *(Adiantum pedatum)*. As a taller backdrop for the two plants, use the dark green needled foliage of yew *(Taxus baccata)*. Amongst these plants, you can set a stone container of pink- and white-leaved caladiums *(Caladium hybrids)*, to add an element of striking contrast which will act as a bright focal point.

Color all year: Most plants have a season or two when they are colorful and the rest of the year they are quietly green or brown. A well-planned garden changes with the seasons, but has color in it year round—you can choose annuals for color all summer, perennials and flowering shrubs for color during particular seasons, and shrubs and trees with bright berries or mottled and colored bark to add interest in winter. And don't forget those all-important evergreen plants whose greenery is welcome throughout the year.

Many flowering shrubs, kurume azaleas *(Rhododendron hybrids)* for example, make sheets of color when in bloom and provide greenery for the balance of the year. The reddish autumn foliage and scarlet berries of heavenly bamboo *(Nandina domestica)* brighten the shaded garden in fall and winter. Variegated forms of *Hosta* light up shaded spots with white-bordered leaves. The vivid red stems of red-twig dogwood *(Cornus stolonifera)* and the green stems of Japanese kerria *(Kerria japonica)* enliven the winter landscape and are especially handsome when dusted with new fallen snow.

FOCAL POINTS

Every garden is more attractive if there is one spot that draws the eye and acts as a focal point. This may be the most colorful plant in an area, the tallest one, or some inanimate object such as a birdbath or statue. If the focal point is a plant, it may change with the seasons—as

Every garden setting is more appealing if there is a focal point such as is provided here by the thornless honey locust tree *(Gleditisia triacanthos inermis* 'Moraine').

Evergreen azaleas *(Rhododendron* sp.) are shade-loving shrubs that make a handsome informal border.

Canadian hemlocks (*Tsuga canadensis*) can be pruned to make an excellent evergreen screen or hedge in shady spots.

A refreshing woodland effect results when azaleas and rhododendrons (*Rhododendron* sp.) are naturalized under tall trees that let light filter through.

one shrub goes out of bloom, your eye may be drawn to another part of the garden where a different shrub is displaying its blossoms.

When arranging the plants in your shade garden, consider what will be the focal points, then design the planting to emphasize them visually. For instance, locating a bird bath in the narrowest part of a curving flower bed makes it seem top-heavy, but placing it in the widest part visually anchors it in the expanse of flowers and foliage. A shrub border is most effectively designed with the tallest shrub positioned about a third of the way from the far end of the bed, with the heights of the other shrubs in the border diminishing in either direction.

SHRUBS IN SHADE GARDENS

Growing at a height intermediate between the ceiling of trees and the carpet of low-growing plants, many shrubs are seen at, or close to, eye level. Whether used as a hedge, screen, accent, background, or foundation planting, shrubs figure strongly in garden design. They are permanent elements of your garden and should therefore be used thoughtfully.

Formal uses: Shaped shrubs are the dominant formal element of many gardens. Sheared hedges of boxwood (*Buxus* species), privet (*Ligustrum* species), and Canadian hemlock (*Tsuga canadensis*) are frequently used to establish garden outlines and property boundaries. Shrubs that are readily trained as espaliers on a wall or fence create a bold, striking formal effect but take up hardly any ground space.

Informal uses: Shrubs pruned to retain their natural shapes can provide substance, texture, and color in a woodland-style garden, an informal shrub border, or a free-form hedge: rhododendrons (*Rhododendron* hybrids), deciduous or evergreen azaleas (*Rhododendron* species and hybrids) and red-twig dogwood (*Cornus stolonifera*) are among many choice woodland shrubs.

SHADE PLANTS IN CONTAINERS

Shady spots are easily and quickly brightened up with plants grown in containers. You can nestle a large planter of white-leaved caladiums (*Caladium* hybrids) in the English ivy (*Hedera helix*) beneath a wide-spreading tree, for instance, to create an eye-catching focal point. Most perennials and annuals make first-rate container plants. You can group or hang them, rearrange and move them as they go in and out of bloom, and change them to follow the seasonal shifting of the sun.

A tub or even a shallow pot of bulbs such as tulips (*Tulipa* hybrids) or daffodils (*Narcissus* hybrids) makes a brilliant accent for a shady spot. It's best after the bulb blossoms fade to move the container to an out-of-the-way sunny spot for the foliage to cure. Spring-blooming bulbs are best kept in planters for only one season. You can plant them in the garden in fall and replant the container with fresh bulbs, if you wish.

Shrubs and small trees can be grown in large tubs and planters and placed on paved areas where there is no open soil. Use them on the front porch on either side of the door to frame the entrance or as focal points on a terrace or patio.

MAKING PEOPLE WELCOME

In landscaped areas where people are meant to walk or sit, a garden set in shade can be a cool, beckoning retreat if it offers some welcome for people as well as for plants. A path leading through a bed of ferns and ivy to a bench beneath a tree can be a simple device that leads the eye and the viewer into the garden.

In woodland settings, paths of shredded bark or tree-trunk rounds have an attractive naturalistic appearance that blends in with the scene. Select wooden or stone benches for such a setting. In more formal gardens, choose brick or flagstone walkways and wrought-iron benches and tables. When the accessories you add to the garden are in keeping with the style of the garden, you create a sense of unity between the plants and their setting.

In deep shade, where the choice of plants is limited, you might consider covering large areas with bricks or flagstones to create a terrace and then using container-grown plants to soften the area and to add interest. This is a low-maintenance alternative that can dress up a garden and create a welcome feeling.

A pleasing addition to any style of shade garden is the sound of falling water. You might wish to create your own brook, complete with waterfall, but an easier way to provide the enjoyment and cooling effect of water in motion is to simply purchase a small bubbling fountain with a recirculating pump from your garden center.

PLANT COMBINATIONS

One of the great pleasures of gardening in the shade is formulating your own plant combinations. Garden designers generally feel that horticulturally compatible plants combine beautifully, no matter what their origin. So unless you are a purist, don't worry about planting North American native plants such as eastern redbud *(Cercis canadensis)* and flowering dogwood *(Cornus florida)* with Asian plants such as Korean dogwood *(Cornus kousa)* and Japanese maple *(Acer palmatum)*. These are adapted to similar environments, even though they are native to different parts of the world, and will look beautiful and grow beautifully together.

A combination often seen in shady gardens in the Southeast is masses of evergreen azaleas *(Rhododendron* hybrids) planted close to an understory of American holly *(Ilex opaca)*, high-pruned eastern redbud *(Cercis canadensis)*, and flowering dogwood *(Cornus florida)*. These are in turn shaded by the sparse-needled branches of tall pines *(Pinus* species), which admits brightness and constantly shifting shadows.

The controlled environment created by lath-screening in a plant room provides ideal growing conditions for a wide range of choice plants.

One of the most pleasing plant combinations seen in shade gardens is azaleas *(Rhododendron* sp.) backdropped by a Japanese maple *(Acer palmatum)*.

17

Caring for Shade Gardens

Gardening in the shade is not quite the same as gardening in the sun. It is no more difficult—the challenge lies only in understanding the special conditions of a shady garden site—but success does depend upon close observation. Soil conditions are different, and water and fertilizer needs are not the same as in sunny areas. Shady, moist conditions may encourage fungus diseases that are rarely seen in sunny locations. The trees whose canopies provide shade plants with the proper light exposure and modify summer temperatures may also pose the problem of greedy tree roots that compete with smaller plants for moisture and nutrients.

Shade changes: Shade can also change subtly over the years without your noticing, so that it suddenly seems one summer to have become dramatically deeper. As trees grow and mature, their limbs reach out more and their trunks grow taller, casting shadows farther. Leaves may grow more thickly and shade is less open. What was once light shade may become more like deep shade, and half shade may turn into all-day shade.

If you observe how the shade changes each year, you can modify your gardening techniques and re-plant, if necessary, with better-suited plants. You may also wish to prune trees to keep them open and to prevent the shade from becoming too dark. The unexpected removal of a tree due to storm damage or disease can suddenly expose a shade garden to full

At left: Lily-of-the-valley shrub (*Pieris japonica*) is a widely adapted ornamental evergreen that blooms profusely in very early spring.

Fancy-leaved caladium (*Caladium x hortulanum*)

Knap Hill/Exbury azalea (*Rhododendron* hybrid)

Burford holly (*Ilex cornuta* 'Burfordii')

Japanese honeysuckle (*Lonicera* sp.)

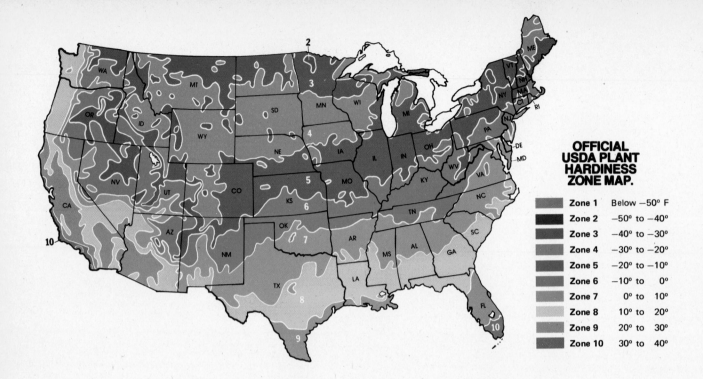

OFFICIAL USDA PLANT HARDINESS ZONE MAP.

	Zone 1	Below −50° F
	Zone 2	−50° to −40°
	Zone 3	−40° to −30°
	Zone 4	−30° to −20°
	Zone 5	−20° to −10°
	Zone 6	−10° to 0°
	Zone 7	0° to 10°
	Zone 8	10° to 20°
	Zone 9	20° to 30°
	Zone 10	30° to 40°

sun; this requires constructing a temporary sunscreen, if valuable flowering trees, shrubs, and perennials are to survive.

CLIMATE

The first step in having a successful shade garden is choosing appropriate plants that are suited to your climate. The USDA plant hardiness map shown above records the average low temperatures that occur throughout the United States and Southern Canada. It divides North America into 10 zones with the average minimum temperature of each zone differing by 10 degrees Fahrenheit. Since a plant's adaptation is often limited by the amount of winter cold it can tolerate, all plants described in this book are identified by the zones where they will give a top-rated performance. Use the map to find your hardiness zone so you can select appropriate plants for your garden.

As every gardener learns, cold hardiness is only one factor of a plant's adaptation. A plant's ability to do well in a certain location depends upon unique combinations of soil type, wind, rainfall, length and time of cold, humidity, summer temperatures, and temperatures in relation to humidity.

The USDA hardiness zone map does not take other climate factors into consideration. To give you additional help in choosing the best plants for your yard and garden, the plants are also identified by which regions of the country they are adapted to. The map on the next page separates the United States and Canada into 10 gardening regions based on climate trends. Find your climate region and then be sure that any plant you choose is recommended for both your USDA zone and your climate region.

Because gardening successfully in the shade depends upon understanding your garden's environment, more help is given here on climate trends. The chart on page 22 shows the percent of sunshine in July. This will help you understand just how much sun your plants are actually getting in the lightly shaded or half-shaded areas of your garden. Shade in the foggy coastal area of Oregon, for instance, is more intense than shade in the cities located in Missouri and Indiana. A plant that may need "full sun" in foggy San Francisco may need "light shade" in Fresno, when the percent of sunshine is taken into consideration.

Knowing the last frost dates in spring and the first frost dates in fall guide you in determining the proper planting times. Statistics for various cities in the United States are listed for last frost in spring, first frost in fall, percent of sunshine for June, July, August, and September, and maximum/minimum temperatures (°F) for the same months.

Obviously the shade beneath a deciduous tree will be different than the shade cast by an evergreen tree. Deciduous trees as a class are out of leaf for five months or more, including the early spring months when temperatures are high enough to encourage flowering of many bulbs and shrubs in the full sun beneath the tree's branches.

Since different tree species leaf out and drop their leaves at various times, the amount of shade beneath different trees can be quite variable. This can affect the vigor of the plants you grow beneath deciduous trees. For instance, early spring-flowering bulbs may do best when planted so as to receive maximum sunshine in spring; they are best planted beneath late-leafing trees. (See the chart on the next page.)

20

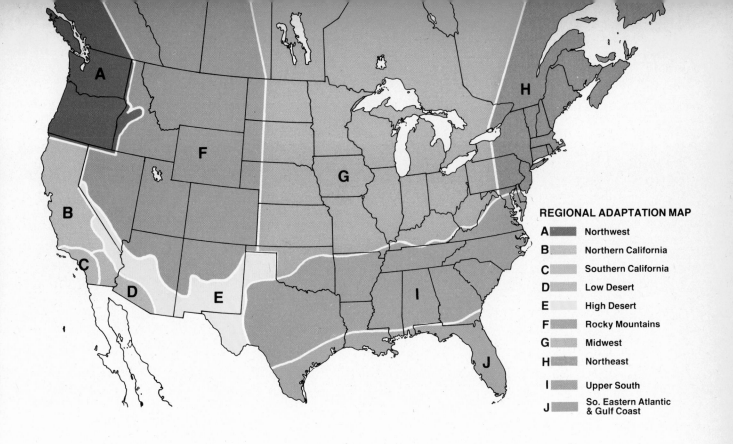

REGIONAL ADAPTATION MAP

A Northwest
B Northern California
C Southern California
D Low Desert
E High Desert
F Rocky Mountains
G Midwest
H Northeast
I Upper South
J So. Eastern Atlantic & Gulf Coast

Leaf-Fall and Leaf-Emergence Dates

The following chart lists the approximate times of leaf-fall and leaf-emergence in Aurora, Oregon, of some popular shade trees as recorded by the North Willamette Experiment Station.

Exact dates in your own area will be different of course, however, differences between each species will be the same number of weeks.

Species	Leaf Fall*	Leaf Emergence**
Carpinus betulus European Hornbeam	4th week November	2nd week April
Celtis occidentalis Common Hackberry	2nd week November	2nd week April
Cladrastis lutea American Yellowwood	1st week November	1st week April
Fraxinus pennsylvanica 'Marshall' Marshall Seedless Green Ash	3rd week October	1st week April
Ginkgo biloba (male) 'Fairmont' Fairmont Maidenhair Tree	3rd week November	4th week April
Koelreuteria paniculata Golden-Rain Tree	2nd week November	1st week April

Species	Leaf Fall*	Leaf Emergence**
Nyssa sylvatica Sour Gum	2nd week November	4th week April
Phellodendron amurense Amur Cork Tree	4th week October	4th week March
Platanus x acerifolia London Plane Tree	3rd week November	2nd week April
Quercus coccinea Scarlet Oak	4th week December	4th week April
Quercus robur English Oak	4th week December	4th week April
Quercus rubra Red Oak	1st week December	4th week April
Tilia cordata Little-Leaf Linden	2nd week November	4th week April

*Defoliation date is date of 100% defoliation.
**Leaf emergence is date when first leaves appear.

Climate Patterns of American Cities

The last spring frost and first fall frost dates, the percent of sunshine, and the maximum/minimum temperatures (°F) for June, July, August, and September are shown below for cities throughout the United States.

WEST COAST

City	June	July	Aug	Sept
Denver, CO	71%	71%	72%	75%
First fall frost: Oct 12	81°/53°F	86°/59°F	85°/58°F	77°/48°F
Last spring frost: May 5				
Fresno, CA	95%	96%	96%	95%
First fall frost: Nov 19	90°/57°F	98°/63°F	96°/61°F	91°/56°F
Last spring frost: Mar 14				
Portland, OR	44%	66%	58%	61%
First fall frost: Nov 24	79°/52°F	85°/53°F	89°/59°F	73°/52°F
Last spring frost: Mar 6				
Red Bluff, CA	89%	96%	94%	92%
First fall frost: Dec 5	89°/62°F	98°/67°F	96°/64°F	91°/60°F
Last spring frost: Mar 6				
Salt Lake City, UT	79%	84%	83%	84%
First fall frost: Nov 1	81°/55°F	91°/63°F	89°/62°F	78°/52°F
Last spring frost: Apr 12				
San Diego, CA	57%	68%	69%	68%
First fall frost: None	71°/60°F	75°/64°F	77°/65°F	76°/63°F
Last spring frost: None				
Seattle, WA	49%	63%	56%	53%
First fall frost: Nov 24	70°/52°F	76°/56°F	74°/55°F	69°/52°F
Last spring frost: Mar 14				
Tucson, AZ	93%	78%	82%	87%
First fall frost: Nov 24	99°/65°F	99°/73°F	97°/71°F	94°/66°F
Last spring frost: Mar 10				

MIDWEST

City	June	July	Aug	Sept
Evansville, IN	73%	76%	76%	70%
First fall frost: Nov 4	85°/64°F	89°/67°F	87°/65°F	82°/59°F
Last spring frost: Apr 2				
Indianapolis, IN	67%	70%	71%	66%
First fall frost: Oct 27	83°/60°F	88°/64°F	86°/62°F	79°/55°F
Last spring frost: Apr 17				
Kansas City, MO	69%	76%	73%	69%
First fall frost: Oct 30	85°/66°F	92°/71°F	90°/69°F	83°/60°F
Last spring frost: Apr 6				
St. Louis, MO	69%	71%	69%	64%
First fall frost: Nov 1	85°/63°F	89°/67°F	87°/66°F	81°/58°F
Last spring frost: Apr 9				
Springfield, MO	66%	70%	72%	71%
First fall frost: Oct 30	85°/63°F	90°/67°F	90°/66°F	83°/58°F
Last spring frost: Apr 12				

EAST COAST

City	June	July	Aug	Sept
Boston, MA	63%	66%	66%	64%
First fall frost: Nov. 7	76°/58°F	81°/64°F	79°/63°F	79°/61°F
Last spring frost: Apr 8				
Burlington, VT	60%	65%	61%	54%
First fall frost: Oct 3	78°/53°F	82°/58°F	80°/56°F	71°/48°F
Last spring frost: May 8				
Hartford, CT	60%	62%	60%	57%
First fall frost: Oct 19	81°/57°F	86°/62°F	83°/60°F	76°/52°F
Last spring frost: Apr 22				
New Haven, CT	64%	66%	64%	63%
First fall frost: Oct 27	75°/56°F	80°/62°F	79°/61°F	73°/54°F
Last spring frost: Apr 15				
Providence, RI	63%	63%	62%	60%
First fall frost: Oct 27	75°/56°F	80°/62°F	79°/60°F	72°/53°F
Last spring frost: Apr 13				
Washington D.C.	64%	63%	63%	62%
First fall frost: Nov. 10	84°/65°F	87°/69°F	86°/68°F	79°/61°F
Last spring frost: Mar 29				

SOUTH

City	June	July	Aug	Sept
Atlanta, GA	67%	62%	65%	63%
First fall frost: Nov 18	87°/66°F	88°/69°F	88°/68°F	83°/63°F
Last spring frost: Mar 21				
Houston, TX	66%	67%	63%	58%
First fall frost: Dec ll	90°/69°F	93°/71°F	92°/71°F	88°/68°F
Last spring frost: Feb 5				
Miami, FL	69%	74%	72%	68%
First fall frost: None	88°/74°F	89°/75°F	89°/76°F	88°/75°F
Last spring frost: None				
Montgomery, AL	66%	63%	66%	62%
First fall frost: Dec 3	90°/69°F	92°/72°F	92°/71°F	88°/66°F
Last spring frost: Feb 27				
New Orleans, LA	67%	57%	55%	60%
First fall frost: Dec 9	90°/71°F	91°/73°F	91°/73°F	87°/69°F
Last spring frost: Feb 20				
Savannah, GA	64%	63%	63%	58%
First fall frost: Nov 29	90°/69°F	91°/71°F	91°/71°F	86°/67°F
Last spring frost: Feb 27				
Shreveport, LA	70%	73%	71%	67%
First fall frost: Nov 15	91°/71°F	93°/73°F	94°/73°F	88°/67°F
Last spring frost: Mar 8				
Tampa, FL	66%	61%	59%	60%
First fall frost: None	89°/72°F	90°/74°F	90°/74°F	88°/73°F
Last spring frost: None				

SHADY MICROCLIMATES

Microclimates are the small climates around your home that differ slightly from the general climate of your area. For instance, the northern side of your house is usually in shadow most of the day. The lack of direct sun there makes the area colder than the southern side of your house, which receives sun all day unless it's shaded by trees.

The shady areas of your garden will of course be cooler than sunny areas of your property, however, you should study your shady garden spots carefully to see if they are influenced in other ways. If air circulation is poor because the prevailing winds are blocked by a building or a hedge, the spot may be unusually humid, inviting fungus diseases. If the spot is low-lying, it may be a frost pocket, because cold air flows and sinks to the lowest spot, much like running water. If a large area of pavement, which heats up from solar radiation, is nearby, the spot may be warmer than expected and could be too hot and dry for some sensitive shade plants.

Understanding how these microclimates modify your garden conditions will increase your success in your shade gardening endeavors. For instance, plants that are borderline hardy for your area may do well if you take protective measures such as providing wind or snow shelters and making use of your property's warm microclimates. Protected plants can often be grown successfully in the next colder zone.

You can create shady microclimates that will function well as shade garden sites by building an overhead shelter, or by a series of simple baffle panels. These cast shade and direct air currents and are easy to construct. They can be as inexpensive as the price of a piece of canvas, a short length of rope, and some 2×4s for framing.

Deciduous trees help conserve energy. In summer they provide cool shade for ornamental plants and for your house itself.

During winter deciduous trees let the sunlight through their bare branches, warming your house and lowering your heating costs.

SOIL FOR SHADE GARDENS

The soil on a forest floor is naturally moist, rich, and crumbly because it is composed of decomposed leaves, twigs, and other plant matter, which forms a natural rich compost. But frequently in home landscapes the soil beneath trees becomes hard and compacted because every autumn a major clean-up effort is carried out and not a fallen leaf is left to remain on the ground. This robs the soil of its natural method of renewal and it becomes depleted of nutrients and inhospitable for gardening.

Beneath a stand of trees, it is advisable not to rake up fallen leaves each autumn. This area is suitable for planting a woodland garden and the fallen leaves will not look unsightly if the area is landscaped with informally grouped shrubs, ferns, and perennials. (Be sure however to remove fallen leaves, if they dropped due to fungus diseases.) If you find the fallen leaves objectionable, then by all means rake them up, but keep the soil covered with a deep mulch. (See mulching on this page.)

Planting in compacted soil: When planting an area of compacted soil for the first time, loosen it up by the gentle use of a garden fork. Spread an inch or two of organic matter across the top of the loosened soil and then hoe it in. Water slowly and deeply with a sprinkler. You are ready to plant in a day or two when the soil has dried slightly.

In areas where thick tree roots are exposed and small roots form a dense mat, you may have difficulty loosening the soil. If this is the case, you can dig out pockets of compacted soil with a garden spade and replace the old soil with enriched soil. Plant ground covers, ferns, or perennials in these pockets of improved soil, where they will get quickly established.

WATERING SHADE GARDENS

Most shade-loving plants are also moisture-loving plants. However, there are no hard-and-fast rules to go by when it comes to watering shade gardens. The key to success is close observation, since each shady site is an individual case.

More often than not, the soil in a shaded site is moist and remains moist for some time after a rain or a watering, because the shaded area is cool. Half-shaded areas, especially those that receive afternoon sun, will be warmer and will dry faster. But beneath the overhang of a house or beneath a densely foliaged tree, rain may be deflected and the shady spot may actually be unusually dry.

Surface tree roots can also quickly rob the topsoil of moisture. Deep-rooted trees do not pose this problem, but surface-rooted ones are difficult to garden under. Where surface-rooted trees are a problem, it helps to water the area deeply and thoroughly, allowing a sprinkler to run gently all day, several times a month during the growing season. This will encourage the roots to grow deeper in search of water. Watering so that only the top several inches of soil is wetted only makes the problem worse. Newly planted trees should be deeply watered to encourage deep roots.

When watering shade plants, it is best to water in early morning so that the plants can dry off before nightfall—this discourages fungus diseases. If possible, drip irrigation systems or hoses that allow water to seep slowly into the soil without wetting foliage is preferable to overhead sprinklers.

How often you should water depends upon how quickly the soil dries. And that in turn depends upon many factors such as the temperature, soil type, and kinds of trees and smaller plants growing in the garden. Most garden plants do best with the equivalent of an inch of rain a week during the growing season. If rain doesn't help you out, then you'll have to supply water when the top inch of soil seems dry. If the soil dries very rapidly, then you aren't supplying enough water for both the tree roots and your garden plants.

FERTILIZER NEEDS IN SHADE GARDENS

Plants growing in the shade cast by trees will need special attention when it comes to fertilizing. Apply a balanced fertilizer, such as 5-10-5 (5% nitrogen, 10% phosphorus, and 5% potassium) several times during the growing season, at the rate recommended for trees. The trees will get most of the nutrients, leaving a modest supply for your other plants.

It's best to apply fertilizer in early spring just before growth begins, and then once a month until midsummer. By the end of summer, plants should be slowing down to prepare for winter dormancy—fertilizing at that time will encourage new growth that may be damaged by fall frosts.

Shade gardens that are shaded by buildings rather than trees will need less fertilizer. Apply fertilizer at the rate recommended for the particular plants you are feeding.

Azaleas, rhododendrons, camellias, and hollies are shade-loving plants that require acid soil. When fertilizing them, it is important to choose a fertilizer that is designed for acid-loving plants. Such a plant food contains its nutrients in chemical forms that these plants can readily absorb.

MULCHING SHADE GARDENS

Mulch is a layer of material spread across the surface of the soil. It may be organic or inorganic and acts to conserve moisture, shade out weeds, and improve the appearance of the garden. An organic mulch, such as shredded bark, sawdust, pine needles, and compost, improves the fertility and texture of the soil as it decomposes. Inorganic mulches, such as pebbles, stones, and gravel, do not improve the soil but are ornamental in certain garden situations and do not need replacing as frequently as do organic mulches.

Shade gardens, like sun gardens, benefit from being mulched. The mulch will help keep roots cool and the soil moist, conditions preferred by most shade plants. Spread mulch about two inches deep over the soil in the planting bed. Add fresh mulch each spring, if needed. In areas with cold winters, an extra application of mulch heaped around borderline hardy plants after the soil freezes in fall will help them survive the winter.

As organic mulches decay, they use nitrogen from the soil. Be sure that you fertilize mulched plants well so they do not suffer from nitrogen deficiency. Rake back the mulch and spread the fertilizer directly on the soil.

Watering

Drip watering systems are efficient. They apply water directly over roots at a rate soil can absorb.

A basin of firmed soil directs water to roots, however periodic repair is required.

Many types of sprinkler heads are available to use with your garden hose. Easy to move where needed.

Mulching

Bark mulch is available in many sizes. Use uniform-size particles to give plantings a neat appearance.

Rock mulch does not wash away and lasts indefinitely, but does not add humus to soil.

Irregular particls of low-cost shredded bark bind together to form a mulch that will hold well on slopes.

Fertilizing

Spray leaves with foliar fertilizer for fastest results.

Time-release fertilizer pellets provide required nutrients for 1 to 5 years, depending on the manufacturer. Read package directions.

Granular fertilizer applied on surface can promote good growth. Do not apply directly over rootball.

Pruning Shrubs and Trees in the Shade Garden

A shrub will lose vigor and become susceptible to disease if it becomes too dense and overgrown.

Improve air circulation and rejuvenate deciduous shrubs by cutting out the oldest stems at ground level, after blooming in spring.

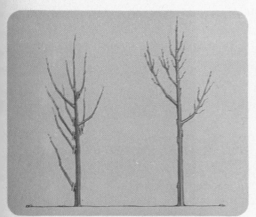

Let in more light by thinning trees to curtail development of new shoots and direct growth. Thinning cuts to be made, shown at left. Resulting growth, shown at right.

Create denser shade by heading a tree to increase the production of new shoots and stiffen main branches. Heading cuts to be made, shown at left. Resulting growth, shown at right.

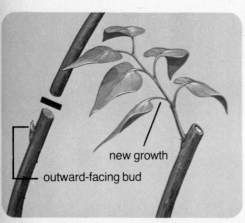

Make pruning cuts above an outward-facing bud to direct new growth outward.

To remove heavy limb (left): 1) undercut, 2) cut through limb, 3) remove stub. To remove dead stub (right): Cut flush with healthy growth, not trunk.

AIR CIRCULATION

Since shaded gardens are often cool and damp, the plants in them are sometimes subject to fungus diseases, which thrive in just such conditions. (See Pests and Problems on page 27.) Improving air circulation will help dry the plants and discourage disease.

One way to ensure good air circulation is to avoid planting shrubs and small trees too closely. Proper spacing that allows air movement between plants is important, especially in muggy climates. Most people tend to plant new plants close together because they are small, but as the plants mature they often crowd each other. If this is the case in your garden, do not hesitate to remove overcrowded shrubs—they can be transplanted elsewhere in the garden if you wish.

Side yards may be either open to the prevailing breezes or protected from them depending upon the location of buildings and fences. If air is stagnant in narrow yards, then open them up, if you can, by removing solid fences and replacing them with lattice-work or some other open style that allows air to pass. Tall hedges and shrubbery may also be blocking the breeze and can be removed or pruned to encourage air movement.

LETTING IN MORE LIGHT

Where shade is too dark to grow the kind of shade garden you want, you don't have to resign yourself to the situation. You can bring in more light where thickly foliaged trees and even the shadow of a building are too dark.

Since most excessive shade results from dense overgrown trees and large shrubs, pruning or occasionally removal often work miraculous transformations. Prune trees high, removing lower limbs, so their branches are far enough above the ground to diffuse rather than block light. In the tree's crown, remove selected branches by *thinning*, a pruning method in which entire main or side branches are removed at their origins. This kind of pruning will allow more light to filter through the tree, brightening the area underneath. If trees are too closely planted to admit light, remove some and thin the remaining ones.

Where excessive shade results from the shadows of buildings, you may think it's an impossible situation to solve. However, there are ways to brighten open shaded areas. The shaded wall or fence, as well as any nearby wall or fence that catches and reflects sunlight, should be painted white or a pastel color. Changing the paint from a dark to a light color can instantly transform a gloomy area suited only to moss and mushrooms into a much brighter spot that fills with reflected light and encourages many beautiful shade-loving plants into blossom.

CREATING SHADE

If you wish to turn a sun-baked area of your yard into a cool, shady one, or if the removal of a tree suddenly throws scorching sunlight down upon your shade garden, you can create instant shade by building garden structures.

Structures to create shade can be easy, straightforward, and inexpensive or expensive and elaborate. Among the least expensive solutions is to erect a structure of posts and beams and make a roof from greenhouse shade cloth, which is available in various densities. A more expensive but more attractive solution is to construct a wooden lath to rest on the rafters. These structures can be used to shade a planting bed, wooden deck, or a flagstone patio.

Intricate lath pergolas and arbors are elegant possibilities for creating shade for people and plants. They are designed to be covered with vines and are right at home in a lightly shaded setting, where they provide a perfect cool retreat.

If you build temporary shade structures, it's a good idea to also plant trees to provide future permanent shade. Select these trees carefully and you will be glad in the years to come. Choose trees that will branch high and provide an airy canopy of foliage, or plant more

heavily foliaged trees and prune them as they mature. The trees described on page 11 have especially good manners in the shade garden.

CARING FOR BULBS

For the long-term benefit of bulbs in your garden, keep an eye out for deepening shade as high-branching trees form heavier canopies. Occasional thinning of branches may be necessary to keep the garden bright enough for the bulbs' foliage to mature properly, especially beneath early-leafing trees.

Spring bulbs, like most bulbs, require well-drained soil. If grading doesn't allow fast run-off, improve soil aeration by blending generous quantities of organic amendments like ground bark, peat moss, well-decayed compost, or nitrogen-supplemented sawdust into the soil to a depth of 4 or 5 inches. Even on slopes with runoff, it is a good idea to amend heavy soil.

Late summer to early autumn is the planting season for spring bulbs. If you must plant later (but never after cold weather has set in), plant deeper than usual and mulch heavily to permit root development in warm soil before winter. If you receive a shipment of bulbs too early for planting, store them in a cool, well-ventilated place until planting time. Refrigerating bulbs in paper (not plastic) bags is a suitable storage method.

Planting depths vary among spring bulbs. A generally sound rule of thumb is to cover them with soil whose depth is 1-1/2 to 2 times the diameter of the bulbs.

Like other plants in gardens shaded by trees, bulbs can suffer when competing with greedy, shallow-rooted trees for moisture and nutrients. The best solution, of course, is to avoid planting near such trees. But if you have no choice, then plant bulbs about 3 inches deeper than usual.

Avoid planting in areas where you will later dig to plant perennials or ground covers, or use stakes or rocks as markers.

Watering is important. When bulbs are planted, soil should be

thoroughly watered unless it is already moist. From the time they sprout above ground level through the flowering period, soil should be moist. For deep bulbs this means thorough watering if soil is dry. Remember that bulbs growing among tree roots are most likely to be dry. When foliage becomes yellow and dry, stop watering for the rest of the season.

PESTS AND PROBLEMS

Certain insect pests and diseases are more troublesome in shady areas. Moist conditions favor fungal diseases such as powdery mildew and botrytis. Most fungal spores need a film of water to germinate in and sometimes even very high humidity will do. If breezes waft through your shade garden, the water on leaf surfaces evaporates and fungal spores don't get much of a chance. But if air circulates poorly and becomes stagnant, diseases will have an easy entrance.

Fungus diseases are best deterred by pruning to increase air circulation (see Air Circulation on page 26) and watering early in the day so flowers and foliage can dry before evening. It is also important to clean up infected plant debris from the ground, since this contains spores that will reinfect the plants.

If fungus diseases do attack, spraying with an appropriate fungicide can sometimes stop the infection. Most fungicides work best, however, at preventing an infection and can't eradicate it completely after it has begun. Where disease has been a recurrent problem, it is advisable to apply a fungicide periodically during the growing season, before any signs of the disease are present.

Plants growing in too much shade often produce softer, larger leaves that are more vulnerable to insect attack. Choosing plants that are well adapted to your climate and to the amount of shade where they are growing will help prevent insect problems. If insect problems occur and appear to be serious, consult your nurseryman for appropriate chemical controls.

Top-Rated Plants for Shady Gardens

The list of plants that flourish in shady gardens is a long one. It includes almost every type of plant from the lowest-growing ground cover to small flowering trees. These plants offer the shade gardener every color in nature from the soft green of ferns to the bright colored blossoms of annuals, perennials, and bulbs.

The shade-loving plants described in the following charts were selected because of their top-rated growth performance and reliability in many areas of the United States. They are widely available in the climate zones where they are adapted.

The charts group the plants according to their most common landscape use, such as lawns and ground covers, or according to set botanical groups, such as ferns, annuals, or perennials. Since some plants fall into more than one category—for instance some ferns can also be used as ground covers and most wildflowers are also perennials—before you decide on which plant to buy, it may be helpful to glance through this entire chapter for additional ideas.

Each chart contains all the pertinent information necessary to select the right plants for your shady garden. The plants are listed in alphabetical order according to botanical name. The USDA zone recommendations and regional adaptation codes (see page 21) are given for each plant, along with cultural information.

Flowering dogwood (*Cornus* sp.) and English ivy (*Hedera helix*) thrive in the shade cast by towering canopy trees.

Wisteria (*Wisteria* sp.)

American holly (*Ilex opaca*)

Star jasmine (*Trachelospermum* sp.)

Variegated euonymus (*Euonymus* sp.)

In mass plantings, the vividly colored foliage of coleus (*Coleus x hybridus*) makes shaded sites glow with living color.

Impatiens (*Impatiens wallerana*) are blanketed with blossoms all summer long, adding visual impact to shaded flower beds.

Annuals

Botanical/ Common Name	Zones and Regions	Type of Shade	Height	Plant Description	Comments/Uses
Antirrhinum majus Snapdragon	2-10 All regions.	Light.	6 in. to 3 ft.	Available in dwarf, semi-dwarf, medium, and tall varieties. Dark green, lance-shaped leaves to 3 in. long. Flowers on tall spikes, sac-like with petals forming upper and lower lips, appearing like dragon's jaws. Blooms from summer to frost, many colors, cinnamon-scented.	Space 6 to 8 in. apart, pinch shoots when young to encourage branching. Squeeze sides of flowers to make "jaws" open. Use for tall borders, background, rock gardens, or cut flowers. Used as a cool-season annual in mild-winter climates.
Begonia (fibrous-rooted) *B. x semperflorens-cultorum* Wax Begonia	2-10 All regions.	Light to half.	6-12 in.	Mounding habit. Leaves to 4 in. long, oval to heart-shaped, glossy, green to bronze, or green variegated with white. Flowers in clusters, single or double, white, pink or red. Blooms almost continuously.	Space 8 to 10 in. apart. Use for bedding, borders, or containers. See page 33 for varieties.
Clarkia amoena Farewell-to-Spring, Godetia	2-10 All regions.	Light to half.	18-24 in.	Sprawling habit. Leaves to 2 in. long, narrow, tapering. Flowers in axils of stems, to 3 in. across, single or double, cup-shaped, white, pink, salmon, purple through red. Blooms summer until frost.	Space 8 to 10 in. apart. Use as bedding plant, in containers, for cut flowers.
Coleus x hybridus Coleus	2-10 All regions.	Light to full.	6-36 in.	Dense habit. Leaves variable, 3-6 in. long, smooth or toothed edges, pointed, splashed with many combinations of colors. Flowers should be pinched off to encourage more leaf production.	Space 10 to 18 in. apart. Grown for unique foliage, not flowers. Use for borders, window boxes, planters, as houseplants. See chart on page 32 for varieties.
Impatiens wallerana Impatiens	2-10 All regions.	Light to full.	6-12 in.	Compact, mounding habit. Leaves are 1 to 3 in. long, oval, dark with lighter undersides. Dazzling flowers held above foliage in almost every shade, some bicolors. Blooms spring to fall.	One of the big 3 annuals for shade gardens. See page 34 for variety descriptions. New Guinea hybrids have brightly colored foliage.
Lobelia erinus Edging Lobelia	2-10 All regions.	Light to half.	6 in.	Trailing habit. Leaves to 1 in. long with serrated edges. Flowers to 3/4 in. across, white, blue, or pink, in summer.	Space 4 to 6 in. apart. Use for ground cover, edging, hanging basket, or borders.

Botanical/Common Name	Zones and Regions	Type of Shade	Height	Plant Description	Comments/Uses
Lobularia maritima Sweet Alyssum	2-10 All regions.	Light.	1 ft.	Mounding habit. Narrow leaves to 2 in. long. Flowers in small clusters, 4-petaled, fragrant, white, pink, rose, or purple. Blooms from summer until frost.	Space 6 to 8 in. apart. Use for borders, edging, planter boxes, rock gardens.
Mimulus species Monkey Flower	2-10 All regions.	Light to full.	1 ft.	Mounding habit. Leaves oval with pointed tips, serrated edges. Tubular, 2-in. flowers on spikes rising well above foliage. Yellow, maroon, or bronze streaked, spotted or splashed with yellow, brown or red, resembling monkey's faces. Blooms in summer.	Space 6 in. apart. Use in planter boxes, rock gardens, hanging baskets, borders. Pinch blooms after first flowering to induce flowering a second time.
Mysotis sylvatica (M. alpestris) Forget-Me-Not	2-10 All regions.	Light.	2 ft.	Clumplike habit. Leaves 2 in. long, narrow, hairy on upright stems. Blue, white, or pink flowers, 1/2 in. across, on stems held above foliage. Blooms in spring.	Space 8 to 12 in. apart. Use as background for spring flowers, in planter boxes, as ground cover. Sow seed in fall. Will self-sow.
Nemophila menziesii Baby-Blue-Eyes	2-10 All regions.	Light to full.	6-10 in.	Mounding habit. Leaves fern-like, finely divided, 2 in. long. Flowers 1-1/2 in. across, fragrant, trumpet-shaped, blue with white centers, at ends of short stems. Blooms in summer.	Space 6 to 9 in. apart. Use in rock gardens, as ground cover, border, edging.
Nicotiana alata Flowering Tobacco, Jasmine Tobacco	2-10 All regions.	Light to half.	2-3 ft.	Bushy habit. Leaves 4-10 in. long. Flowers are long, star-shaped, trumpetlike tubes that stand at right angles from the stem. Colors range from white through green to pink and lavender. Fragrant flowers appear from summer until frost.	Space 1 ft apart. Some varieties open only at night or on overcast days, others open midday. Plant where fragrance can be appreciated. Use massed in large beds, for borders, large containers.
Nierembergia species Cupflower	2-10 All regions.	Light.	6 in. to 3 ft.	*N. hippomanica:* compact, mounding habit, 6-12 in. high. Leaves narrow, stiff to 1/3 in. long. Flowers profuse, cup-shaped, 1 in. wide, violet-blue. Blooms in summer. *N. scoparia:* bushy, 2-3 ft high. Leaves to 3/4 in. long, narrow, stiff. Flowers profuse, cup-shaped, 1 in. across, blue with white tinge. Blooms in summer.	*N. hippomanica:* use as ground cover, rock gardens, edging or container plant. *N. scoparia:* use for planter boxes, rock gardens, backgrounds.
Nigella damascena Love-in-a-Mist	2-10 All regions.	Light.	1-2-1/2 ft.	Branching habit. Leaves thread-like, forming a collar under flowers. Blossoms single, at ends of stems, to 1-1/2 in. across, white, red, or blue. Blooms spring through summer. Fruit follows: globular seedpod, green with reddish markings.	Space 8 in. apart. Airy looking. Seeds used in flavoring foods. Flowers used for bedding and in cut arrangements.
Pelargonium species Geranium	2-10 All regions.	Light.	10 to 36 in.	Habit varies by type from bushy to trailing. Lobed green leaves often marked with contrasting zones or rings of dark or lighter green, bronze, pink, or white. Bright colored round flowers clusters in many shades of white, pink, and red held above the foliage on strong stems. Perennial in Zones 9-10.	Space 12 to 24 inches apart. Many species available some with scented leaves. Lady Washington, Geranium, *P. x domesticum* is very popular in warm climates. Ivy geranium, *P. peltatum,* has a sprawling habit; excellent as a ground cover or hanging basket. All geraniums are beautiful border or pot plants and flower best in full sun but also do well in partial shade.
Petunia x hybrida Petunia	2-10 All regions.	Half to light.	12-14 in.	Downy leaved, mounding or cascading plants bear brightly colored, single or double trumpet-shaped blossoms in almost every color; many bicolors. Blooms from late spring to frost.	Divided into 2 types; multifloras (more but smaller flowers) and grandifloras (larger but fewer flowers.) Many varieties available. Some have cascading habits ideal for containers. Space 8 to 12 inches apart. Pinch back and fertilize if plants get too leggy.

Annuals (continued)

Botanical/ Common Name	Zones and Regions	Type of Shade	Height	Plant Description	Comments/Uses
Primula malacoides Fairy Primrose	2-10 All regions.	Light to full.	12-15 in.	Low-growing rosette of rounded hairy leaves. Flowers on slender stems in whorls, delicate appearance. Blooms in soft shades of lavender, pink, white, and red in early spring.	Grows best in cool, moist conditions. Excellent woodland plant or combined with early spring bulbs.
P. x polyantha Polyanthus Primrose	2-10 All regions.	Light to full.	6-12 in.	Basal rosette of 4- to 6-in. tongue-shaped leaves with rich green crinkled texture. Fragrant flowers 1 to 2 inches across in large clusters, on thick, erect stems. Pure red, purple, yellow, pink, bronze, apricot, and maroon. All with yellow eye, some gold-edged, or double. Blooms in spring.	A most popular bedding or pot plant. Space 6 to 12 inches apart. Plants short-lived but divide easily every 1 to 2 years. Plants die back, resprout in early spring. Best in cool, moist areas.
Salvia splendens Scarlet Sage	2-10 All regions.	Light to half.	1-3 ft.	Bushy, branching habit. Leaves 3 in. long, oval, pointed, glossy, deep green. Flowers on spikes, held above foliage, 1 in. long, tubular, white, rose through scarlet to lavender, from early summer until frost.	Space 8 to 12 in. apart. Use massed in shade garden, borders, edging, planter boxes.
Torenia fournieri Wishbone Flower, Bluewings	2-10 All regions.	Light to full.	12 in.	Loose, clumplike habit. Leaves 2 in. long with toothed edges. Flowers 1 in. across, on winged stalks, are divided into light purple upper lip, dark purple lower lip. Yellow throat has wishbone-shaped stamens. Blooms from summer until frost.	Space 6 to 8 in. apart. Use for borders, edging, planter boxes, houseplant.

Coleus

CAREFREE
Small leaves, deeply lobed.

DRAGON
Large leaves, moderately lobed.

FIJI
Large leaves, delicately fringed.

PONCHO SERIES
Cascading, for hanging baskets.

RAINBOW
Large leaves, heart-shaped.

RAINBOW, FRINGE-LEAVED
Similar to Rainbow, leaves fringed.

SABER
Long, saber-shaped leaves.

WIZARD
Large leaves, heart-shaped.

Wax begonia (*Begonia x semperflorens-cultorum*)

Hybrid tuberous begonia (*Begonia x tuberhybrida*)

Hybrid tuberous begonia (*Begonia x tuberhybrida*)

Begonia

Series or Variety	Height	Foliage	Flowers
WAX BEGONIA			
Cocktail series:			
'Brandy'	6-8 in.	Bronze.	Light pink.
'Gin'	6-8 in.	Bronze-green.	Rose.
'Vodka'	6-8 in.	Bronze.	Deep scarlet.
'Whisky'	6-8 in.	Bronze.	White.
'Gladiator'	12-18 in.	Bronze-tinted green.	Red.
Glamour Series	8-10 in.	Green.	Pink, red, rose, white, and white edged with rose. Large.
'Indian Maid'	6-8 in.	Bronze.	Scarlet.
'Linda'	6-8 in.	Green.	Deep rose.
'Othello'	6-8 in.	Dark bronze.	Scarlet-orange.
'Scarletta'	6-8 in.	Green.	Large, scarlet.
'Snowbank'	8-10 in.	Green.	White.
Thousand Wonders (Tausendschon) Series	6-8 in.	Green.	Scarlet, white.
'Viva'	6-8 in.	Green.	White.

Series, Variety, or Type	Form	Colors	Comments
HYBRID TUBEROUS			
Camellia	Upright.	White, pink, red, yellow, orange, scarlet, salmon, deep red, apricot.	Large, ruffled double flowers resemble camellias.
Carnation	Upright.	Deep red, pink, white, orange, yellow.	Large, ruffled, frilly flowers resemble carnations.
Crispa Marginata	Upright.	Bicolors: yellow edged with crimson, white edged with crimson.	Large, frilled single flowers.
Multiflora Maxima	Upright.	Orange, yellow, red, white, pink.	Multitudes of 2-in. single or double flowers on sun-tolerant plants; excellent for beds or pots.
Nonstop	Upright.	Yellow, red, orange, pink, rose, apricot, salmon.	Double, semidouble, and a few single flowers on same plants. Compact growth habit. Very free-flowering.
Picotee Double	Upright.	Bicolors: white edged with pink, red, or apricot. 'Flamenco' speckled red and white. 'Sunburst' yellow edged with red.	Flowers are large and ruffled.
Rose Form	Upright.	Apricot, pink, yellow, white, red, salmon.	Edges of petals smooth, center petals furled like center of rose.
Ruffled Double (Ballerina)	Upright.	Apricot, yellow, white, pink, scarlet.	Flowers heavily ruffled, 6 to 8 inches wide.
Hanging Basket	Pendulous.	Pink, red, yellow, orange, apricot; picotee types: assorted pastel colors with red or pink edge.	Many Belgian hybrids have slender leaves and wide-open flowers with attractively slender petals. American hybrids have rounder petals. Various Hanging Basket begonias sometimes marketed as Lloydii or Lloydii Pendula begonias.
Happy End	Pendulous.	Red, orange, salmon, white.	This series of pendulous begonias has a mixture of single and double flowers.
Sensations	Pendulous.	Red, yellow, copper, white, pink.	This series of pendulous begonias has large double flowers.

Impatiens (*Impatiens wallerana*) is a choice plant for creating a sparkling display of vibrant color in shady garden areas. Blossoms blanket plants all during the summer season.

Impatiens

Series or Variety	Colors	Comments
DWARF (8-10 in.)		
Super Elfin	Fuchsia, orange, orchid, rose, pink, hot pink, scarlet, salmon, red, white, bicolors.	Profuse flowering, good branching at base of plants, and very compact habit make this series especially suitable for hanging baskets and pots as well as beds. 'Blush' is delicate pink with red eye; 'Lipstick', deep rose with white eye. Others are named for colors. Super Elfin varieties are also sold as a mix.
INTERMEDIATE (10-12 in.)		
Futura	Burgundy, coral, orange, orchid, pink, red, rose-pink, scarlet, white, pale rose.	The all-time favorite series, useful for hanging baskets, planters, and beds. Growth habit is compact and mounding. Varieties are named for colors; often sold as a mix. 'Wild Rose' is especially iridescent.
Novette	Bright orange, deep orange ('Scarlet'), orange, deep rose, pink, red, salmon, violet, white, bicolor.	Same growth habit and uses as Futura series. 'Rose & White Star' is bicolored. 'Bright Orange' has bronze leaves.
Twinkles	White-star pattern on fuchsia, red, rose, scarlet.	Same growth habit and uses as Futura and Novette series. Sold by color names or as a mix.
TALL (12-16 in.)		
'Blitz'	Intense scarlet.	Other impatiens have 1- to 2-in. flowers, but 'Blitz' has 2-1/2-in. ones. Bronze foliage. Excellent in beds and hanging baskets. An award winner.
Duet	White with red, scarlet, and deep rose.	Double and semidouble bicolored flowers on large, relatively upright plants. Useful for beds and large containers. Sold as a mix. Can grow taller than other tall impatiens—to 18-20 in.
Grande	Coral, orange, orchid, purple, red, rose, white.	Large flowers on plants suitable for all uses. Sold by color names or as a mix.
'Tangeglow'	Very bright orange.	Suitable for all uses.
Zigzag	White with scarlet, orange, pink, rose, salmon, or purple.	Striking bicolors sold as a mix. Suitable for all uses.

Biennials and Perennials

Botanical/ Common Name	Zones and Regions	Type of Shade	Height	Plant Description	Comments/Uses
Aconitum carmichaelii Monkshood	See wildflowers page 40.				
Alyssum montanum Madwort *A. saxatile* — see *Aurinia*	4-10 All regions.	Light.	6-10 in.	Mounding habit. Leaves silvery-gray, covered with dense hairs. Bright yellow, fragrant flowers on stems held above foliage. Blooms spring into summer.	Space 6 in. apart. Use for edging or rock gardens.
Anchusa azurea Alkanet, Bugloss	4-10 All regions.	Light.	3-5 ft.	Open, spreading habit. Leaves to 6 in. long, oval to lance-shaped, covered with stiff hairs. Flowers in clusters, 3/4 in. across, bright blue. Blooms in summer.	Space 1 to 2 ft apart. Use for borders, as bedding plants.
Anemone x hybrida (*A. hupensis japonica*) Japanese Anemone	6-9 All regions.	Light to half.	2-1/2 ft.	Clumplike habit. Leaves to 5 in. long, deeply lobed (maple-like) with toothed edges, dark green. Flowers on tall stems held well above foliage, 3 in. across, white to pink. Blooms late summer until frost.	Space 6 to 15 in. apart. Use for borders, background, rock gardens, containers, and cut flowers.
Aquilegia x hybrida Columbine	3-9 A-I	Light.	2-3 ft.	Erect, branching habit. Leaves lobed, blue-green, lacy. Flowers to 3 in. across with spurs. Wide range of colors including bicolors. Blooms in early summer.	Space 1 to 2 ft apart. Use for borders, rock gardens, under trees, as cut flowers. Hummingbirds attracted to blooms.
Arabis caucasica Rock Cress	6-10 All regions.	Light.	6 in.	Mounding to matlike habit. Leaves soft, gray-green. Flowers to 1/2 in. across, fragrant, white, in spring.	Space 10 to 12 in. apart. Use for borders, edging, rock gardens, walls.
Aster species Asters, Michaelmas Daisy	4-10 All regions.	Light.	9 in. to 6 ft.	Mounding to bushy habit. Leaves variable—1/2 to 5 in. long. Flowers to 2 in. across, daisy-like. Blooming season variable, according to species.	Space 12 to 15 in. apart. Use for rock gardens, borders, containers, cut flowers. *A. alpinus:* 9 in. high, flowers white, lavender, or blue. Blooms in late summer. *A. novae-angliae:* 3-5 ft high, leaves to 5 in. long, flowers red to purple. Blooms in late summer. *A. novi-belgii:* 3-4 ft high, flowers white, pink, lavender, or blue. Blooms in fall.
Astilbe x arendsii False Spiraea	4-9 A,B,F, G,H,I	Light to full.	6-30 in.	Mounding habit to 1-1/2 ft high. Leaves fernlike, with toothed edges. Fluffy, white, pink to red flowers held on spikes above foliage. Blooms in summer.	Space 1 to 2 ft apart. Use for borders, as cut flowers, can be dried. Effective near pools.
Aurinia saxatilis Basket-of-Gold	3-10 All regions.	Light.	6-12 in.	Mounding habit. Leaves silvery-gray, covered with dense hairs. Flowers on stems held above foliage, bright yellow. Blooms in spring.	Space 6 in. apart. Use for edging or rock gardens.
Begonia (rhizomatous-rooted) *B. x rex-cultorum* Rex Begonia	2-10 All regions.	Light to half.	10-18 in.	Leaves emerge from stems at or slightly below ground level. Leaves 8-12 in. long, heart shaped with toothed edges, very showy with many colors in exotic designs. Flowers insignificant, white to pink.	Space 12 in. apart. Requires humidity. Use in containers and as houseplant.
Bergenia cordifolia Heartleaf Bergenia	2-10 A,B,C,F, G,H,I,J	Light to full.	12-18 in.	Clumplike habit. Leaves to 10 in. wide, thick, heart-shaped to round (similar to cabbage), dark green with crisped, wavy edges. Flowers to 3/4 in. across, in clusters on thick stems, at or just above foliage. Colors range from white through rose-pink to purple.	Space 12 to 15 in. apart. Use for rock gardens, borders, near ponds. Requires humidity.

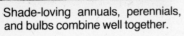
Shade-loving annuals, perennials, and bulbs combine well together.

Foxglove (*Digitalis purpurea*)

Forget-me-not (Mysotis sp.)

Biennials and Perennials (continued)

Botanical/ Common Name	Zones and Regions	Type of Shade	Height	Plant Description	Comments/Uses
Brunnera macrophylla Siberian Bugloss	3-10 All regions.	Light to half.	1-1/2 ft.	Clumplike habit. Leaves 6-8 in. long, heart-shaped, dark green. Flowers on thin stems held above foliage, 1/4 in. across, in small clusters, blue with yellow centers. Blooms in spring.	Space 12 to 18 in. apart. Use under trees, in between evergreen shrubs for touch of color.
Campanula species Bellflower	3-8* A,B,C, F,G,H,I	Light to half.	From 6 to 48 in. high, rounded to spreading.	Leaves to 1 in. long, heart-shaped with serrated edges. Flowers bell-shaped to star-shaped, pale blue to white.	Many species available. *C. glomerata* reaches 1-1/2 to 2-1/2 ft and is spreading. Blooms spring to midsummer and is a good cut flower. *C. isophylla* reaches 2 ft high and blooms midsummer to fall. *C. medium*, a biennial, grows 6 to 12 in. high with tall flower stalks from spring to midsummer. For other species see the ground cover chart on page 54.
Cyclamen species Hardy Cyclamen	5-10 A,B,C, F,G,H,I	Light to half.	To 10 in.	Small clumplike habit. Leaves to 3 in. wide, round to heart-shaped, variegated with silver, light and dark green. Flowers 1-2 in., nodding, petals reflexed. Succulent stems carry flowers above foliage. Colors range from white through pink to purple. Some varieties are fragrant. Blooms in spring and fall.	Space 3 to 6 in. apart. Use for borders, rock gardens, containers. Many species available.
Dicentra spectabilis Bleeding-Heart	4-8 A,B,C,F, G,H,I,J	Light to half.	2-3 ft.	Mounding habit. Soft green leaves on arching stems, finely cut with smooth edges.	Space 2 ft apart. Better as single plant than massed. Also a good chocie for wildflower garden.
Digitalis purpurea Common Foxglove	4-10 All regions.	Light to full.	To 5 ft.	Basal clump of large oval leaves with pointed leaf tips, dark green above, light green beneath. Tubular, 3-in.-long, white, yellow, pink, purple, or red flowers with spotted throats on tall spikes. Blooms spring and summer.	Space 15 to 24 in. apart. Use for background, borders, as cut flowers. All plant parts poisonous. Stake flower spikes individually. May act as biennial or perennial.
Doronicum cordatum Leopard's-Bane	4-10 A,B,F, G,H,I,J	Light.	2-3 ft.	Clumplike habit. Leaves 3-5 in. long, heart-shaped with toothed edges. Single, 2- to 3-in., daisylike, bright yellow flowers on long stems. Blooms in spring and summer.	Space 12 to 15 in. apart. Use for borders, rock gardens, as cut flowers.
Helleborus niger Christmas Rose	4-10 A,B,C, D,E,F, G,H,I	Light to half.	1-1/2 ft.	Clumplike habit. Leaves divided into 7-9 toothed, dark green leaflets. Flowers 2-4 in. across, roselike, white to pink with yellow-tipped stamens, fall through spring.	Best used as single plants, not massed. Sensitive to transplanting. Mix with other shade-loving plants for fall and winter bloom.

Botanical/ Common Name	Zones and Regions	Type of Shade	Height	Plant Description	Comments/Uses
Hemerocallis hybrids Daylily	3-10 All regions.	Light to half.	2-5 ft.	Clumplike habit. Leaves 1-2 ft long, narrow, arching. Lily-like flowers, 3-5 in. across, on tall spikes, arising from mound of foliage. Colors range from yellow, orange, pink through red to maroon. Blooms in summer, each flower lasting only 1 day, but a profusion of flowers over a long season.	Space 18-36 in. apart. Use for borders, under deciduous trees, near pools, etc. Choose early, mid-, or late season varieties.
Heuchera sanguinea Coralbells	4-10 All regions.	Light to half.	2 ft.	Mounding habit. Leaves 1-2 in. wide, heart-shaped with scalloped edges. Flowers on tall wiry stems, 1/2 in. across, bellshaped, pink to red. Blooms in summer.	Space 9 to 15 in. apart. Use for edging, rock gardens, cut flowers.
Hosta ventricosa *(H. caerula)* Blue Plantain Lily	4-9 A,B,C, D,F,G, H,I,J	Light to full.	3 ft.	Clumplike habit. Leaves to 9 in. long, heart-shaped, shiny blue-green. Spikes of violet or blue, bell-shaped, 2-in., flowers on 3-ft-tall spikes. Blooms in late summer.	Space 1 ft apart. Use for ground cover, edging, borders, containers. Valued primarily for striking foliage. See ground covers (page 55) for other hosta species.
Iberis sempervirens Edging Candytuft	4-10 All regions.	Light.	12 in.	Compact, mounding habit. Leaves to 1-1/2 in. long, narrow, dark green. White flowers in clusters above foliage, spring into summer, sometimes repeating in fall.	Space 6 to 9 in. apart. Use for ground cover, edging, borders, rock gardens, or containers.
Iris kaempferi Japanese Iris	5-9 A,B,F, G,H,I,J	Light to half.	3-5 ft.	Upright habit. Leaves sword-shaped, 3 ft long. Flowers on stems growing above foliage, to 8 in. across with reflexed sepals on a horizontal plane. Colors range from white through pink to purple and blue. Blooms in summer.	Space 18 in. apart. Excellent for cut flowers, borders, rock gardens, along fences. Needs moisture and grows in boggy soil at edge of pond.
Lobelia cardinalis Cardinal Flower	4-10	Light to half.	3 ft.	Upright habit. Leaves 4 in. long, narrow, pointed with serrated edges, along upright stems. Flowers at tops of stems, tubular, intense red, in summer.	Space 15 to 18 in. apart. Requires moist soil. Use for borders, edging, along streams.
Mertensia virginica Virginia Bluebells	See wildflowers page 41.				
Myosotis scorpioides *(M. palustris)* Forget-Me-Not	4-10 All regions.	Light.	1-1/2 ft.	Upright habit. Narrow, 2-in.-long leaves along upright stems. Flowers 1/4 in. across, bright blue with white, yellow or pink centers. Blooms in summer.	Space 8 to 12 in. apart. Spreads by creeping stems. Use for background, edging, ground cover, planter boxes.
Paeonia hybrids Chinese Peony, Common Garden Peony	5-8 A,B,F, G,H,I,J	Light.	2-4 ft.	Clumplike habit. Leaves large, divided or lobed, with narrow leaflets. Flowers held on stems above leaves, 1-8 in. across, single to double, white through pink to red. Blooms in summer.	Old-fashioned favorite. Use for borders, background, excellent cut flower. Best in cool-summer climates.
Polygonatum odoratum Solomon's-Seal	See wildflowers page 41.				
Saxifraga stolonifera Strawberry Geranium, Mother-of-Thousands	8-10 B,C,J,I	Light to half.	1-1/2- 2 ft.	Low mound to matlike habit. Hairy leaves to 4 in. across, in rosettes, white-veined with reddish undersides. Young plantlets form on ends of slender runners as with strawberries. White, 1-in. flowers in clusters on tall branching stems. Blooms in spring.	Space 6 to 12 in. apart. Use for ground cover, in hanging baskets, rock gardens, as houseplant.
Trollius europaeus Globeflower	5-10 All regions.	Light to full.	1-2 ft.	Bushy habit. Dark green leaves divided into 3-5 lobes. Flowers 1-3 in. across, globe shaped, yellow to orange on ends of long stems. Blooms spring through summer.	Space 1 ft apart. Use near pools and ponds, to brighten shade areas, as cut flowers. Needs ample moisture.
Viola odorata Sweet Violet	See wildflowers page 41, and ground covers page 57.				

Tender Bulbs

Botanical/ Common Name	Zones and Regions	Type of Shade	Height	Plant Description	Comments
Agapanthus species Lily-of-the-Nile	Perennial in 9-10. Annual elsewhere.	Light to half.	15-48 in.	Dark green, straplike leaves. Clusters of bright blue, trumpet-shaped flowers borne on tall stalks in summer.	*A. orientalis* grows to 48 inches high. *A.* x 'Peter Pan' reaches only 15 inches.
Begonia (tuberous-rooted) *B.* x *tuberhybrida*	Perennial in 9-10. Annual elsewhere.	Light to half.	12-18 in. Pendulous.	Leaves emerge from tubers, to 6 in. long, round to heart-shaped, pointed with crisped edges, dark green. Flowers to 8 in. across single or double; white, vivid yellow, pink, apricot, orange, or red.	Space 8 to 10 in. apart. Requires humidity. Use in hanging baskets, for borders, as houseplant. Stake upright types. See page 33 for varieties.
Caladium x *hortulanum* Fancy-Leaved Caladium	Perennial in 10. Annual elsewhere.	Light to full.	12-24 in.	Grown for its dramatic heart-shaped leaves mottled or blotched in shades of white, green, red, pink, or bronze.	Must have well-drained soil.
Zantedeschia aethiopica Calla Lily	Perennial in 8-10. Annual elsewhere.	Light to half.	36-48 in.	Beautiful dark green, arrow-shaped leaves. Large white, funnel-shaped flowers in spring and summer.	Best in moist soil. Some dwarf forms often available.

Spring-Blooming Bulbs

Botanical/ Common Name	Zones and Regions	Type of Shade	Height	Plant Description	Comments
Chionodoxa luciliae Glory-of-the-Snow	3-8 A,B,F, G,H,I	Light to half.	6 in.	Each plant produces 2 or more ribbonlike leaves. Bright blue, star-shaped flowers with white centers borne in early spring.	Naturalizes freely from seed. *C. sardensis* has darker blue flowers.
Clivia miniata Kaffir Lily	9-10 B,C,D,J	Light to full.	12-18 in.	Mounding, dense habit. Leaves lilylike, to 18 in. long, 3 in. wide, fleshy, dark green. Flowers in big clusters on stems just above foliage, 2-3 in. across, intense orange with yellow-tipped stamens, in spring.	Use for planter boxes, containers, as best bloom occurs when tuberous roots are crowded.
Convallaria majalis Lily-of-the-Valley	See ground covers page 54.				
Crocus Crocus species	3-10 in. All regions.	Light.	5 in.	Small grasslike leaves. Cupped flowers in a multitude of colors. Blooms in early spring or fall.	Many species available. Best in cold climates.
Endymion hispanicus Blue Bells	4-10 All regions.	Light.	18 in.	Bright green straplike leaves. Tall spikes of bright blue, bell-shaped flowers in spring.	Often sold as a species of *Scilla*.
Eranthis hyemalis Winter Aconite	4-8 A,B,F, G,H,I	Light to half.	4 in.	Delicate, finely cut foliage. Small buttery yellow, cup-shaped flowers in mid- to late winter.	Blooms through snow. Naturalizes quickly.
Galanthus species Snowdrops	3-9 A,B,F, G,H,I	Light.	9-12 in.	Grasslike foliage. Nodding white flowers are dotted green on inner petals. Bloom in early spring.	Two species most common are *G. nivalis* with 3/4 to 1 inch long flowers and leaves 1/4 inch wide; and *G. elwessi* with clumps of 1-1/2-inch-long flowers and 3/4-inch-wide leaves.
Leujocum vernum Spring Snowflake	5-8 A,B,F, G,H,I	Light.	9-12 in.	Bright green grass-like leaves. White, bell-shaped flowers, spotted green bloom in early spring.	Very similar to snowdrop. Naturalizes freely.
Muscari species Grape Hyacinth	3-10 All regions.	Light.	6-12 in.	Thin, grasslike leaves. Short spikes of sweetly scented, blue to purple flowers in spring.	Several species of similar plants. Naturalizes freely.
Narcissus species Daffodil, Jonquil, Narcissus	5-10 All regions.	Light.	5-20 in.	Bright green, grasslike foliage. A multitude of flower shapes and sizes. May be fragrant. Blooms in spring, primarily in shades of white, yellow an orange.	A large family of very popular bulbs. Some naturalize.

Caladium (*Caladium x hortulanum*) Grape hyacinths (*Muscari* sp.) Easter lily (*Lilium longiflorum*)

Botanical/ Common Name	Zones and Regions	Type of Shade	Height	Plant Description	Comments
Scilla siberica Siberian Scilla, Siberian Squill	3-8 A,B,F, G,H,I	Light.	6 in.	Bright green, grasslike foliage. Delicate, bell-shaped blue flowers on short spikes in early spring.	Naturalizes quickly in moist soil.
Tulipa species Tulip	5-9 All regions.	Light.	8-30 in. inches.	Short, straplike leaves. Single blooms on tall stems borne in a rainbow of colors and many shapes. Blooms from spring into summer depending on type.	Many species and hybrids available. Requires cold storage before planting to bloom in mild climate.

Bulbs That Bloom in Late Spring, Summer, or Fall

Botanical/ Common Name	Zones and Regions	Type of Shade	Height	Plant Description	Comments
Cyclamen species Hardy Cyclamen	5-10 A,B,C, F,G,H,I	Light to half.	To 10 in.	Small clumplike habit. Leaves to 3 in. wide, round to heart-shaped, variegated with silver, light and dark green. Flowers 1-2 in., nodding, petals reflexed. Succulent stems carry flowers above foliage. Colors range from white through pink to purple. Some varieties are fragrant. Blooms in spring and fall.	Space 3 to 6 in. apart. Use for borders, rock gardens, containers. Many species available.
Fritillaria imperialis Crown Imperial Fritillaria	5-8 A,B,F, G,H,I	Light.	2-4 ft.	Unusual foliage arranged in a pineapplelike tuft. Clusters of orange, red, or yellow nodding flowers on tall stalks in late spring.	*F. meleagris*, bears a purple checked flower in spring.
Lilium species Lilies	4-10 All regions.	Light to half.	1-7 ft.	Erect stalks lined with thin green leaves. Trumpet-shaped flowers in a variety of colors; some fragrant. Blooms in summer.	The classic summer-blooming bulb. Many species and hybrids available. Grows best in moist soil.
Lycoris squamigera Magic Lily	6-10 All regions.	Light.	15-24 in.	Thin, strapped-shaped leaves. Spidery clusters of fragrant rose-pink flowers borne atop tall stalks in fall.	Best in well-drained soil that dries out in summer.
Nerine bowdenii Nerine	8-10 A,B,C, I,J	Light.	15-20 in.	Straplike foliage appears with or after flowers. Clusters of star-shaped, pink to magenta flowers on tall stalks in late summer.	Best in dry, sandy soil. Good in containers.
Ornithogalum umbellatum Star of Bethlehem	5-10 A,B,C, D,E,G, H,I,J	Light.	12 in.	Grasslike foliage. Clusters of white, star-shaped flowers borne on tall stalks in late spring.	Spreads rapidly. May be weedy in neat gardens.

Columbine (*Aquilegia* species), a charming and widely adapted wildflower, blooms in late spring and early summer.

The beguiling fringed flowers of bleeding heart (*Dicentra eximia*) lend sparkling color to shady spots all during their extended blooming season.

Wildflowers

Botanical/ Common Name	Zones and Regions	Type of Plant	Type of Shade	Height	Plant Description	Comments
Aconitum carmichaelii Monkshood	4-9 A,B,F, G,H,I	Perennial.	Light to half.	3-4 ft.	Leaves dense, 2-6 in. long, leathery, deeply lobed, coarsely toothed near leaf tips, dark green. Spikes of helmet-shaped, bluish-purple flowers. Blooms late summer to fall.	All plant parts poisonous if eaten. Space 12 to 16 in. apart. Difficult to transplant. Use under trees, bordering shade garden, near water.
Aquilegia species Columbine	3-9 A,B,C, D,E,F, G,H,I	Perennial.	Light.	8 to 48 in.	Delicately lobed soft green leaves on a clumping plant. Stunning shooting-starlike flowers with back-sweeping, spurred petals bloom in late spring and early summer. Available in a rainbow of single and bicolored shades.	Many species available native to different parts of America. Choose local kinds. Sow seed in fall or use transplants in spring.
Cornus canadensis Bunchberry	2-7 A,B, F,G,H	Perennial.	Light to full.	6 to 10 in.	Whorls of bright green leaves on erect branches originate from vigorously spreading underground stems. White flowers with 4 to 6 petals appear in late spring followed by bright red berries.	Useful woodland ground cover in moist acid soils. Spreads rapidly.
Dicentra species Bleeding Heart	4-8 A,B,F, G,H,I	Perennials.	Light to half.	12 to 60 in.	Mounding habit. Soft green to grayish-green finely cut leaves. Pink to rose, yellow or white flowers on arching stems in spring and summer.	Several native species from different parts of the country. Try the rose-flowered fringed bleeding heart *(D. eximia)* in the East; Golden teardrops *(D. chrysantha)* or Western bleeding heart *(D. formosa)* in the West.
Erythronium dens-canis Dog-Tooth Violet	3-9 G,H,I		Light to half.	6 in.	Straplike leaves with reddish-brown mottling. Gracefully nodding, rose or purple, lily-like flower in spring.	Best in cool, moist soil. Other species sometimes available.

Wild sweet William (*Phlox divaricata*) spreads by underground shoots to form tidy mounds. Its copious blossoms are colorful and softly scented.

Sweet violets (*Viola odorata*) form a lush carpet of colorful blooms in spring, and seem most at home in the light shade of a natural woodland setting.

Botanical/ Common Name	Zones and Regions	Type of Plant	Type of Shade	Height	Plant Description	Comments
Mertensia virginica Virginia Bluebells	4-8 A,B,F, G,H,I	Perennial.	Light to full.	1 to 2 ft.	Upright habit. Leaves along stems to 7 in. long, lance-shaped with rounded ends. Nodding, 1-in.-long, trumpet-shaped flowers in clusters at ends of stems open pink maturing to light blue. Blooms in spring.	Space 8 to 12 in. apart. Plants die back by midsummer. Use interplanted with ferns. Requires moist soil.
Phlox divaricata Blue Phlox, Wild Sweet William	3-9 A,B,F, G,H,I,J	Perennial. May be evergreen.	Light.	12 to 18 in.	Oval leaves arising from spreading underground shoots. Loose clusters of violet-blue, pink, lavender or white flowers blanket plants in midspring. Lightly scented.	Beautiful ground cover. Plant from root cuttings in moist acid soil.
Polygonatum odoratum Solomon's-Seal	4-8 A,B,F, G,H,I	Perennial.	Light to full.	1-1/2 ft.	Erect, arching stems display 4-in.-long leaves alternately. One-in.-long, tubular flowers in pairs hang beneath leaf axils along stem; fragrant, greenish-white, in spring.	Space 12 to 18 in. apart. Spreads from creeping under-ground stems. *P.o.* 'Varie-gatum': leaves with white edges. Use with hosta, ferns for low-growing shade garden focal points. Best in cool-summer climates.
Sanguinaria canadensis Bloodroot	4-7 A,F, G,H,I	Perennial.	Light to full.	6 to 8 in.	Deeply lobed grayish-green leaves arising from spreading underground stems which exude a red juice when cut. White to pinkish flowers borne atop short stalks in spring.	Grows best in moist, acid soils. Propagate from seed or division.
Trillium species Wake Robin	4-8 A,B,F, G,H,I	Perennial.	Full.	6 to 18 in.	Fleshy underground stems produce a whorl of 3 oval leaves. White to greenish white, yellow or pinkish flowers in spring followed by often colorful berries. Some flowers fragrant.	Many species native to several areas of North America. Look for locally adapted types. Most grow best in moist acid soil. Grow from seeds or root cuttings.
Viola odorata Sweet Violet	6-10 All regions.	Perennial.	Light to half.	8 in.	Broadly clumping habit. Leaves 2-8 in. long, heart-shaped with toothed margins. Flowers 1 in. across, bright to deep blue, fragrant. Blooms in spring.	Spreads by rooting runners. Use for borders, edging, rock gardens, woodlands, beneath high-shade shrubs.

Also see *Primula* in the annual chart, page 32, and *Campanula* in the perennial chart, page 36 and the ground cover chart on page 54.

Ferns

Botanical/ Common Name	Zones and Regions	Evergreen/ Deciduous	Type of Shade	Size and Form	Plant Description	Comments/Uses
Adiantum pedatum Maidenhair Fern	3-8 A,B,F, G,H,I	Deciduous.	Light to half.	10 to 20 in., creeping.	Fronds finely divided. Black, wiry stems fork at ends, making graceful arching U-shape. Leaflets fan-shaped, notched, bluish-green.	One of many maidenhair ferns. Beautiful, lacy effect. Use in rock gardens, borders, wild-flower garden.
Asplenium bulbiferum Mother Fern	9-10 B,C,J	Evergreen.	Light to full.	1 to 3 ft, rounded.	Fronds to 3 ft, arching, finely divided, light green.	Usually grown as houseplant. Plantlets grow on upper sur-face of fronds, can be removed and planted. Exotic looking.
A. nidus Bird's-Nest Fern	10 C,J	Evergreen.	Light to full.	1 to 4 ft.	Fronds to 4 ft long, undivided, stiff, upright, soft green, often with wavy edges.	Usually grown as houseplant. Fronds combine in a pattern to look somewhat like bird's nest. Fronds turn brown if handled.
A. trichomanes Maidenhair Spleenwort	3-8 A,B,C, D,E,F, G,H,I	Evergreen.	Light to full.	1 ft, upright.	Fronds once-divided, to 8 in. long, 3/4 in. wide. Leaflets round, 1/3 in., sometimes toothed. Stems black.	Withstands dryness for short periods. Unusually hardy. Often used in crevices of rock walls.
Athyrium filix-femina Lady Fern	3-8 A,B,C,D, E,F,G,H	Deciduous.	Light to half.	To 3 ft, creeping.	Fronds finely divided, upright, light green. Leaflets toothed.	Many cultivars available. Hardy. Can take full sun. Spreads by underground stems. Use for filling gaps between woodland plants.
Cibotium glaucum Hawaiian Tree Fern, Hapu	10 B,C,J	Evergreen.	Light to half.	15-ft tree fern.	Trunk covered with lustrous, yellowish-brown, matted hairs. Fronds long, finely divided, arching, smooth with no hairs, gray-green beneath.	Can be propagated by sec-tions of trunk placed upright in moist medium until roots sprout. Majestic-looking accent plant for landscapes.
Cystopteris bulbifera Berry Bladder Fern	4-9 A,B,F, G,H,I	Deciduous.	Light to full.	1 to 3 ft.	Long fronds taper daintily, their undersides covered with bulblets which form new plants if planted during summer. Foliage is deep green.	Will grow in boggy and lime-stone soils. In natural habitat, grows in boggy soil along streams and in moist lime-stone cliffs.
Cyrtomium falcatum Holly Fern	8-10 B,C,I,J	Evergreen.	Light to full.	To 3 ft, upright, rounded.	Fronds to 3 ft long, with coarse hairs along stem. Once-divided. Leaflets to 5 in. long, holly-like, dark green and glossy.	Tolerates sun if kept moist. Use where bold, not lacy, effect is desired.
Davallia trichomanoides Squirrel's-Foot Fern	10 B,C,J	Evergreen to semi-deciduous.	Light to half.	1 ft, creeping.	Rhizomes covered with white to tan-brown hairs, hence the name. Fronds finely divided to 12 in. long, half as wide.	Epiphyte, usually grown in hanging baskets or as ground cover in Southern California.
Dicksonia antarctica Tasmanian Tree Fern, New Zealand Tree Fern	8-10 B,C,I,J	Evergreen.	Light to half.	To 30 ft, tree fern.	Trunk brown, covered with hairs. Fronds to 6 ft, finely divided, deep green.	Hardiest of tree ferns. In coastal areas can take full sun if kept moist. Protect from wind. Can be grown in tubs.
Dryopteris austriaca spinulosa Spinulose Wood Fern, Toothed Wood Fern	5-10 All regions.	Evergreen to semi-deciduous.	Light to full.	To 3 ft.	Fronds to 2 ft long, finely divided. Leaflets spiny-toothed.	Used by florists for cut-flower arrangements.
D. erythrosora Japanese Shield Fern, Wood Fern	5-10 All regions.	Evergreen.	Light to full.	To 3 ft, erect, spread-ing.	Fronds to 2 ft long, finely divided, reddish when unfurl-ing, later turning deep green. Leaflets toothed.	Drought tolerant, hardy. Use as accent plant in landscape.
Humata tyermannii Bear's-Foot Fern	10 B,C,J	Deciduous.	Light to full.	To 1 ft, creeping.	Rhizomes covered with white, shiny, scale-like hairs, hence its name. Fronds to 12 in. long, finely divided, growing from rhizome.	Usually grown as houseplant, in hanging baskets. Brownish rhizomes indicate over-watering.
Matteuccia struthiopteris Ostrich Fern	3-8 A,B,F, G,H,I	Evergreen.	Light to full.	To 5 ft, upright, vase shaped.	Fronds plumelike, to 5 ft long, once-divided, dark green with toothed leaflets.	Because of size, recom-mended for outdoors only. Hardy native. Use for back-ground or specimen against fence, wall.
Microlepia strigosa Lace Fern	9-10 B,C,J	Evergreen.	Light to half.	To 3 ft, mound-ing.	Rhizomes clumplike. Fronds to 3 ft long, 1 ft wide, finely divided, light green.	Divide rhizomes at end of growing season. Can be grown in containers.
Nephrolepis exaltata Sword Fern	10 C,J	Evergreen.	Light to full.	To 5 ft, erect.	Fronds to 5 ft long, 6 in. wide, once-divided, bright green. Leaflets sometimes toothed.	Many cultivars available. Effective in pots raised on plantstands for arching fronds to be appreciated. *N. exaltata* 'Bostoniensis' (Boston Fern): wider, more arching fronds.

Maidenhair fern (*Adiantum pedatum*) lends itself well to many different uses in a variety of situations and thrives in varying degrees of shade.

Sword fern (*Nephrolepis exaltata*) is widely grown in shade gardens in regions where the climate is mild year round.

Botanical/ Common Name	Zones and Regions	Evergreen/ Deciduous	Type of Shade	Size and Form	Plant Description	Comments/Uses
Osmunda cinnamomea Cinnamon Fern, Fiddleheads	3-8 A,B,F, G,H,I	Deciduous.	Light to full.	To 5 ft, vase shaped.	Two types of fronds: sterile—to 5 ft long, twice-divided, green. Fertile—arise from center of plant, leaflets compact near stem, turning brown.	Fertile fronds turn brown and wither early. Can take sun if kept moist. Young, expanding fronds edible, arising very early in spring. Use for background.
O. regalis Royal Fern, Flowering Fern	3-10 All regions.	Deciduous.	Light to full.	To 6 ft, spreading, vase shaped.	Fronds to 6 ft, twice-divided, toothed leaflets, expanding in shades of pink to yellow to red, maturing to green. Fertile leaflets brown, in clusters at end of frond.	One of the largest native ferns. Can take full sun. Use in background of shade garden. Best in cool-summer areas.
Platycerium bifurcatum Staghorn Fern	7-10 B,C,I,J	Evergreen.	Light to half.	To 3 ft.	Two kinds of fronds: sterile—flat, overlapping, clinging tenaciously to support; fertile—growing from center of sterile fronds, to 3 ft long, leathery gray-green, forked at ends, resembling antler.	Epiphyte—usually grown on pieces of wood hung vertically to allow fronds to arch gracefully. Striking decoration for lanai, patio.
Polypodium vulgare European Polypody, Common Polypody, Wall Fern	3-8 A,B,C, D,E,F, G,H,I	Evergreen.	Light to full.	To 1 ft, rounded.	Rhizomes form thick mats. Fronds to 2 ft long, 4 in. wide, once-divided, deep green. Leaflets with wavy edges.	One of many polypody ferns. Rhizomes edible, sweet. Many cultivars. Use in rock gardens where rhizomes creep among rocks.
Polystichum acrostichoides Christmas Fern	3-8 A,B,E, F,G,H,I	Evergreen.	Light to full.	To 2-1/2 ft.	Fronds to 2 ft long, 5 in. wide, once-divided. Leaflets to 3 in. long with irregular bumps on upper edge, near stem.	Very popular. Used as ground cover, in woodland garden.
P. munitum Western Sword Fern, Giant Holly Fern	7-10 A,B,C, D,E,I,J	Evergreen.	Light to full.	To 3 ft, rounded.	Fronds to 3 ft long, 10 in. wide, once-divided, leathery, dark green. Leaflets with rough edges or sharp teeth.	Many landscape uses. Mature plants may become large, with over 100 fronds.
P. setiferum Hedge Fern, Soft Shield Fern	7-10 A,B,I,J	Evergreen.	Light to half.	To 2 ft, spreading.	Fronds arching, to 2 ft long, 6 in. wide, twice-divided, dark green.	Lacy effect. Mix with other shade-loving plants.
Rumohra adiantiformis Leatherleaf Fern	7-10 B,C,I,J	Evergreen.	Light to half.	To 3 ft, rounded.	Fronds 3 ft long, leathery, angular in shape, finely divided. Leaflets coarsely toothed.	Can take full sun. Fronds triangular, become stiff with age. Used by florists for arrangements.
Sphaeropteris cooperi (*Alsophila australis/ A. cooperi*) Australian Tree Fern	9-10 B,C,J	Evergreen.	Light to half.	To 20 ft, tree fern.	Fronds to 10 ft long, fan-shaped, finely divided, light green with yellowish scale-like hairs on underside.	Fast growing. Can take full sun if kept well watered. Protect from wind. Can be grown in containers. Scalelike hairs irritating to skin.
Woodwardia fimbriata Giant Chain Fern	7-10 A,B, C,I,J	Deciduous.	Light to full.	To 9 ft, creeping, upright.	Creeping rhizomes invasive, give rise to fronds up to 9 ft long, twice-divided. Leaflets deeply lobed.	Requires constant moisture. Fast growing when established. Interesting silhouette against wall.

Shrubs

Botanical/ Common Name	Zones and Regions	Evergreen/ Deciduous	Type of Shade	Size and Form	Plant Description	Comments/Uses
Abelia x grandiflora Glossy Abelia	6-10 A,B,C, D,E,G, H,I,J	Evergreen.	Half.	3 to 5 ft with equal spread. Mounding, arching branches.	Dense growth. Leaves small, glossy, opening bronzy, turning to green in summer, then reddish-brown in fall. Flowers tubular, pink to white, from summer to fall.	Use for unclipped informal hedge. 'Edward Goucher' is smaller, flowers deeper pink.
Acanthopanax sieboldianus Makino, Five-Leaved Aralia	5-10 A,B,F, G,H,I,J	Deciduous.	Light to full.	6 to 8 ft. Erect with slender, arching branches.	Spiny branches. Leaves composed of 5 leaflets. Flowers small, greenish-white, in summer.	Showy leaves make this quite useful in landscape.
Amelanchier species Serviceberry, Shadbush	4-10 A,B,F, G,H,I,J	Deciduous.	Half.	3- to 30-ft shrub or tree.	Leaves downy, clear green, turning to orange and bronze in fall. Flowers white, star-shaped bloom in early spring. Fruit dark purple or black, edible, in late spring.	Shrub or tree. Use for showy spring flower display. *A. alnifolia:* 3-20 ft, leaves 2 in. wide, serrated. *A. canadensis:* to 30 ft, berries red. *A. laevis:* to 35 ft, berries dark blue. Not for hot, dry climates.
Aronia arbutifolia Red Chokeberry	4-9 A,B,F, G,H,I,J	Deciduous.	Light to full.	6-9 ft with 3- to 5-ft spread. Open, erect habit.	Leaves to 3 in., turn rich red in fall. Small, pink-to-white flowers, in clusters bloom in spring. Fruit 1/4 in., brilliant red, in fall.	Use to brighten borders of shade gardens, woodland. Fruit holds on through fall—showy together with red leaves.
Berberis species Barberry	4-9* A,B,F, G,H,I	Deciduous or evergreen.	Light to full.	4-6 ft with equal spread. Upright. arching branches.	Spiny branches. Leaves variable in size, green turning yellow and red in fall. Flowers yellow. Blooms in spring. Berries showy in fall and winter.	Use as thorny hedge or impenetrable barrier. *B. julianae* (Zones 6-8): bluish-black berries. *B. thunbergii* (Zones 4-9): bright red berries.
Buxus species Boxwood	5-10* A,B,F, G,H,I,J	Evergreen.	Light to half.	2-20 ft with equal spread. Dense and rounded.	Dense growth. Leaves small, light green. Flowers inconspicuous.	Use for border, hedge, topiary. Protect from wind. *B. microphylla japonica* (Zones 7-10): to 5 ft unpruned, 1 ft sheared. *B. sempervirens* (Zones 5-10): to 20 ft.
Camellia species Camellia	7-10 A,B, C,I,J	Evergreen.	Light to half.	6-10 ft with equal spread. Upright.	Leaves shiny dark green. Flowers 2 to 6 in. across, red, pink, white, or any combination. Bloom season from fall through late spring.	Protect from hot sun. Full shade inhibits flowering. Use as background plant, espalier, or informal hedge. *C. japonica:* leaves large; may grow to 20 ft tall. *C. sasanqua:* leaves small; may grow to 12 ft tall.
Chaenomeles japonica Flowering Quince	5-9 A,B,D,E, F,G,H,I	Deciduous.	Light to half.	2-8 ft with equal spread. Form variable.	Thorny branches. Leaves tinged with red when young. Flowers white, pink, red, or orange. Fruit small, greenish-yellow.	Very early bloom, often in January. Use for hedge or barrier.
Chamaecyparis obtusa (dwarf forms) Dwarf Hinoki Cypress	5-9 A,B, G,H,I	Evergreen.	Half.	6 in. to 3 ft with up to 2-ft spread.	Dark green foliage is dense. Branchlets display leaves in horizontal layers.	Very slow growing, ornamental. Use for border, in rock garden.
Clethra alnifolia Summer Sweet, Sweet Pepperbush	7-10 A,B,F, G,H,I,J	Deciduous.	Light to half.	6 to 9 ft. Upright.	Dense foliage to 4 in. long, serrated. Flowers white to pink, fragrant, long lasting. Blooms in summer.	Tolerates wind, seashore conditions. Can be used as a sheared hedge.
Cornus species Dogwood	2-9* A,B,C,F, G,H,I,J	Deciduous.	Light to half.	10-20 ft. Variable spread.	Leaves to 4-5 in. long turn red in fall. Flowers surrounded by large bracts of creamy white to yellow, opening often before leaves develop. Fruit white, red, blue, or black, hanging well into winter.	*C. alba* (Zones 2-8): blood-red bark, white fruit. *C. kousa* (Zones 6-9): late blooming, red fruit. *C. mas* (Zones 4-8) scarlet-red fruit, to 3/4 in. long. *C. sanguinea* (Zones 4-7): dark red bark, black fruit. *C. stolonifera* (Zones 2-9): bright red bark in winter, white fruit.
Cotoneaster salicifolius Willow-Leafed Cotoneaster	6-10 A,B,C,E, G,H,I,J	Evergreen.	Half.	15 ft with equal spread. Arching branches.	Leaves narrow, to 3 in. long, glossy green. Flowers to 1/2 in. across, white to pinkish, early summer. Fruit round, 1/4 in., bright red.	Branches dark reddish brown, showy in fall with fruit and yellowing leaves. Use for screens or backgrounds.

Glossy abelia (*Abelia x grandiflora*)

Winter daphne (*Daphne odora*)

Wintercreeper (*Euonymus fortunei*)

Botanical/ Common Name	Zones and Regions	Evergreen/ Deciduous	Type of Shade	Size and Form	Plant Description	Comments/Uses
Cycas revoluta Sago Palm	9-10 B,C,D, I,J	Evergreen.	Light to half.	3 to 10 ft with age. Rounded.	Fernlike to palmlike. Leaves 2-3 ft long, featherlike.	Related to conifers. Very slow growing. Good for containers. Creates a tropical effect.
Daphne species Daphne	5-10* A,B,C, G,H,I,J	Evergreen or deciduous.	Light to half.*	To 4 ft, spreading wide. Form variable.	Leaves to 3 in. long, dark green. Flowers fragrant pink to purple, flowers in spring. Fruit scarlet.	Use as ground cover, in rock gardens. *D. cneorum:* (Zones 5-9) 1 ft high, spreading to 3 ft wide. *D. mezereum* (Zones 5-9): deciduous, grows to 4 ft. *D. odora* (Zones 8-10): evergreen, grows to 4 ft. Fragrance permeates garden.
Deutzia gracilis Slender Deutzia	5-8 A,B,F, G,H,I	Deciduous.	Light to full.	3 ft with 5 ft spread. Stems gracefully arching.	Leaves to 2-1/2 in. long, serrated edges. Flowers in clusters, white, in May.	Use for unclipped hedge.
Elaeagnus pungens Silverberry	7-10 A,B,C, D,H,I,J	Evergreen.	Light to half.	6-12 ft. Sprawling.	Thorny branches. Leaves to 3 in., gray-green with wavy edges. Flowers inconspicuous. Fruit oval, 1/2 in. long, red with silver bloom.	Use as clipped hedge or barrier. Variegated forms also available.
Enkianthus campanulatus Redvein Enkianthus	5-9 A,B,F, G,H,I	Deciduous.	Light.	6-20 ft, eventually half as wide. Horizontal branches.	Leaves to 3 in., dull green, with serrated edges, turns brilliant red-orange in fall. Flowers 1/2 in. long, yellow veined red. Blooms in May.	Showy clusters of bell-shaped flowers appear before leaves and good fall color make this a good choice for background plant.
Euonymus species Euonymus	3-9* All regions.	Evergreen or deciduous.	Light to half.	6-20 ft, variable spread. Compact, rounded.	Leaves to 3 in. long, deciduous types turn red in fall. Flowers inconspicuous, followed by pink, orange, or red fruit.	*E. alatus* (Zones 3-9): deciduous, to 10 ft high, equal width. Fruit red-orange. Use for hedge or screen. *E. europaea* (Zones 4-9): deciduous, to 20 ft high. Fruit pinkish, splitting open. Use singly for unusual effect. *E. japonicus* (Zones 7-9): evergreen, to 10 ft with 6-ft spread. Use as hedge or screen. *E. kiautschovica* (Zones 6-9): evergreen to 8 ft. Fruit pink, seeds red. Good formal hedge, screen, or espalier.
Fothergilla species Fothergilla	5-9 A,B,F, G,H,I	Deciduous.	Light to half.	3 to 9 ft. Form variable.	Leaves round to oval, 4 in. long. Yellow to scarlet fall color. Flowers to 2 in. across, brush-like, fragrant, white. Blooms in spring.	Use displayed in front of evergreens. *F. gardenii:* to 3 ft, flowers in spring before leaves open. *F. major:* to 9 ft, flowers in spring with opening leaves.

*Varies by species.

Shrubs (continued)

Botanical/ Common Name	Zones and Regions	Evergreen/ Deciduous	Type of Shade	Size and Form	Plant Description	Comments/Uses
Hamamelis species Witch Hazel	4-9* A,B,F, G,H,I	Deciduous.	Light to half.	6 to 30 ft. Form variable.	Leaves round, to 5 in. long, dark green above, grayish beneath, yellow in fall. Flowers 1 in. across, golden-yellow, fragrant, late winter to early spring.	Use for background. *H. mollis* (Zones 2-8): 6-10 ft, zigzag branching, blooms December to spring. *H. x intermedia:* (Zones 6-8) 15 to 18 ft, yellow flowers January to February. Showiest of witch hazels. *H. virginiana:* (Zones 4-9) 20 to 30 ft, spreading wide. Blooms October to December with yellow fall foliage.
Hibiscus syriacus Shrub Althaea, Rose-of-Sharon	5-10 A,B,E,F, G,H,I,J	Deciduous.	Light.	8-12 ft with 6-10 ft spread. Erect, round topped.	Leaves to 3 in. long, 3 lobed, coarsely toothed. Late to leaf out in spring, one of first to drop in fall. Flowers many colors, single or double, late summer until frost.	Use for unclipped hedge, screen. Tolerates seashore conditions.
Hydrangea species Hydrangea	5-10* All regions.	Deciduous.	Light to half.	6 to 20 ft. Rounded.	Dense growth. Leaves to 8 in. long. Flowers in clusters, June until frost, usually white.	Use for background, along walkways, under trees. *H. macrophylla* (Zones 6-10): blooms blue in acid soil, pink in alkaline soil. *H. arborescens (Zones 5-9):* oval leaves. *H. quercifolia* (Zones 6-9): lobed leaves turn red in fall. *H. paniculata* (Zones 5-9): grows taller, can be trained as a tree or hedge. Blooms later.
Hypericum calycinum Aaron's Beard, Creeping St.-John's-Wort	See ground covers page 55.					
Ilex species Holly	6-10* A,B,C,F, G,H,I,J	Evergreen.	Light to full.	3 to 20 ft. Form variable.	Leaves dark green, glossy, most often with spines. Flowers inconspicuous. Berries on female plants bright red, long-lasting.	Use for clipped hedges, barriers, etc. *I. aquifolium:* (Zones 6-9) to 20 ft. *I. cornuta* 'Burfordii': (Zones 6-10) to 10 ft, nearly spineless, large berries. *I. crenata:* (Zones 6-10) to 3-4 ft, berries black.
Jasminum species Jasmine	7-10* All regions.	Evergreen to semi-deciduous.	Light to half.	3 to 10 ft. Form variable.	Leaves divided into 3-5 leaflets. Flowers yellow, 1/2 in. to 2 in. across, fragrant or not, blooming throughout the year.	Use for hedges, train on trellis. *J. floridum:* (Zones 7-10) 3-4 ft, partially deciduous. *J. mesnyi:* (Zones 9-10) 6-10 ft, arching branches.
Juniperus species Juniper	2-10 All regions.	Evergreen.	Light to half.	1 to 15 ft. Form variable.	Needlelike to scalelike foliage, gray-green, blue-green, yellow-green, or dark green.	Best in full sun but tolerates partial shade. Use for ground covers, hedges, screens, windbreaks, bonsai.
Kalmia latifolia Mountain Laurel	5-9 A,B,F, G,H,I	Evergreen.	Light to full.	5 to 10 ft. Open, rounded.	Leaves oval, dark green, glossy, to 5 in. Flowers pinkish-white to deep pink, in clusters. Blooms late spring.	Keep mulched year round. Grows well with rhododendrons. If winter-damaged, will regrow after being cut to ground.
Kerria japonica Japanese Kerria	5-9 A,B,F, G,H,I	Deciduous.	Light to full.	6 to 8 ft with equal spread.	Green stems. Leaves to 4 in. long, coarsely toothed, turn yellow in fall. Flowers roselike, bright yellow. Blooms in spring.	Prune after flowering. Variety 'Pleniflora' has double yellow flowers. Use where full shade and poor soil exist.
Leucothoe fontanesiana Drooping Leucothoe	5-8 A,B, G,H,I	Evergreen.	Light to full.	2 to 5 ft. Arching branches.	Leaves to 6 in. long, oval, open bright green to bronze, turn purple in fall. Fragrant flowers resemble lily-of-the-valley. Blooms in spring.	Can be pruned to make high ground cover on shady slopes.
Ligustrum amurense Amur Privet	4-10 All regions.	Deciduous.	Light to half.	10 to 12 ft. Open, spreading.	Leaves 2 in. long, oval, dark green. Flowers small, creamy white, in summer. Blue-black berries follow.	Use for clipped hedge or screen. *L. obtusifolium regelianum:* to 6 ft, horizontal branching. Summer flowers white; blue-black berries follow, lasting into winter. Best deciduous privet.
Lonicera species Honeysuckle	3-10* A,B,C,F, G,H,I,J	Deciduous or evergreen.	Light to half.	6-8 ft. Form variable.	Leaves 1/2 to 3 in. long. Flowers 1/2 in. across, white to pink, fragrant, spring through summer.	*L. fragrantissima:* (Zones 6-10) deciduous, red fruit. Use as clipped hedge. *L. nitida:* (Zones 8-10) evergreen, 1/2-in.-leaves, bluish-purple fruit. *L. tatarica:* (Zones 3-9) deciduous, pink flowers, red fruit. Use for screen, windbreak.

46

Dwarf Chinese holly (*Ilex cornuta* 'Rotunda') thrives in shade, adds evergreen beauty to the garden, and is easy to care for.

The leaves of heavenly bamboo (*Nandina domestica*) offer color interest, changing from pink to green, then to crimson and purple in winter.

As a screening plant for shaded gardens in mild climates, Japanese pittosporum (*Pittosporum tobira*) is unsurpassed.

Botanical/ Common Name	Zones and Regions	Evergreen/ Deciduous	Type of Shade	Size and Form	Plant Description	Comments/Uses
Magnolia virginiana Sweet Bay	6-10 A,B, H,I,J	Evergreen.	Light to half.	40 ft with 20 ft spread. Loose open habit.	Leaves to 5 in. long, grayish beneath. Flowers 3 in. across, fragrant, white, mid- to late summer. Fruit conelike, red.	Often semideciduous. Bush-like in North, more treelike in South. Use as patio tree, or single specimen.
Mahonia aquifolium Mahonia	5-9 All regions	Evergreen.	Light to half.	5 to 7 ft. Spreading.	Glossy green leaves have thorns; turn yellow and red in fall. Yellow flowers held above foliage. Blooms early spring. Berries blue-black.	Best fall color develops with some sun. Dramatic effect in landscape. Use for background, along borders.
Nandina domestica Heavenly Bamboo	6-10 A,B,C,D, E,H,I,J	Evergreen.	Light to half.	6 ft. Vertical growing.	Leaves divided into many leaflets, 1-2 in. long, opening pinkish to red, maturing to light green and turning dark red to purple in fall. Flowers small, white. Blooms in summer. Bright red berries follow.	Use for hedge, screen, containers, group plantings.
Osmanthus fragrans Sweet Olive	8-10 A,B,C,F, G,H,I,J	Evergreen.	Light to half.	To 10 ft with equal spread. Rounded.	Dense growth. Leaves oval, glossy-green, often with serrated edges, to 4 in. long. Flowers inconspicuous, white, very fragrant. Blooms spring through summer.	Can be sheared. Use for hedge, screen, in containers, or prune to small tree.
Philadelphus coronarius Mock Orange	5-8 A,B,D.	Deciduous.	Light to full.	10 to 12 ft with equal width.	Leaves oval, to 3 in. long. Flowers in clusters, 1-1/2 in. across, fragrant, white, in June.	Use for hedge, screen, or wherever fragrance is appreciated. 'Aureus': smaller, with golden leaves. Best in cool-summer climates.
Pieris species Andromeda	5-9 A,B,F, G,H,I	Evergreen.	Light to half.	3 to 10 ft. Rounded.	Leaves narrow, to 3 in. long. Flowers in clusters, white to pink.	Good companion plant for rhododendrons and azaleas. *P. floribunda:* new growth light green. Flowers white, fragrant, in spring. *P. japonica:* new growth bronzy-red. Flowers pinkish in pendulous clusters, early spring.
Pittosporum tobira Japanese Pittosporum	8-10 A,B,C, D,E,I,J	Evergreen.	Light to half.	6 to 12 ft. Broad, loose.	Leaves rounded at ends, to 4 in. long, leathery, shiny, dark green or variegated. Flowers in clusters, fragrant, creamy yellow. Blooms in early spring. Fruit round, green to brown.	Use for screens, border plantings, small tree, or in containers.

*Varies by species.

Botanical/ Common Name	Zones and Regions	Evergreen/ Deciduous	Type of Shade	Size and Form	Plant Description	Comments/Uses
Pyracantha coccinea 'Lalandei' **Laland Firethorn**	5-9 All regions.	Evergreen.	Light to half.	10-20 ft. Irregular form.	Thorny branches. Leaves rounded, glossy-green, to 2 in. long, 3/4 in. wide. Small, white, fragrant, flowers in clusters. Blooms in spring. Berries orange, in fall and winter.	Birds attracted to berries. Use for dense hedge, impenetrable barrier, espalier. Can train against wall. Better fruit with some sun.
Rhododendron species **Azaleas and Rhododendrons**	4-10 A,B,C,F, G,H,I,J	Evergreen and deciduous.	Light to full.	2-20 ft. variable.	Great variety of size and form, from low and compact to tall and open. Plants vary in leaf shape, size, and texture. Rhododendrons are generally larger shrubs, azaleas are lower and more compact with smaller leaves. Blossoms also vary in color, season, form, and number. Rhododendrons usually produce larger but fewer flower clusters. Azaleas produce an abundance of smaller flowers.	These are the most exciting spring-flowering shrubs for shady gardens. Hundreds of species and types are available. For more information see page 49. Must have acid soil and ample moisture. Colors include many shades of white, yellow, pink, red, lavender, and purple. Some are blotched or striped. Main bloom season is early-to-midspring.
Symphoricarpos albus **Snowberry**	3-10 All regions.	Deciduous.	Half to full.	To 6 ft, with equal spread. Arching branches.	Leaves round, to 2-1/2 in. long. Flowers in clusters, small, bell shaped, in June. Berries large, white, in fall.	Forms thicket. Birds attracted to berries. Invasive roots control erosion.
Taxus species **Yew**	4-9* A,B,C, D,H,I	Evergreen.	Light to full.	2 to 12 ft. Spreading.	Leaves needlelike to 2 in. long, dark green on top, light green beneath. Berries produced on female plants, red, poisonous if eaten.	*T. baccata* 'Repandens': (Zones 6-9) to 3 ft with horizontal spreading branches. *T. canadensis*: (Zones 4-9) to 3 ft, needles light green. Best for deep shade. *T. x media* 'Hatfieldii': (Zones 5-9) to 10 ft, columnar. Needles dark green. Use for hedge.
Ternstroemia gymnanthera **Ternstroemia**	7-10 A,B,C, D,I,J	Evergreen.	Light to full.	To 4 ft. Wide-spreading.	Leaves oval, to 3 in. long, bronzy when developing, red in fall and winter—especially in some sun. Flowers small, fragrant, white, in summer. Fruit yellow to orange.	Use for informal hedge. Related to camellias.
Tsuga canadensis **Canadian Hemlock**	5-9 A,B, G,H,I	Evergreen.	Light to full.	To 50 ft. pyramidal with drooping branches.	Leaves needlelike, dark green, 1/2 in. long. Long-lasting cones 1 in. long.	Long-lived plants. Use as hedge or screen in shady areas.
Vaccinium corymbosum **Highbush Blueberry**	4-8 A,B,F, G,H,I	Deciduous.	Light to half.	6 to 12 ft, with equal spread.	Leaves to 3 in. long, bluish-green when expanding in May, turning shades of yellow, bronze through red in fall. Flowers borne in profusion with expanding leaves, white. Edible dark blue berries in summer.	Must have acid soil. Prune to shape, prevent overflowering. Use fruit fresh or for pies, jams.
Viburnum species **Viburnum**	3-9* A,B,C,F, G,H,I,J	Deciduous.	Light to full.	4 to 15 ft. Varible widths.	Leaves to 4 in. long, dark green, serrated, turn red in fall. Small, white flowers in flat or rounded clusters, 2-4 in. across. Blooms spring or early summer. Fruit color varies, showy fall through winter. Fruit attractive to birds.	*V. acerifolium*: (Zones 3-8) to 6 ft, fruit purple-black. *V. dentatum*: (Zones 3-8) grows 10-15 ft with up to 8-ft spread. Fruit blue-black. Use as screen or background. *V. plicatum tomentosum*: (Zones 4-9) to 9 ft with equal spread, horizontal branching. Bright red fruit. *V. prunifolium*: (Zones 3-9) to 10-15 ft with equal spread, horizontal branching. Fruit blue-black. Can be trained as small tree.
Viburnum species **Viburnum**	7-10* A,B,C, I,J	Evergreen.	Light to full.	3 to 10 ft. Variable widths.	Leaves to 6 in. long, glossy, dark green. White flowers in clusters to 4 in. across. Blooms in spring. Fruit color varies. Showy fall through winter.	Use for informal hedges. *V. davidii*: (Zones 7-10) to 3 ft, wide spreading. Berries light blue. *V. japonicum*: (Zones 7-10) to 8 ft. Fruit red. *V. suspensum*: (Zones 9-10) to 10 ft with equal spread. Fruit red to black.

*Varies by species.

Azaleas (*Rhododendron* sp.) with their colorful flowers mix companionably with plantain lily (*Hosta* sp.) as a shade garden border.

The brilliant burst of floral color provided by azaleas (*Rhododendron* sp.) in spring transforms a shaded garden area into a dramatic garden picture.

Azaleas

Type	Zones	Evergreen or Deciduous	Comments
Belgian Indica Hybrids	8-10 Hardy to 20°F.	Evergreen.	Developed for greenhouse forcing, these plants have lush foliage and produce copious quantities of large double and semidouble flowers. Usually under 3 feet high.
Gable Hybrids	6-8 Hardy to 0°F.	Evergreen to semi-deciduous.	Hardy version of Kurume hybrids. Compact plants with heavy bloom of single or double flowers in midspring. Range from 3 to 6 feet high.
Ghent Hybrids	5-8 Hardy to −25°F.	Deciduous.	Among the most cold hardy azaleas. Single or double flowers, some fragrant, on plants about 6 feet high.
Girard Hybrids	6-8 Hardy to −5°F.	Evergreen.	Introduced in recent decades. Developed for hardiness. Double or single flowers on plants from 3 to 5 feet high.
Glenn Dale Hybrids	7-8 Hardy to 5°F.	Evergreen.	Bred primarily for hardiness. Includes a great number of varieties with differing plant sizes and flower types.
Kaempferi Hybrids	6-8 Hardy to −10°F.	Evergreen.	Vigorous upright or spreading plants reaching upwards of 6 to 8 feet high.
Knap Hill/Exbury Hybrids	5-8 Hardy to −20°F.	Deciduous.	Produce brilliantly colored, large blossoms in huge clusters. Some are fragrant. Beautiful fall color. Plants usually reach 5 to 6 feet high.
Kurume Hybrids	7-10 Hardy to 5°F.	Evergreen.	Compact plants with dense, small leaves and masses of small flowers. Branches often layered in tiers. Generally between 3 and 5 feet high.
Mollis Hybrids	5-8 Hardy to −20°F.	Deciduous.	Clusters of red, orange, or yellow flowers on 4- to 6-foot high plants. Good heat tolerance.
Rutherfordiana Hybrids	8-10 Hardy to 20°F.	Evergreen.	Originally developed for greenhouse forcing. Attractive, small bushy plants with handsome foliage and abundant single, semidouble, or double blossoms. Usually 3 to 4 feet high.
Satsuki/Macrantha Hybrids	7-10 Hardy to 5°F.	Evergreen.	Late blooming, small plants which can tolerate full sun. Large, single flowers often frilly. Seldom grow over 3 feet high.
Southern Indica Hybrids	8-10 Hardy to 20°F.	Evergreen.	Tough, outdoor, taller versions of the Belgian Indicas. Produce small to medium-sized single blossoms in midspring. Plants grow between 3 and 6 feet high and are upright or spreading. Can take full sun.

Five-leaf akebia (*Akebia quinata*) is a widely adapted vine that makes a fine shade garden ground cover when not trained to a trellis.

American bittersweet (*Celastrus scandens*) spreads quickly in a shade garden, has amber-colored autumn foliage and bright berries that are attractive after leaves fall.

Jackman clematis (*Clematis x jackmanii*) produces copious quantities of velvety-purple blooms over a long season from summer into fall.

Vines

Botanical/ Common Name	Zones and Regions	Evergreen/ Deciduous	Type of Shade	Size	Plant Description	Comments/Uses
Akebia quinata Five-Leaf Akebia	4-10 All regions.	Semidecid-uous to evergreen.	Light to half.	20 to 30 ft.	Leaves divided into 5 leaflets, 3 to 5 in. long. Dull-purple flowers in clusters, 1/2 to 1 in. across. Fruit to 4 in. long, fleshy, purple, edible.	Regrows quickly when cut to ground. Requires support or trellis to twine on.
Ampelopsis brevipedunculata Blueberry Climber	4-10 All regions.	Deciduous.	Light to half.	To 20 ft.	Leaves to 5 in. wide, 3-lobed, coarsely toothed, dark green. Flowers insignificant. Fruit berrylike, in clusters, 1/4 in. across, changing from yellow to bright blue, in fall.	Climbs by tendrils. Use against walls, provide strong support.
Aristolochia durior Dutchman's-Pipe	4-10 All regions.	Deciduous.	Light to full.	To 20 ft.	Leaves to 12 in. long, kidney-shaped, dark green. Flowers 2 to 4 in. long, shaped like a pipe, greenish-brown to purple. Blooms in summer.	Flowers hidden by large leaves. Use for covering porch or trellis, or as a screen. Often grown as an annual in mild climates.
Celastrus scandens American Bittersweet	3-9 A,B,F, G,H,I	Deciduous.	Light to half.	10 to 20 ft.	Leaves to 4 in. long, oval, light green, turning bright yellow in fall. Flowers small, greenish-white, in late spring. Yellow-and-red berries showy in fall and winter.	Climbs by twining. Invasive. Prune in early spring before leaves emerge. Use for covering trellis, fence, or arbor.
Clematis armandii Evergreen Clematis, Armand Clematis	8-10 A,B,C, D,I,J	Evergreen.	Light to half.	15 to 20 ft.	Leaves 4 to 6 in. long, divided into 3 leaflets. Flowers 1 to 2-1/2 in. across, fragrant, white, in early spring. Seedpods long, plump, in early summer.	Mulch and shade roots to keep them cool. Blooms on old wood. Prune after flowering. Use for background or accent. 'Apple Blossom' has light-pink flowers.
C. x jackmanii Jackman Clematis	5-10 A,B,C, D,F,G, H,I,J	Evergreen or deciduous.	Light to half.	12 to 15 ft.	Leaves similar to *C. armandii*. Flowers abundant, 4 to 6 in. across, flat, deep velvety-purple. Blooms from summer to fall.	Mulch and shade roots to keep them cool, moist. Blooms on new wood. Prune back to 2 ft in early spring before new growth begins. Requires support or framework. Use on arbors and trellises.
C. texensis Scarlet Clematis	4-10 All regions.	Deciduous.	Light to half.	6 to 10 ft.	Leaves divided into 3 to 8 leaflets, each 1 to 3 in. long. Flowers bell-shaped, 1 in. across, scarlet. Blooms from summer to frost. Seedpods silvery, feathery at tips, follow blossoms.	Protect from wind. Can tolerate dry periods briefly. Blooms on new wood. Prune in early spring before new growth begins. Forms a lush mass suitable for low fences.

Botanical/ Common Name	Zones and Regions	Evergreen/ Deciduous	Type of Shade	Size	Plant Description	Comments/Uses
Distictis buccinatoria **Blood-Red Trumpet Vine**	9-10 B,C,J	Evergreen.	Light to half.	20 to 30 ft.	Oval leaves 2 in. long. Flowers in clusters, held out from the foliage, 4 in. long, trumpet-shaped, crimson with a yellow throat. Blooms from late spring through fall.	Climbs by tendrils. Provide strong support. Use for covering fence or arbor. Prune after flowering. Tends to become top-heavy.
D. laxiflora **Vanilla Trumpet Vine**	9-10 B,C,J	Evergreen.	Light to half.		Leaves divided into 2 to 3 oblong leaflets, each 2-1/2 in. long. Trumpet-shaped, 3-in.-long flowers have the fragrance of vanilla and open purple, fading to orchid and white before dropping. Blooms in warm season.	Climbs by tendrils. Can bloom up to 8 months of the year in some areas. Use as a light screen for fences, against walls, or for arbors; excellent for patios where fragrance can be enjoyed.
Euonymus fortunei **Wintercreeper, Evergreen Bittersweet**	4-8 A,B,D, E,G,H,I	Evergreen.	Light to full.	To 20 ft.	Leaves 1 to 2 in. across, rounded to oval with scalloped margins, forming neat, glossy green carpet over branches. Mature plant has larger leaves, flowers are inconspicuous, followed by scarlet fruit.	Vines do not need support, cling by root-like holdfasts. Use for coverings walls, fences and bare ground. Many varieties available.
Hedera helix **English Ivy**	See ground covers, page 55, and variety chart on page 53.					
Hydrangea anomala petiolaris **Climbing Hydrangea**	5-9 All regions.	Deciduous.	Light to half.	To over 50 ft.	Leaves to 5 in. long, heart-shaped, fine-toothed, bright green when appearing in spring. Flowers in clusters 6 to 8 in. across, on stems 1 to 3 ft long, white, in early spring.	Climbs by aerial rootlets, clinging to almost any surface. Use for covering large surfaces such as masonry walls, tall chimneys, large trees. Support vine or it may become a rambling, creeping shrub.
Jasminum nitidum **Angel-Wing Jasmine**	10 B,C,D,J	Evergreen.	Light to half.	10 to 20 ft.	Leaves to 3 in. long, oval, leathery-textured, glossy. Flowers 1 to 1-1/2 in. across, shaped like pinwheels, white above, purplish underneath, fragrant, in clusters of 3. Blooms from spring through summer.	Requires support. Use as backdrop for perennial bed. Tie to an arbor or trellis, or use in containers. Prune in spring before growth begins, or after flowering in fall.
J. officinale **Common White Jasmine, Poet's Jasmine**	7-10 B,C,D,I,J	Semideciduous to evergreen.	Light to half.	To 30 ft.	Leaves divided into 5 to 7 leaflets, each to 2 in. long. Flowers in clusters, star-shaped, 1 in. across, very fragrant, white, bloom all summer.	Climbs by twining. Use to cover arbor or trellis. 'Aureo-variegatum' has leaves variegated yellow.
J. polyanthum **Chinese Jasmine, Pink Jasmine**	8-10 B,C, D,F,J	Evergreen.	Light to half.	To 20 ft.	Leaves divided into 5 to 7 lance-shaped leaflets, each to 3 in. long. Flowers small, starlike, white with rose-pink on the outside, in dense clusters on side branches.	Use for covering large fence or trellis, as ground cover, or in containers.
Lonicera hildebrandiana **Giant Burmese Honeysuckle**	9-10 B,C,J	Evergreen.	Light to half.	40 to 80 ft.	Leaves 4 to 6 in. long, oval, dark green. Flowers tubular, 7 in. long, fragrant, creamy white to golden yellow, in summer. Fruit small, berry-like, dark green, following blooming season.	Requires space, sturdy support. Use for espalier against fence, along tops of walls, or as ground cover on slopes. Prune after flowering.
L. japonica **Japanese Honeysuckle**	4-10 All regions.	Semideciduous to evergreen.	Light to half.	15 to 30 ft.	Leaves 3 in. long, oval, dark green. Flowers in pairs, 1-1/2 in. long, fragrant, purple in bud opening to white, aging to yellow. Blooms in summer.	Clings by twining; requires support. Use for fragrant screen, or unsupported to control erosion on steep slopes. 'Halliana': white flowers, leaves green, vigorous. 'Gold-Net' Honeysuckle: yellow-variegated leaves.
L. sempervirens **Trumpet Honeysuckle**	4-10 All regions.	Semideciduous to evergreen.	Light to half.	To 40 ft.	Leaves to 3 in. long, oval, blue-green beneath. Flowers tubular, 2 in. long, not fragrant, coral to red. Blooms throughout summer. Scarlet fruit in fall.	Climbs by twining. Use on fence or trellis for screen. Requires support, if unsupported, becomes shrubby ground cover.

Low-maintenance vines that thrive in the shade, jasmines (*Jasminum* sp.) are easy to train and bear fragrant white star-shaped flowers in summer.

A twining vine that is excellent for shade garden use, Japanese honeysuckle (*Lonicera japonica*) bears masses of fragrant blossoms in summer.

The most popular wisteria in American gardens, Chinese wisteria (*Wisteria sinensis*) is delicate in appearance, but requires a strong support.

Vines (continued)

Botanical/ Common Name	Zones and Regions	Evergreen/ Deciduous	Type of Shade	Size	Plant Description	Comments/Uses
Parthenocissus quinquefolia Virginia Creeper	4-10 All regions.	Deciduous.	Light to full.	To 75 ft or more.	Leaves divided into 5 leaflets, each 2 to 6 in. long with coarsely toothed margins, tinged purple when opening in spring, maturing to dark green, then turning brilliant scarlet in fall. Flowers insignificant. Fruit berrylike, bluish-black, long lasting.	Clings by adhesive disc-tipped tendrils that require rough surface. Use for covering trellis, fences, or sides of buildings. Also good ground cover for steep slopes; branches form roots.
P. tricuspidata Boston Ivy	4-10 All regions.	Deciduous.	Light to full.	To 60 ft.	Leaves 3-lobed, to 8 in. across, opening purplish, maturing to dark green, then turning fiery scarlet and yellow in fall. Flowers insignificant. Fruit berrylike, dark blue, long lasting.	More tenacious than *P. quinquefolia,* clings to almost anything. Use for covering large areas of wall, along fences or as ground cover. Tolerates dust and exhaust fumes.
Polygonum aubertii Silver Lace Vine, China Fleece Vine	5-10 All regions.	Deciduous or evergreen.	Light to half.	15 to 30 ft.	Leaves arrow-shaped, to 2 in. long, glossy with wavy margins. Flowers in dense, upright clusters, greenish-white. Blooms from late summer to fall.	Climbs by twining. Use for fence cover, patio cover, or to cascade over tops of walls. Somewhat drought tolerant.
Trachelospermum jasminoides Star Jasmine, Confederate Jasmine	8-10 B,C,D, E,I,J	Evergreen.	Light to half.	To 20 ft.	Leaves 3 in. long, oval, glossy, dark green. Flowers 1 in. across, star-shaped with twisted petals, fragrant, white, from spring through summer.	Climbs by twining. Use for covering arbors, fences, or as a screen for small gardens. Drape over walls or planters for cascading effect.
Wisteria sinensis Chinese Wisteria	5-9 All regions.	Deciduous.	Light to half.	To 25 ft.	Leaves divided into 7 to 13 leaflets, each 2 to 3 in. long. Flowers in pendulous clusters 6 to 12 in. long, slightly fragrant, blue-violet, opening simultaneously from April to May, just before leaves emerge. Seedpods velvety, 3 to 6 in., follow blossoms.	This is the most-often-seen wisteria in North American gardens. Varieties are also available with white, violet, single or double flowers. Use to twine over fence, arbor, pergola, or patio. Provide sturdy support.

English ivy (*Hedera helix*) is a hardy multipurpose evergreen vine that is unsurpassed as a lush evergreen ground cover in the shade. Enormously versatile, it can be found planted under trees, bordering a walk, or companion-planted with tender plants, such as bougainvillea (*Bougainvillea* sp.), to provide protection from frost.

Hedera helix
English Ivy

English ivy, a vining plant that is often used as a ground cover, comes in a great number of varieties that increase its usefulness in the shade garden. The varieties listed below vary in growth rate, leaf shape, and leaf color. They make excellent container subjects and their restrained growth makes them a better choice as small-scale ground covers or to create an interesting pattern on a wall or fence.

Variety Name	Description
'Aureo-variegata'	Leaves are variegated with yellow.
'Baltica'	Leaves are about half the size of the species, have whitish-green veins that pick up a purplish tinge in winter. One of the hardiest varieties.
'Bulgaria'	Cold-hardy in Zone 5 and somewhat drought-tolerant.
'California Gold'	Small light green leaves are flecked and striped yellow.
'Deltoidea'	Small medium green leaves are closely spaced and heart shaped.
'Digitata'	Leaves have 5 to 7 lobes.
'Fan'	Light green leaves with rounded lobes look like hand fans.
'Fluffy Ruffles'	Small leaves with wavy margins. Good in small spaces.
'Hahn's Self-Branching'	Small, deep green, sharply pointed leaves densely cover a compact plant. Excellent in containers or hanging baskets.
'Glacier'	Light green or gray-green, triangular leaves are edged white.
'Gold Heart'	Small green leaves with a gold or white heart in the center.
'Green Feather'	Very small, deeply cut leaves resemble a bird's foot.
'Needlepoint'	Densely branched and heavily foliaged. Dark green leaves have 3 pointed lobes.
'Sulphurea'	Slightly ruffled or curved heart-shaped leaves speckled and edged with yellow.
'238th Street'	One of the most cold hardy ivies and not subject to sunburn. Has heart-shaped leaves.

Ground Covers

Botanical/ Common Name	Zones and Regions	Evergreen/ Deciduous	Type of Shade	Size, Form and Planting Distance	Plant Description	Comments/Uses
Ajuga reptans Carpet Bugle, Bugleweed	4-10 A,B,C,F, G,H,I,J	Evergreen perennial.	Light to full.	6 in. high. Space plants 6 to 12 in. apart.	Spreads by runners to form a dense mat. Leaves 2 to 4 in. wide (larger in full shade) dark green, bronze, purplish, or variegated. Flowers blue, pink, or white on 6-in. spikes. Blooms in spring.	Can take full sun, especially varieties with bronze leaf tones. Use for large-scale plantings, under shade trees, along pathways.
Anemone x hybrida Japanese Anemone, Windflower	6-9 All regions.	Deciduous perennial.	Light to half.	1-2 ft high. Clumps spread to 3-4 ft. Space plants 3 to 4 ft apart.	Dark green lobed leaves form a clump. Flowers at tips of 2 to 4-ft stems, 1 to 3 in. across, single to double, white through pink to rose. Blooms in fall.	Swaying of flowers on stem-tips in breeze gives plant its name. Use along fences, walls, or foreground of tall shrubs.
Arctostaphylos uva-ursi Kinnikinick, Bearberry	2-8 A,B,C, F,G,H,I	Evergreen shrub.	Light to half.	To 10 in. high with 15-ft spread. Space plants 3 ft. apart.	Creeping branches root, forming thick mat. Leaves oval, 1 in. across, leathery, bright glossy green, turning reddish in cold weather. Flowers urn-shaped, 1/3 in. long, white to pink. Blooms in spring. Red fruit attracts birds.	Drought resistant. Use on steep slopes, trailing over walls, in rock gardens.
Asarum species Wild Ginger	4-10* A,B,F, G,H,I,J	Deciduous or evergreen perennial.	Light to full.	6 to 10 in. high with equal spread. Space plants 8 to 15 in apart.	Leaves heart-shaped, 2 to 7 in. across, green turning purple in cold weather, forming a mat. Flowers bell-shaped, purple-brown, hidden by leaves. Blooms in spring.	Requires moisture. Use combined with flowers or underneath evergreen shrubs. *A. canadense*: (Zones 4-10) Deciduous. Leaves soft, hairy. *A. caudatum*: (Zones 5-10) Evergreen. Leaves shiny, dark green. *A. europaeum*: (Zones 5-10) Evergreen leaves glossy 2 to 3 ft across.
Astilbe chinensis 'Pumila'	4-9 A,B,F, G,H,I	Deciduous perennial.	Light to half.	To 4 in. high. Wide-spreading. Space plants 1-1/2 ft apart.	Leaves to 4 in. long, serrated, forming a mat. Pink flowers in spikes to 15 in. high in summer.	Long-lasting flowers. Can be grown in containers. Especially beautiful near ponds or streams, wherever it makes a beautiful contrast to other plants.
Bergenia crassifolia Siberian Tea	4-10 A,B,C,F, G,H,I,J	Evergreen perennial.	Light to half.	To 1-1/2 ft high, rounded. Space plants 12 to 15 in. apart.	Leaves 8 in. across, leathery with wavy and serrated edges. Flowers in spikes held above foliage, white, pink or rose. Blooms in early spring.	Use for borders, rock gardens and among other shade-loving plants. Deciduous in coldest areas.
Campanula species Bellflower	3-8* A,B,C, F,G,H,I	Perennials.	Light to half.	To 1 ft high, rounded to spreading. Space plants 10 in. apart.	Leaves to 1 in. long, heart-shaped with serrated edges. Flowers bell-shaped to star-shaped, pale blue to white.	Use for small areas, bordering pathways, rock gardens. *C. elatines garganica*: (Zones 6-8) Flowers star-shaped, bright blue, summer through fall. *C. portenschlagiana*: (Zones 6-8) Flowers bell-shaped, bright blue, summer. *C. poscharskyana*: (Zones 3-8) Flowers star-shaped, blue, spring through summer.
Convallaria majalis Lily-of-the-Valley	3-7 A,B,F, G,H,I	Deciduous perennial.	Light to half.	To 10 in. high, slender, lily-like. Space "pips" 6 to 10 in. apart in clumps 1 to 2 ft apart.	Leaves to 8 in. high, 3 in. wide, dark green and tapering. White, bell-shaped, fragrant flowers on thin stalks to 8 in. Blooms in spring.	Plants spread by underground stems, dense, slow-spreading. All parts of plant poisonous. Not for mild-winter areas. Use under rhododendrons, azaleas, with ferns, at base of deciduous trees.
Epimedium species Barrenwort, Bishop's Hat	4-8 A,B,F, G,H,I	Evergreen to semi-deciduous. perennial.	Light to full.	To 15 in. high, spreading. Space plants 8 to 10 in. apart.	Leaves to 3 in. across, heart-shaped, leathery, dark green, turning reddish in fall. Flowers to 1 in., cup-shaped with a spur, various colors. Blooms in spring.	Use under trees in containers, or with ferns. Tolerates root competition. *E. grandiflorum*: Flowers white to rose. *E. pinnatum*: Flowers yellow with red spurs. *E. x youngianum* 'Niveum': Flowers pure white.
Euonymus fortunei Wintercreeper	4-8 A,B,D, E,G,H,I	Evergreen vine.	Light to full.	Vine to 1 ft high with 20-ft spread. Space plants 1 ft apart.	Leaves to 2 in. long, leathery with toothed edges, dark green. Flowers pink, insignificant.	Forms dense cover. Use for erosion control on steep slopes, banks. Can take full sun, desert heat.

54

In most climates, bugleweed (*Ajuga reptans*) forms a dense mat brightened by spikes of flowers in spring and early summer.

Aaron's beard (*Hypericum calycinum*) forms a low shrub brightened with yellow flowers all summer.

Ground-hugging, wide-spreading varieties of juniper (*Juniperus* sp.) make excellent ground covers for gardens in shade.

Botanical/ Common Name	Zones and Regions	Evergreen/ Deciduous	Type of Shade	Size, Form and Planting Distance	Plant Description	Comments/Uses
Galax urceolata (*G. aphylla*) Wandflower	4-8 A,B,F, G,H,I	Evergreen. Perennial.	Half to full.	To 6 in. high, rounded. Space plants 1 ft apart.	Spreads by underground stems. Leaves in rosettes, to 5 in. across, heart-shaped, green turning bronze in fall. White flowers on 2-1/2-ft spikes, spring through summer.	Use in rock gardens, under medium-sized shade-loving shrubs. Best in cool-summer climates.
Gaultheria procumbens Wintergreen, Teaberry, Checkerberry	4-8 A,B,F, G,H,I	Evergreen.	Light to half.	To 6 in. high with 18-in. spread. Space plants 1 to 2 ft apart.	Creeping stems give rise to woody branchlets with glossy oval, 2-in.-long leaves. Flowers small, white. Blooms in summer. Berries to 1/2 in. across, red, in fall.	Oil of wintergreen derived from leaves, fruit. Use under rhododendrons and azaleas, as ground cover in woodland gardens. Grows well with mosses.
Hedera helix English Ivy	5-10 All regions.	Evergreen vine.	Light to full.	Vine to over 50 ft. Planting variable depending on use: space close for small areas, 1-2 ft apart for large-scale covering.	Leaves to 5 in. across, leathery with 3-5 lobes, dark green. When mature, leaves heart-shaped. Flowers only on mature plants, yellow-green, 2 in. wide. Fruit similar to peas in shape, black.	Many different varieties; see page 54. Aerial rootlets on creeping stems attach plant securely to fences, walls, brick, etc. Controls erosion with deep roots. Many landscape uses.
Hosta species Plantain Lily	3-9 A,B,C, D,F,G, H,I,J	Deciduous perennial.	Half to full.	6-36 in. high, rounded to spreading. Space plants 1 to 2 ft apart.	Leaves 6-15 in. long, blue-green, heart-shaped with large, prominent veins. Flowers displayed on long spikes, lily-like, often fragrant, white through lavender to purple, in summer.	Many varieties. Very hardy plants, long-lived. Use for borders, under trees, in containers.
Hypericum calycinum Aaron's Beard, Creeping St.-John's-Wort	5-10 All regions.	Evergreen perennial.	Light to half.	To 12 in. high with equal spread. Space plants 12 to 18 in. apart.	Leaves to 4 in. long, color varies. Flowers to 3 in. across, petals bright yellow with tufts of gold-tipped yellow stamens in center.	Plants become invasive. Roots help control erosion on banks and hillsides. Mow in spring every couple of years to rejuvenate plantings.
Juniperus species Juniper	2-10 All regions.	Evergreen shrub.	Half.	4 in. to 3 ft high, wide spreading. Variable according to species. Generally 3 to 4 ft apart.	Leaves needlelike, green, blue, silver, or plumlike tints.	Heat and drought tolerant when established. Many varieties. Use as large-scale cover, in rock gardens, on hillsides, or cascading over walls.

*Varies by species.

Botanical/ Common Name	Zones and Regions	Evergreen/ Deciduous	Type of Shade	Size, Form and Planting Distance	Plant Description	Comments/Uses
Liriope species Lily Turf	5-10* B,C,D, G,H,I,J	Evergreen perennial	Light to half.	6 in. to 2 ft high. Grass-like clumps. Space *L. muscari:* 12-18 in. apart. *L. spicata:* 8-12 in. apart.	Leaves to 2 ft long, 1/2 in. wide. Light blue flowers on spikes 6-10 in. long. Blooms in late summer. Sparse blue-black berries follow.	Use for mass planting, edging for pathways and borders. *L. muscari:* (Zones 7-10) Leaves to 2 ft, some forms variegated. *L. spicata:* (Zones 5-10) Leaves to 10 in. long, spreads by underground stems.
Lysimachia nummularia Moneywort, Creeping Jennie	4-10 A,B,C,F, G,H,I,J	Evergreen perennial.	Light to half.	2-6 in. high with 2-ft spread. Forms dense mat. Space plants 10 to 12 in. apart.	Rooting stems. Leaves 1 in. across bright green. Flowers 3/4 in. across golden yellow. Blooms spring through summer.	Use near pools, allowing to creep over bricks and around rocks. Thrives on moisture. 'Aurea': leaves golden, takes full shade.
Mahonia repens Creeping Mahonia	4-10 All regions.	Evergreen shrub.	Light to half.	2 to 3 ft high with equal spread. Space plants 12 in. apart.	Spreads by underground runners. Leaves 2 in. long, spiny, gray-green when ex-ing in spring, bright red in fall, turning to bronzy-green through winter. Yellow flowers in 1-3 in. clusters. Blooms in spring. Blue-black berries attract birds.	Drought tolerant when estab-lished. Creeping underground runners help control erosion on banks, hillsides. Use for borders, around patio, in rock gardens.
Ophiopogon species Mondo Grass	6-10 B,C,D, G,H,I,J	Evergreen perennial.	Light to half.	8 in. to 3 ft high. Grass-like clumps Space plants 6 to 12 in. apart.	Leaves to 3 ft long, 1/2 in. wide. Flowers small, white to purple, hidden by leaves, in summer. Fruit follows, pea size, dark blue.	Use for borders, under trees, in containers. *O. jaburan:* Leaves to 3 ft, some forms variegated. *O. japonicus:* Leaves 8 in. long, dark green.
Oxalis oregana Redwood Sorrel	8-10 A,B,C, I,J	Evergreen perennial.	Light to full.	10 in. high. Spreads wide. Space plants 12 to 24 in. apart.	Spreads by underground runners. Leaves divided into 3 cloverlike leaflets, 2-4 in. across, yellow green. Flowers to 1 in. across, veined petals white to pink. Blooms in spring and sometimes fall.	Moisture-loving. Goes well with ferns, underneath rho-dodendrons, azaleas, along shady pathways.
Pachysandra terminalis Japanese Spurge, Pachysandra	4-9 A,B,C,F, G,H,I,J	Evergreen perennial.	Light to full.	6-10 in high. Spreading. Space plants 6 to 12 in. apart.	Spreads by underground runners. Leaves 2-4 in. long, oval, veined, dark green to yellow, toothed near leaf tips. Fluffy, fragrant, white flowers on spikes. Blooms in summer. Fruit small, white, in fall.	Leaves turn yellow when exposed to full sun. Most widely planted evergreen ground cover. Use for large areas under trees, as lawn substitute.
Paxistima species Cliff-Green, Mountain-Lover, Oregon Boxwood	5-9 A,B,C,F, G,H,I,J	Evergreen shrub.	Light to half.	1 to 4 ft high, compact. Space plants 12 to 14 in. apart.	Leaves to 1 in. long, serrated toward tips, becoming bronze in fall and winter. Flowers insignificant, reddish-brown. Blooms in spring.	Excellent under azaleas and rhododendrons, around bases of trees, in rock gardens. *P. canbyi:* native to East Coast, 9-12 in. high. *P. myrsinites:* native to Pacific Northwest, 1-1/2-4 ft high and easily kept low by trimming.
Sagina species Irish Moss, Scotch Moss	4-9 A,B,C, F,G,H,I	Evergreen perennial.	Light to half.	3-4 in. high, in dense tufts. Space plants 6 in. apart.	Mosslike with slender leaves. Flowers single, up to 1/4 in. across, white.	Use between paving, under ferns, on mounds, in rock gardens, or bordering ponds. Keep free of fallen leaves or rot may occur. *S. subulata* (Irish Moss): leaves dark green. *S. subulata* 'Aurea' (Scotch Moss): leaves light green.
Sarcococca hookerana humilis Sweet Box	7-10 A,B,C, H,I	Evergreen shrub.	Light to full.	To 2 ft high, with 6-ft spread. Space plants 9 to 12 in. apart.	Spreads by underground runners. Leaves to 3 in. long, narrow, pointed, glossy, dark green. Flowers small, fragrant, white, hidden by foliage. Blooms in spring. Black berries follow.	One of the best ground covers for heavy shade. Use under trees, whenever neat, clean appearance is desired.

Redwood sorrel (*Oxalis oregana*) thrives in moist spots in shady gardens. Bright white to pink flowers are borne in spring often with a second flush of blooms in fall.

Widely adapted Irish moss (*Sagina subulata*) forms a ground-hugging carpet of lush green foliage that is attractive year round in shady sites.

Periwinkle (*Vinca minor*) is a low-maintenance ground cover outstanding for carpeting large shady areas. Lavender-blue flowers appear in spring.

Botanical/ Common Name	Zones and Regions	Evergreen/ Deciduous	Type of Shade	Size, Form and Planting Distance	Plant Description	Comments/Uses
Soleirolia soleirolii Baby's-Tears	8-10 B,C,D, E,I,J	Evergreen perennial.	Light to full.	1-6 in. high spreading, forming a dense carpet. Space plants 6 to 12 in. apart.	Mosslike, creeping. Leaves tiny, round, light to golden green. Flowers insignificant.	Damaged by foot traffic, but recovers rapidly. Use under ferns, rhododendrons, camellias, other shade-loving shrubs. Requires moisture.
Taxus baccata 'Repandens' Spreading English Yew	6-9 A,B,C, G,H,I	Evergreen shrub.	Light to half.	To 2 ft high with eventual 10-ft spread. Space plants 3 to 5 ft apart, if mass effect is desired.	Horizontal branching. Leaves needlelike, shiny dark green on top, white underneath. Flowers insignificant. Berries red, produced on female plants.	Both leaves and fruit are poisonous. Can use individually rather than in mass plantings. Can be made compact by pruning. Effective cascading over a wall.
Vancouveria hexandra American Barrenwort, Vancouver Fern	6-9 A,B, G,H,I	Deciduous perennial.	Light to full.	To 1 ft high. Space plants 12 to 18 in. apart.	Spreads by underground runners. Leaves divided into 3 leaflets, each to 2 in. long, apple-green. Drooping, white, 1-1/2 in. flowers on spikes held above foliage. Blooms in spring.	Leaflets have fernlike appearance, hence common name. Use with ferns under coast redwoods, oaks. Best in cool climates.
Vinca minor Periwinkle	5-10 All regions.	Evergreen perennial.	Light to full.	To 6 in. high. spreading wide. Space plants 1 ft apart.	Creeping stems form roots. Leaves to 3/4 in. long, glossy, dark green. Flowers 1 in. across, lavender-blue. Blooms in spring.	Varieties with white flowers available also. Mow periodically to force more vigorous, attractive growth. Use for large, shady areas and under trees. More restrained than its very invasive relative *V. major*.
Viola odorata Sweet Violet	See wildflowers page 41.					

*Varies by species.

St. Augustine grass (*Stenotaphrum secundatum*) grows rapidly to form a dense mat that crowds out weeds; adapted to both dry or humid areas of the southern states.

Red fescue (*Festuca rubra*) makes a choice grass for northern gardens, where it produces a deep green, fine-textured lawn under shady conditions.

Warm-Season Lawn Grasses

Warm-season grasses and dichondra grow best in regions of the southern United States with warm summers. They are dormant in winter except in frost-free areas.

Botanical Name/Common Name	Description	Comments
Dichondra micrantha Dichondra	Not a true grass. Forms a dense, low mat of small round leaves, about a 1/2 inch in diameter.	Tolerates light to half shade. Hardy to 25°F. In the Southwest and Southern California it is an indispensable lawn plant. Give ample water.
Stenotaphrum secundatum St. Augustine Grass	Light green, rough texture. Fast growing.	Excellent for half to light shade in dry or humid southern areas. Fast, tight growth crowds out weed growth. 'Floratum' resists pests and disease but isn't hardy. 'Seville' is hardier.
Zoysia species Zoysia Grass	Forms a wiry, dark green mat.	Accepts light shade. Tolerates heat and drought, resists pests and disease.

Cool-Season Lawn Grasses

Cool-season grasses grow best in the cool months of spring and fall. Unless you live in a northern climate where summers are mild, cool-season grasses go dormant or grow slowly during summer. They can, however, be kept green by watering regularly in summer.

Botanical Name/Common Name	Description	Comments
Festuca rubra Red Fescue	Dependable, dark green and fine textured.	Accepts light to half shade. Dislikes heat and moist rich soil. Shade fescue (*F. rubra heterophylla*) is especially good.
Lolium perenne Turf-type Perennial Ryegrass	Dark green and fine textured.	Grows best in light to half shade and the cool summers and mild winters of coastal areas. Very quick to establish — can be walked on 3 weeks after planting. Sometimes used for winter over-seeding in southern areas.
Poa pratensis Kentucky Bluegrass	Lush dark green. Slightly bolder texture than ryegrass.	Prefers moist, mild summer areas but holds its own over most of the continent except the hottest southern areas. Best varieties for light shade include: 'Bensun' (A-34), 'Bristol', 'Eclipse', 'Glade', 'Nugget', and 'Touchdown'.

A ruggedly beautiful specimen tree, Japanese maple (*Acer palmatum*) brings richly colored leaves and a visually interesting form to shade garden situations.

Shadbush (*Amelanchier canadensis*) is a tree of many virtues for shady sites, offering star-shaped, early spring flowers, showy berries, and colorful fall foliage.

Understory Trees

Botanical/ Common Name	Zones and Regions	Evergreen/ Deciduous	Type of Shade	Size	Plant Description	Comments/Uses
Acer circinatum Vine Maple	6-9 A,B,G,H,I	Deciduous.	Light to full.	10 to 30 ft, depending on light, with equal spread.	Round-topped to vinelike habit. Branches often horizontal, sprawling, twisted. Leaves to 6 in. across with 7 to 11 shallow lobes. Red-tinged in spring turning to green, then yellow and orange in fall. Reddish-purple flowers in clusters, emerge before leaves appear in spring. Red-winged seed capsules are showy in fall.	Grows low, vinelike in shade, tall in sun. Can train branches to form an espalier, or place in front of dark background to display irregular structure.
A. palmatum Japanese Maple	6-8 A,B,C, F,G,H,I	Deciduous.	Light to half.	To 20 ft with equal spread.	Round-topped. Branches form close to ground. Leaves 2-4 in. long with 5-11 toothed lobes. Red-tinged, turning green, then yellow and red in fall. Some varieties have red leaves all season. Flowers insignificant.	Many varieties available. The most delicate and lacy of all maples. Protect from dry wind. Use for grove plantings, under taller trees, for entryways, near pools, as specimens.
Amelanchier canadensis Shadbush, Saskatoon, Serviceberry	4-8 A,B,F, G,H,I,J	Deciduous.	Light to half.	To 30 ft with 20-ft spread.	Round-topped, usually multi-trunked. Branches thin, graceful. Leaves round to oval, 3 in. wide, green turning to yellow, orange and red in fall. Flowers on short spikes, 1 in. across, star-shaped, in early spring before leaves expand. Fruit like miniature apples, purple-red, edible, late spring through summer.	Young leaves covered with gray down. Birds fond of berries. Effective against evergreen background when in bloom. Use under taller trees, in woodland plantings, in clumps to display bare stems.

Understory Trees (continued)

Botanical/ Common Name	Zones and Regions	Evergreen/ Deciduous	Type of Shade	Size	Plant Description	Comments/Uses
A. laevis **Shadbush, Shadblow, Allegheny Serviceberry**	4-8 A,B,F, G,H,I,J	Deciduous.	Light to half.	To 25 ft with 15- to 20-ft spread.	Spreading habit. Leaves oval, opening purplish, turning green, then yellow and red in fall. Fragrant, white flowers in drooping clusters. Blooms in early spring before leaves expand. Fruit bluish-purple, edible, late spring through summer.	Use similar to *A. canadensis*. You can make jams or preserves from fruit, if birds do not strip tree first.
Arbutus unedo **Strawberry Tree**	7-10 A,B,C, D,I,J	Evergreen.	Light to half.	10 to 35 ft with equal spread.	Rounded crown, multi-stemmed, often shrubby habit. Bark showy, red-brown, cracking. Leaves narrow, oval, 2 to 3 in. long, glossy dark green. Flowers 1/4 in. long, urn-shaped, white to pinkish, fall through winter. Fruit 3/4 in. across, yellow to red, persistant, edible but bland and mealy. Has flowers and fruits simultaneously.	Natural bonsai-like habit when mature. Fruit attracts birds. Best used where it can be looked up into.
Cercis canadensis **Eastern Redbud**	4-7 A,B,F, G,H,I	Deciduous.	Light.	25 to 40 ft with equal spread.	Rounded crown becomes flat-topped with age. Often multi-stemmed. Leaves 3 to 5 in. wide, heart-shaped, opening reddish-purple, turning dark green, then yellow in fall. Flowers in clusters along stems, pealike 1/2 in. across, pink to purplish-pink, in early spring before leaves.	Use for accent tree, or in group planting with dogwood—both bloom at same time. Dramatic as patio tree against light-colored background. Good in containers.
Chionanthus virginicus **Fringe Tree**	5-9 A,B,G, H,I,J	Deciduous.	Light to half.	To 30 ft with equal spread.	Open, spreading habit. Leaves 3 to 7 in. long. Flowers in clusters to 8 in. long, dainty with fringelike petals, fragrant, white, from late spring to early summer.	Late to leaf out in spring. Needs acid soil. Use for accent tree or in group plantings.
Cornus alternifolia **Pagoda Dogwood, Green Osier**	3-7 A,B,F,G,H	Deciduous.	Light to half.	To 20 ft with equal spread.	Upright habit. Branches in flat tiers, spreading horizontally. Leaves to 5 in. long, oval to pointed, expanding light green turning red in fall. Flowers in clusters, small, white, in spring. Fruit dark blue, follows flowers.	Leaves arranged opposite on stems, unique in the *Cornus* alliance. Use for unusual accent plant in woodland planting of shade garden. 'Argentea': leaves variegated white.
C. florida **Flowering Dogwood**	5-9 A,B,C, G,H,I,J	Deciduous.	Light to half.	20 to 40 ft with equal or slightly greater spread.	Flat-topped with horizontal spreading branches. Bark has checkered pattern. Leaves 3-6 in. long, oval, light green turning to red in fall. Flowers small, greenish-white, surrounded by large white or pink bracts 3 to 6 in. across, in spring before leaves appear.	Beautiful winter silhouette. Good as patio tree or under taller shade trees. Very showy when in bloom.
C. kousa **Japanese Dogwood**	6-9 A,B,C, G,H,I	Deciduous.	Light to half.	To 20 ft.	Vase-shaped when young, becoming rounded with age. Mottled bark. Flowers surrounded by large white bracts, pointed at ends. Later-blooming than flowering dogwood. Fruits, to 1 in. across, resemble raspberries.	Same landscape uses as flowering dogwood. 'Chinensis' (Chinese Dogwood): 10 to 12 ft tall, very large bracts, blooms for over 1 month.
C. mas **Cornelian Cherry**	4-8 A,F,G,H,I	Deciduous.	Light to full.	15 to 20 ft with equal spread.	Open, twiggy habit. Leaves 2 to 4 in. long, oval, expanding green, turning yellow to red in fall. Small yellow flowers in clusters along bare branches. Blooms very early spring. Fruit 3/4 in. across, bright scarlet, hanging like cherries, in late summer.	Fruit used in making jams and jellies. Airy habit casts light shade. Use in woodland planting in front of evergreens where bloom is best displayed. Drought tolerant.

Strawberry tree (*Arbutus unedo*) is an evergreen tree that bears tiny flowers fall into winter, bright fruit nearly year-round.

Eastern redbud (*Cercis canadensis*) can have many uses in the shade garden and is an excellent patio tree. Flowers appear before leaves emerge and foliage exhibits yellow fall color.

Japanese dogwoods (*Cornus kousa*) put on a brilliant floral show for a month in early summer.

Botanical/ Common Name	Zones and Regions	Evergreen/ Deciduous	Type of Shade	Size	Plant Description	Comments/Uses
Corynocarpus laevigata New Zealand Laurel	10 B,C,J	Evergreen.	Light to half.	20 to 30 ft with 15- to 20-ft spread.	Upright with rounded crown. Leaves to 7 in. long, oblong, leathery, glossy dark green. Flowers in small clusters, white, not showy. Fruit 1 in. across, bright orange, follows flowers, poisonous.	Slow-growing. Use for screens, hedges. Moisture-loving.
Crataegus crus-galli Cockspur Thorn	5-9 A,B,E, F,G,H,I	Deciduous.	Light.	18 to 25 ft. Wide spreading.	Flat-topped when mature. Leaves to 3 in. long, glossy dark green, turning orange-red in fall. White flowers bloom in spring. Fruit red, long lasting.	Takes well to shearing; use for hedge. Very hardy. Thorns to 3 in. long. *C. c. inermis* is thornless.
C. laevigata English Hawthorn	5-9 A,B,E, F,G,H,I	Deciduous.	Light.	18 to 25 ft with 15- to 18-ft spread.	Upright, rounded crown. Leaves variable, 2-3 in. long with 3 to 7 deep, toothed lobes. Flowers variable, single, double, white, pink, or red. Blooms in spring. Bright red fruit, summer to fall.	Use for impenetrable hedge. Not recommended for humid areas. Many varieties available.
C. phaenopyrum Washington Hawthorn	5-9 A,B,E, F,G,H,I	Deciduous.	Light.	To 30 ft with 20-ft spread.	Columnar, later developing rounded canopy. Leaves 2 to 3 in. long, glossy with 3 to 5 pointed lobes, turning scarlet to orange in fall. White flowers in clusters. Blooms in late spring. Fruit, 1/4 in. across, follows blossoms, lasting into winter.	Thorns to 3 in. long. Best hawthorn for fall color. Delicate appearance. Useful in shady lawns.
Franklinia alatamaha Franklin Tree	6-8 A,G,H,I	Deciduous.	Light.	20 to 30 ft with 10-ft spread.	Upright to pyramidal habit. Leaves 4 to 6 in. long, oval, bright green, turning orange to red in fall. Flowers camellia-like, 3 in. across, white with yellow centers. Blooms in late summer when leaves change color.	Protect from wind. Needs moist, acid soil. Often a companion for rhododendrons and azaleas. A rare and expensive tree.

American holly (*Ilex opaca*) adds evergreen beauty to shady gardens.

Japanese snowbell (*Styrax japonicus*) makes a lovely small specimen or lawn tree featuring white bell-shaped flowers in late spring; colorful foliage in fall.

Understory Trees (continued)

Botanical/ Common Name	Zones and Regions	Evergreen/ Deciduous	Type of Shade	Size	Plant Description	Comments/Uses
Ilex x altaclarensis 'Wilsonii' Wilson Holly	6-10 A,B,C, D,E,J,I	Evergreen.	Light to full.	To 40 ft with 30-ft spread.	Pyramidal habit. Leaves to 4-1/2 in. long, 3 in. wide, glossy green with spiny-toothed edges. Flowers insignificant. Berries bright red, abundant.	Can use for espalier or clipped hedge.
I. aquifolium English Holly, Christmas Holly	6-9 A,B,C, H,I,J	Evergreen.	Light to full.	To 35 ft with 20-ft spread.	Pyramidal habit. Leaves 1-1/2 to 3 in. long, deep glossy green. Berries on female plants bright red, abundant. Needs male and female plants for berries.	Traditional Christmas holly used for wreaths. Varieties available without spiny leaves, others variegated.
I. opaca American Holly	6-9 A,B,C, H,I,J	Evergreen.	Light to full.	To 50 ft with 30-ft spread.	Pyramidal habit. Leaves to 3 in. long, dull, dark green with spiny-toothed edges. Berries red or orange. Needs male and female plants for berries.	Varieties available without spiny leaves. Use for screens, tall hedges.
Magnolia virginiana Sweet Bay Magnolia	6-10 A,B, H,I,J	Semi-deciduous.	Light to half.	To 45 ft with 20-ft spread.	Usually multi-stemmed, dense. Leaves to 5 in. long, gray-green above, light beneath. Flowers 2-3 in. across, fragrant, creamy white. Blooms throughout the summer.	Use as patio tree. Prefers moist, acid soil.
Oxydendrum arboreum Sourwood, Sorrel Tree	6-9 A,B,G, H,I,J	Deciduous.	Light.	15 to 20 ft with 10- to 15-ft spread.	Narrow to pyramidal habit. Usually multi-trunked. Leaves 4 to 8 in. long, opening tinged red, turning dark green, then scarlet in fall. Flowers in drooping 10-in. clusters, bell-shaped, creamy white, in mid-summer. Ornamental brown seedpods follow blossoms.	Requires moist, acid soil. Plant with azaleas and rhodo-dendrons. Not for hot dry climates.
Styrax japonicus Japanese Snowbell	6-9 A,B,C, E,G,H,I	Deciduous.	Light to half.	To 30 ft.	Flat-topped with horizontal branching. Leaves to 3 in. long, oval, dark green, angling upwards. Flowers hang from undersides of branches, bell-shaped, white, from late spring to early summer.	Needs acid soil. Use as patio tree or in woodland plantings.
Tsuga canadensis Canadian Hemlock	5-9 A,B,G,H,I	Evergreen.	Light to half.	To over 60 ft.	Dense, broad, pyramidal habit. Branches droop horizontally. Dark green needlelike leaves with white stripes on the undersides, to 3/4 in. long, arranged in 2 rows on stems. Cones to 3/4 in. long, brown.	Use for trimmed hedges, screens or windbreaks. Needs acid soil.
T. caroliniana Carolina Hemlock	5-7 A,B,F, G,H,I	Evergreen.	Light to half.	40 to 70 ft.	More slender, less symmetrical than Canadian hemlock. Needles 3/4 in. long, grass-green, encircle stems. Cones 1 to 1-1/2 in. long.	Tolerant of air pollution. Uses same as Canadian hemlock. Needs acid soil.

Index

Page numbers in bold type indicate the main entry for a plant. Page numbers in italics refer to photographs or illustrations.

AZALEAS & RHODODENDRONS

Executive Producer: Richard M. Ray
Contributing Authors: Alvin Horton, Michael MacCaskey
Consultants: Fred Galle, Past President American Rhododendron Society, Pine Mountain, GA; Carl A. Totemeier, Jr., Old Westbury Gardens, Long Island, NY.
Photography: Michael Landis
Art Director: Richard Baker
Book Design: Judith Hemmerich
Research Editor: Randy Peterson
Copy Editors: Greg Boucher, Miriam Boucher
Production Editor: Kathleen Parker
Book Production: Lingke Moeis
Illustrations: Charles Hoeppner, Roy Jones
Typography: Linda Encinas
Additional Photography: William Aplin, Susan A. Roth
Cover Photo: Michael Landis
Acknowledgements: Ed Egan, Editor, American Rhododendron Society, Tigard, OR; Fran Egan, Secretary, American Rhododendron Society, Tigard, OR; Green Bros. Landscaping, Inc. Smyrna, GA; Dr. H.G. Hedges, Secretary-Treasurer, Canadian Rhododendron Society, Ontario, Canada; Longue Vue Gardens, New Orleans, LA; Nuccio's Nursery, Altadena, CA; Dr. Harold Pellett, University of Minnesota Landscape Arboretum, Chaska, MN; Planting Fields Arboretum, Oyster Bay, NY; Robert L. Ticknor, Past President American Rhododendron Society, Canby, OR.
Notice: This publication is designed to provide accurate and authoritative information in regard to the subject matter covered. Any recommendations or suggestions are made without guarantee. The authors and publisher disclaim all liability.

Top-Rated Azaleas and Rhododendrons

Springtime commences in this country in the Deep South and the far West about St. Valentine's Day, and slowly advances northward until by Memorial Day the entire continent appears to be in full bloom. Everywhere, flowering trees and shrubs fill the landscape with masses of welcome color, finalizing the transformation from winter into spring. Throughout most of the United States azaleas are the heralds of spring.

When azaleas are in bloom, their delicate flowers appear so profusely that they entirely blanket the plants with color, completely obscuring the foliage and branches. Their blooms come in such an array of colors and forms that it staggers the imagination. In old Southern gardens, where azaleas are synonymous with spring, enormous, spreading plants with layers of branches and masses of flowers may be as old as a hundred years. Estate and public gardens that feature these impressive plants attract visitors from around the world. The peak of their blooming season is celebrated by festivals in many of the old Southern cities, such as Charleston, South Carolina; Wilmington, North Carolina; and Savannah, Georgia.

Rhododendrons, close relatives of azaleas and generally more cold hardy, are just as awe-inspiring. Usually blooming later in spring, they are admired for their large bouquet-like clusters of flowers, called trusses, that crown the branch tips. Colorful azaleas and rhododendrons are planted to beautify

At left: Azaleas are in their glory planted in a woodland setting growing under the dappled shade of high-branched trees.

'Gibraltar' (Knap Hill/Exbury Hybrid)

'Sappho' rhododendron

'Rosebud' (Gable Hybrid)

Knap Hill/Exbury Hybrid azalea

Pontic azalea *(R. luteum)*

'Snow' (Kurume Hybrid)

Knap Hill/Exbury Hybrid azalea

home landscapes throughout most of the country and rank high as all-time garden favorites.

No other flowering shrub—not even roses—creates the seasonal splendor and year-round appeal that azaleas and rhododendrons do. There are azaleas and rhododendrons to suit every taste and almost every climate, over 10,000 named varieties. So many in fact that some avid gardeners specialize in collecting azaleas and rhododendrons. But you don't have to be a plant collector to enjoy these very special shrubs—they are easy to grow once you understand how to provide for their particular needs.

Top-Rated Azaleas and Rhododendrons is designed to help you select the azaleas and rhododendrons best-suited to your needs and to ensure your success in growing them. The 200 species and varieties described here were specially chosen as being top-rated plants. A group of experienced gardeners and professional horticulturists from throughout the United States and Canada selected these plants from the thousands that are available. Their choice was based on beauty, versatility, cold hardiness, durability, availability, and special considerations such as late season of bloom or unusual flower color.

Their rhododendron choices also take into consideration ratings made by the American Rhododendron Society, a group of azalea and rhododendron hobbiests and professionals. The society's ratings represent years of testing, often beginning well before a variety is commercially available. So it's no coincidence that top-rated azaleas and rhododendrons are the most reliable, attractive, and popular ones. But since a variety top-rated for Delaware is not necessarily top-rated for Oregon, regional recommendations are given for all selected rhododendron varieties and species; and for all major azalea hybrid groups and species.

A HISTORY ALL THEIR OWN

Azaleas and rhododendrons are native to moist woodlands and forests of North America, Europe, and Asia. Scores of rhododendron species grace the forests of the eastern Himalayas where the monsoon rains keep the soil and air moist, and the steep slopes provide for excellent drainage. Abundant also in Southeast Asia and Malaysia, rhododendrons are mostly understory trees and shrubs, enjoying the filtered sunlight that passes through the open network of overhead foliage. Several rhododendron species are native to the Appalachian Mountains.

Azaleas are found growing wild mostly in the mountain forests of Eastern Asia and North America. North America has an impressive offering of native azaleas, and many of these are graceful, colorful plants that are superb in many home landscape situations.

Compared to the rose, whose cultivation dates back to the beginning of history, azaleas and rhododendrons are recent arrivals to cultivated gardens. Though valued in the Orient for centuries, azaleas and rhododendrons were first discovered by Western gardeners in the 18th Century. At that time, avid English plant collectors explored and collected new and exotic plants from around the world.

Imported from Asia Minor, the golden-flowered and spicely-fragrant pontic azalea, *R. luteum*, was being grown in England by the time of the American Revolution. By the end of the 18th Century, many native American azaleas, including the yellow-flowered flame azalea, *R. calendulaceum*, and the pink-flowered swamp azalea, *R. viscosum*, were cultivated in Europe. Also, many new azalea species and natural hybrids had arrived from the Orient.

From the Appalachian Mountains four native American rhododendrons came to English gardens by the mid-1700's. These included the catawba rhododendron, *R. catawbiense*, with its masses of pink or lavender blossoms, and the rose-bay rhododendron, *R. maximum*, a massive plant bearing rose or purplish-pink flowers in late June.

During the 19th Century, scores of azaleas and rhododendrons arrived in Europe from Asia and America. All of these American and Asian rhododendrons and azaleas were eagerly embraced by English, Belgian, Dutch, and French horticulturists, who crossed and interbred them in attempts to create even more spectacular plants.

The heyday of plant exploration was during the mid-1800's. During that time many daring explorers and collectors ventured into China and Japan, areas where few Westerners had ever set foot. In the mid-1800's, Dr. Joseph Hooker, son of the first director of Kew Gardens in London and ultimately his successor, trekked in the Himalayas and returned to England with more than 40 new species of rhododrons. In 1843, Scottish plant collector Robert Fortune set out on a plant-hunting expedition in China. He discovered only a few azaleas and rhododendrons, but one of them, *R. fortunei*, has contributed its huge, fragrant, rosy-lilac blossoms to countless beautiful hybrid rhododendrons.

Perhaps the most famous plant explorer was Ernest H. Wilson, who, in the employ of an English nursery, made four journeys to China during the early part of this century in search of new and exotic plants. His exploits earned him the nickname of "Chinese" Wilson. From the high altitudes of southern and southwestern China, he introduced more than 400 new species of azaleas and rhododendrons. He found the elevation of 11,000 feet offered the most diversity, though he collected rhododendrons from even as high as 15,000 feet.

Explorer, plant collector, and author, Frank Kingdon-Ward, spent a half-century searching regions such as Assam, Burma, Tibet, and western China for rhododrons. George Forrest, a Scottish plant collector who made seven trips to western China, was perhaps the most daring of all the explorers, risking his life to collect plants. He explored the interiors of China and Tibet by learning local languages and employing local people as guides and bearers. Somehow, he managed to survive warfare, malaria, and other tropical ills, as well as the ordinary rigors of mountain climbing. Many of Forrest's introduced species are important parents of today's popular hybrids.

During a span of two centuries, English plant explorers introduced hundreds of Asian and American azaleas and rhododendrons—both evergreen and deciduous species— to Europe. As Japan slowly became open to Western trade, hybrids created by Japanese gardeners were offered to the Western world as well, and their traits were drawn upon in the creation of newer hybrids. A fervor of plant breeding that began in Europe in the 1700's and that is still going on today is responsible for thousands of named hybrids and varieties.

HYBRIDS TODAY

Today the thousands of named varieties of azaleas and rhododendrons in existence offer a confusing array of plants to gardeners. Azaleas especially seem a confusing lot. There are deciduous kinds and evergreen kinds, and the named varieties fall into many hybrid groups. Rhododendron hybrids are perhaps less confusing because they fall into no hybrid groups, but this lack of organization provides no guidance in selecting from the thousands of varieties.

The first azalea species available to plant breeders were deciduous kinds. They were hybridized to create new color and fragrance combinations. When evergreen azaleas from the Orient became available, these were crossed with the deciduous kinds in an attempt to increase the color range and cold hardiness of the evergreen azaleas.

Once only plants for southern American gardens, today evergreen azaleas are grown as far north as Boston, thanks to the dedication of several hybridizers. The aim in azalea breeding is toward creating ever more cold hardy evergreen azaleas that can retain their foliage in the cold northern climates. And though deciduous azaleas come in the full spectrum of colors including yellow, red, and clear orange, the evergreen azaleas offer only an assortment of shades of pink, purple, red, and white.

THE GENUS RHODODENDRON

In 1753 when the famous biologist Linnaeus published his classification of all the plants and animals in the world, he had classified azaleas and rhododendrons in two separate genera—the genus *Azalea* and the genus *Rhododendron*. At that time he had seen only a few species, and those were from the New World. Today botanists recognize that these plants, though they appear quite different at first glance, have many similarities. They now are both grouped into a single huge genus, the genus *Rhododendron*.

Botanists look at these plants and see that they have the same kind of floral structure, pollen, and seeds. They all cross freely with each other and are therefore closely related. Modern plant classification places azaleas and rhododendrons in the same genus. Some botanists divide the genus into 43 series with azaleas making up one series. Other botanists divide the genus into 8 subgenera, with deciduous azaleas making up one subgenus and evergreen azalea another subgenus.

Gardeners, however, continue to think of them as separate kinds of plants. They think of azaleas as low plants covered with masses of flowers in spring and fine-textured evergreen or deciduous leaves. To a gardener, a rhododendron is a large plant with whorls of big evergreen leaves and distinct clusters of flowers.

Because gardeners continue to think of azaleas and rhododendrons as different kinds of plants, many nurseries label azaleas with the out-of-date genus name *Azalea*. For instance, the pink-flowered royal azalea, *Rhododendron schlippenbachii,* is often labelled *Azalea schlippenbachii.*

Using Azaleas and Rhododendrons in Your Garden

There are no hard-and-fast rules when it comes to landscaping—taste is an individual matter—but most home gardeners find that following some general guidelines can help in creating an attractive, functional landscape. Success in landscaping depends upon selecting plants that serve a particular use, that are enjoyable to look at, and that can adapt to the conditions of their planting site.

Azaleas and rhododendrons are among the most beautiful and useful ornamental plants. To show them off to best advantage, it helps if you understand just what makes them so lovely and what makes them different from each other. Keeping in mind their shape, texture, and color throughout the year, you will be able to effectively situate them and combine them with other plants.

SEEING AZALEAS AND RHODODENDRONS

It goes without saying that these are spectacular plants, but just what do you *see* when you look at these shrubs? Everyone admires the beautiful splashes of color they create in spring and early summer, but if you really study them, you'll see that each azalea and rhododendron has an individual character that is best taken into account when deciding what to plant and where to plant it.

At left: 'Hinodegiri' (Kurume Hybrid) is attractive year-round, making it an excellent choice for use in shrub borders or foundation plantings.

'Nova Zembla' rhododendron

'Toucan' (Knap Hill/Exbury Hybrid)

'Herbert' (Kaempferi Hybrid)

Knap Hill/Exbury Hybrid azalea

'Gumpo White' (Satsuki/Macrantha Hybrid) is effectively backdropped by red Japanese maple *(Acer palmatum 'Dissectum')*.

Plantings of color-coordinated azaleas create dramatic visual impact.

'Purple Gem' is a dwarf rhododendron useful in small-scale gardens.

EVERGREEN AZALEAS

When in bloom, a well-grown evergreen azalea is blanketed with brightly colored blossoms and hardly a leaf is visible. Even a single large shrub creates a dramatic impact for the two weeks it's in flower. Planted en masse, azaleas are, quite simply, boisterous. Though some kinds have small, dainty flowers and others have large, showy flowers, the sheer abundance of blossoms overrides any textural impact the size of the flowers might create. A blooming azalea is anything but subtle.

Out of bloom, evergreen azaleas return to their quiet, elegant character. Their leaves are generally fine-textured, ranging in size from 1/2 to 4 inches long. The more cold hardy kinds, such as the Gable Hybrids, have the smallest leaves. Southern and Belgian Indicas offer larger, more lush-looking foliage. In fall and winter, foliage may take on beautiful glossy reddish, purplish, or bronze hues. This is especially true of the kinds with deep-colored flowers. White-flowered kinds have dark green foliage in winter.

Different varieties retain varying amounts of foliage during winter. Generally, plants near their limit of cold hardiness lose most of their inner leaves, keeping only a whorl or two of leaves near the branch tips. Azaleas that have strong evergreen characteristics make the best plants for foundation plantings and privacy hedges.

Evergreen azaleas can have a variety of shapes. Some are tall and wide, others are low and spreading. Branches may be dense and random, or arranged in distinct layers. It's best to choose a plant whose size and shape fits in with its landscape situation. Tall wide plants make better screening hedges, while low, spreading ones are better for foundation plantings.

Because evergreen azaleas are fine-textured and dense and display such a bold show of color, they are best in formal kinds of landscape situations. They make excellent foundation plants, and are perfect for shrubbery borders on the edge of a lawn, either mixed with other shrubs or planted in groups. They also make effective hedges.

Azaleas have been significant plants in Oriental gardens for centuries, pruned into elegant bonsai shapes, or pruned to accentuate their layered branches. At one time during the history of Oriental gardening, azaleas were not allowed to flower. They were kept pruned into artistic shapes and admired for their foliage and branch structure.

DECIDUOUS AZALEAS

Flowers of deciduous azaleas usually appear in large clusters at branch tips. Though flower size can be large and clusters can contain as many as 15 or more flowers, especially in the Knap Hill/Exbury Hybrids, the floral show is more subtle than with the evergreen azaleas. This is because the bold-textured flower clusters are not massed together as they are with the evergreen azaleas, and shrubs are looser and more open.

Most deciduous azaleas have tall, vase shapes made up of many upright stems. They are loose and open, giving a light airy feeling. When bare of leaves in winter, they have an especially delicate texture due to their slender, upright branches. The light touch is not lost when plants are in bloom, because flowers usually appear before the new leaves emerge, or if foliage is present, it is sparse.

Summer foliage does not obscure the branch structure and the shrubs maintain their graceful character. Leaves measure four or five inches long and are oval and pointed. They are bright green and frequently change to beautiful reds, oranges, and golds in fall before dropping, creating a second season of color.

The nature of their flowers, foliage, and branch structure gives deciduous azaleas a more informal character than evergreen azaleas. Because they are so open, they make poor foundation plants, except against rustic or modern-style houses with wood siding right down to the ground. They are best grouped in a shrubbery border, with a fence or other dense shrubs as a backdrop, or scattered in a woodland setting. They also make effective specimen plants beside a pond or in an Oriental garden.

SPECIES AZALEAS

These lovely, delicate-flowered plants have many things in common with the deciduous hybrids. They are usually airy shrubs that bloom before foliage emerges in spring. Their clusters of blossoms are frequently made up of funnel-shaped flowers whose long, curving stamens extend beyond the petals.

Most species have a graceful beauty that is best shown off in a natural woodland setting or a wildflower garden. Though their color impact in spring and fall is excellent, species azaleas do not blend well with evergreen azaleas. The explosion of color of the evergreen hybrids overpowers the exquisite grace of their wild cousins.

RHODODENDRONS

Many rhododendrons, especially old-time ones, are large plants with big, leathery leaves and balls of flowers at the branch tips. Such plants have a bold texture that commands attention. Large rhododendrons need plenty of growing room, but they also need spacious quarters so their texture doesn't become oppressive. Newer hybrids feature shrubs with more compact growth and smaller leaves, though flower cluster size usually remains the same. These plants are more suitable for small landscapes. Dwarf shrubs offer a medium texture and compact size that is useful in many gardens.

The big rhododendrons are excellent screening shrubs planted as a hedge on a large property or in the background of a shrubbery border. Their large, dense evergreen foliage blocks views and viewers year-round, and their stunning

Azaleas and rhododendrons have unlimited landscape uses in regions where their growth requirements can be met.

Pontic azalea, from Asia, *(R. luteum)* produces very fragrant yellow-orange blooms in midseason.

9

Azaleas and rhododendrons appear to best advantage in naturalized settings that echo their native growing environment, as shown above and below.

'Redwing' (Rutherfordiana Hybrid), bears masses of brilliant red flowers in midseason; has attractive foliage year-round.

clusters of speckled flowers provide dramatic displays. They also look at home planted in groups or singly under trees in woodland settings.

Though sometimes planted as foundation shrubs, large-growing rhododendrons grow too big too fast to be good along most houses. They will quickly block windows and crowd other shrubs. For foundation plantings, try compact or dwarf rhododendrons. Their coarse foliage looks best against wood shingles or stucco, and may look too busy when set off in quantity against bricks or stone.

DESIGN BASICS

The visual impact a plant makes depends upon its size and shape, the texture and color of its flowers, and the texture and color of its foliage. Plants are not static, and these attributes change throughout the growing season. For instance, deciduous azaleas have a medium texture during the summer when in full foliage, but when leafless in winter, their bare twigs are fine-textured. Skillful garden designers consider all these aspects when they select and locate shrubs.

Texture: Fine-textured plants are more restful to look at. When seen from a distance they appear smaller and farther away than they really are. When used in small or enclosed areas they make the space seem larger. Bold-textured plants have the opposite effect. When viewed from a distance they appear closer and larger than they really are. Planted in quantity in an enclosed space, they may seem too busy and overpowering.

Fine textures and bold textures can be combined to good effect, the contrasting textures creating visual excitement. Many garden designers group fine-textured plants at one end of the garden and bold-textured ones at the other end, so there is a visual progression from fine to bold textures. They also use larger groups of fine-textured plants, progressing toward smaller groups of bold-textured plants. This keeps the visual effect from becoming too busy.

If you want the area to seem larger, plant the fine-textured azaleas in the distance and the bold-textured rhododendrons nearby. Do just the reverse if you want a large area to seem more intimate.

It's usually better not to mix deciduous and evergreen shrubs in a haphazard manner. Though in the summer they may have the same texture, in winter the deciduous ones will be fine-textured and appear weak mixed in with the evergreen shrubs. Plant the deciduous ones in groups among, and in front of, evergreen kinds.

Color: Considered alone, almost any flower has a beautiful color. But that beautiful color has to look good with the rest of the colors in the landscape. When choosing azaleas and rhododendrons, you'll be choosing from a full spectrum of colors including every hue and shade imaginable. When set side-by-side, many of these otherwise attractive colors will clash. Selecting plants when they are in bloom may help you keep color mistakes to a minimum.

Some azalea fanciers plan a border of azaleas around a color scheme. The pure pinks, purples, and magenta-reds are grouped together and separated from the warmer corals, oranges, and orange-reds by groups of white azaleas, or by other kinds of shrubs that won't be in bloom at the same time.

It is also a good idea to select shrubs that bloom at different times of the season. The flowering season of all the top-rated azaleas and rhododendrons included in this book is given in their descriptive entries. Choose a balance of early, mid, and late season shrubs so you will have a long, beautiful color display. You may wish to group the plants according to season so different parts of the garden are in bloom during different times. This gives the best show and avoids a polka dot look.

Many gardeners plant several shrubs of the same color together. This gives a more pleasing effect than a hodgepodge of random colors with each vying for attention.

When choosing flower colors, be sure to think about the colors already in the landscape. In a foundation planting, the flowers will be set off against the house. Magenta-red azaleas and rhododendrons look dull and dark against red brick, but are stunning against white clapboard. Other spring-flowering shrubs and trees will be in bloom at the same time and their blossoms should harmonize and complement one another. Favorite combinations are: pink azaleas and white dogwood; magenta azaleas and white spiraea; and purple rhododendrons and pink mountain laurel. Plant white azaleas with yellow forsythia and white rhododendrons with golden-chain tree for an elegant yellow-and-white garden.

Size and Shape: Little plants become big plants, rhododendrons and azaleas not excepted. Some grow more slowly than others and of course they ultimately reach different heights depending upon the variety. The temptation is always to plant new shrubs close together because they look best that way. But they only look good for a few years, then they become crowded and overgrown-looking.

Plan ahead and consider a plant's mature height and spread when you plant it. Put large-growing plants where there will be room for them in 10 years and small-growing plants where space is limited. (See page 58 for more about spacing.)

Low, spreading shrubs with horizontal branches, such as the Satsuki/Macrantha Hybrid azaleas, soften upright lines of houses and fences and keep your eye moving along the lines of the branches. Upright vase shapes, like those of the Knap Hill/Exbury Hybrid azaleas, stop your eye and break up monotonous horizontal lines. Plant several shrubs of the same shape in a group, and vary the groups to create visual excitement.

Mass plantings of azaleas of the same color produce a bold and dramatic effect.

The fact that many azaleas and rhododendrons achieve statuesque size at maturity should be considered when making plant selections for your garden.

White-flowering azaleas, planted en masse, offer a bright display in shady areas under densely branched trees.

Evergreen azalea hybrids enhance a formal entryway year-round; add visually refreshing color when they flower in spring.

'Sherwood Orchid' (Kurume Hybrid) has a spreading growth habit; bears violet-red flowers in midseason.

A WOODLAND GARDEN

Azaleas and rhododendrons grow naturally as shrubs in open forests on mountain slopes. There they enjoy the dappled light that diffuses through the branches of tall trees, and the moist but fast-draining, organically rich soil. It's quite feasible to create this natural setting, even on a small scale, in a typical suburban home landscape. A wooded setting of any size will display rhododendrons and azaleas like jewels against velvet.

To create a woodland garden, you need an area of your property shaded by high-branched trees planted fairly close together, similar to the manner they would grow in a woods. Trees must be deep-rooted, so they won't compete for water with the shrubs, and they should cast light filtered shade. (See the chart on page 14 for appropriate trees.) Evergreen shrubs and trees should be planted on the north side of the woodland, if the area is open to wind, to provide natural wind protection in areas with cold winters.

Depending upon the scale of your planting, choose large or small rhododendrons and azaleas. Plant them in scattered groups beneath the trees, adhering to the design principles outlined earlier on texture, color, and size.

The woodland garden is the perfect setting for native American azaleas and rhododendrons, though hybrids can be very effective too. You can interplant the azaleas and rhododendrons with smaller shrubs that bloom at different times of the year to create a longer color show. Wildflowers, spring-blooming bulbs, and ferns will be at home blanketing the open ground between the shrubs. (See pages 15 and 17 for companion shrubs and flowers that grow in acid soil in filtered shade.)

Such a natural woodland garden requires practically no attention once it is established. You should not even rake up fallen leaves since they add to the mulch that is so important in keeping soil rich, moist, and naturally acid.

A SHRUB BORDER

The borders of many yards are planted with shrubs to mark the boundaries and provide privacy, and simply because the borders of a property provide convenient planting sites for attractive plants. This bed of shrubs is called a shrub border and it can be as elaborate or as simple as the homeowner wishes. If the property border offers conditions suitable for azaleas and rhododendrons (see pages 19 to 22), this is an ideal place to display them.

Where there's room, the most effective borders are several shrubs deep and have curving shapes. Outlines with gentle curves where in-curves are balanced by out-curves are the most attractive. Arrange shrubs at several depths, creating a foreground, a midground, and a background. The plants in the front should be lower than those in the back, but it's best to avoid planting in rigid rows.

The shrub border can be planted only with azaleas and rhododendrons, in which case locate the taller, bolder rhododendrons as a dark green background for evergreen or deciduous azaleas, or plant them together at one end of the border. It's best to arrange several plants of one kind with harmonizing colors together, as described under the section on design basics. Shrub borders are most pleasing if they have a background such as a fence, wall, or backdrop of greenery from tall evergreens.

Choosing azaleas and rhododendrons that bloom at different times of the season will keep the border colorful. You may also wish to incorporate other flowering shrubs for variety and to keep the border in bloom throughout the summer. The chart of companion shrubs on page 15 lists plants that have the same requirements as azaleas and rhododendrons.

Borders of shrubs may also be planted along a house wall as a foundation planting or to accent a walkway or patio. In these cases, be extra careful to select plants that won't grow too tall or too wide, or they will soon outgrow the spaces intended for plants and crowd the spaces intended for people.

AN ORIENTAL GARDEN

An Oriental garden, despite its subtly formal elements, is really a simplified or stylized natural terrain. It could be thought of as a woodland garden pared down to its bare essentials. Few Westerners possess the knowledge or ability to construct an authentic Oriental garden with all its intricacies and symbolism. But the essential simplicity and serenity can be reproduced to please Western tastes.

Azaleas and rhododendrons are used sparingly as accents in Oriental gardens. You might group three low, fine-textured Kurumes that are sheared or pinched for compactness where they can mound over rocks. Satsuki/Macranthas and Kurumes are often pruned to accentuate their layered 'cloud' form. Locate a single deciduous azalea near a pool or fountain, or plant several of the same color in a mass. However, open space is essential and must strike a pleasing balance with planted areas.

COMPANION PLANTS

Plants that harmonize with azaleas and rhododendrons both culturally and aesthetically make good garden companions. When you consider possible companion trees, shrubs, ground covers, or perennials for azaleas and rhododendrons, follow these criteria: Companion plants should thrive in shade and acid soil and have water and fertilizer needs similar to those of azaleas and rhododendrons. A tree or large shrub should have a taproot rather than shallow, matting roots, which compete for water and nutrients. The companion plant's color and texture should not clash with the azaleas or rhododendrons you have in your garden.

On the following pages are lists of choice companion trees, shrubs, ground covers, and bulbs, 18 to 20 of each. The lists are by no means exhaustive.

The light airy branches of Mollis Hybrid azaleas create a graceful effect in Oriental gardens.

Spectacular color displays may be achieved by combining azaleas with flowers in complementary shades.

13

Japanese maple *(Acer palmatum)*, a small graceful tree, is a visually pleasing backdrop for azaleas.

Dogwood trees *(Cornus sp.)* add a natural woodland feeling to azalea and rhododendron plantings.

COMPANION PLANTS: TREES

Name	Deciduous/ Evergreen	Height	*Recommended Zones:	Comments
Acer palmatum Japanese Maple	D	variable, to 20 ft	6-9 W 6-8 E	Beautiful graceful trees. Some have elegant deeply cut leaves, others have dark purple foliage. Beautiful red or yellow fall color. Trees may be too small to provide useful shade, but make exquisite companions. Protect from wind and drying sun in hot climates.
Amelanchier sp. Shadblow, Serviceberry	D	35 ft, or taller	4-8	Masses of fine-textured white flowers in early spring. Beautiful red fall color. Pinkish-gray trunk bark. Good shade from open, upright tree.
Cercis sp. Redbud	D	25-40 ft	5-9 W 4-8 E	Twigs, branches, and trunk bear clusters of small purplish-pink pealike flowers before heart-shaped leaves. White-flowering variety available.
Cornus sp. Dogwood	D	20-40 ft	5-9	Flowering dogwood, *C. florida*, blooms with azaleas. Clouds of white or pink blossoms. Prune high if used as shade, low for background. Japanese dogwood, *C. kousa*, produces white flowers a month later. Red fall color.
Eriobotrya japonica Loquat	E	20 ft	7-10	Large dark green leaves cast dense shade. Use as background. Golden fruits produced in early spring are edible and ornamental.
Gleditsia triacanthos inermis Thornless Honey Locust	D	60-90 ft	4-10 W 4-9 E	Airy tree with finely divided leaves. Casts light shade. Tolerates heat and drought. Leaves require little cleanup.
Ilex opaca American Holly	E	30-50 ft	6-9	Shiny, spiny foliage makes dense cover on pyramidal tree. Use as background and as windbreak. Berries form on female trees if pollinated.
Laburnum x watereri Golden-Chain Tree	D	25-30 ft	6-9 W 6-7 E	Long clusters of yellow wisterialike flowers in late spring. Prune to a single trunk to grow tall and cast light shade. Seeds are poisonous.
Larix sp. Larch	D	70-100 ft	5-8	Needles provide soft texture and light shade spring through fall; drop in autumn after changing to gold color. Several species available.
Magnolia x soulangiana Saucer Magnolia	D	20-25 ft	5-10	Large, fragrant white, pink, or purplish flowers in spring. Bold-textured leaves. Plant with azaleas and rhododendrons of compatible color.
Metasequoia glyptostroboides Dawn Redwood	D	75-85 ft	4-10	Small fine-textured needles drop in fall. Upright, open shape casts light shade. Fast-growing and graceful.
Oxydendrum arboreum Sourwood	D	15-25 ft, or taller	6-9	Clusters of tiny bell-like flowers in spring and ornamental seedpods in summer. Glossy green leaves turn scarlet in fall.
Pinus strobus White Pine	E	100-150 ft	2-8	Long bluish needles make fine-textured background. Tree casts light shade and makes good windbreak.
Pittosporum undulatum Victorian Box	E	15 ft, or taller	9-10	Handsome dark glossy green foliage. Makes good background and windbreak. Small inconspicuous flowers in spring are highly fragrant.
Prunus caroliniana Carolina Cherry Laurel	E	20-40 ft	7-10	Lush dark green background. May be sheared into hedge.
Pyrus calleryana 'Bradford' Bradford Pear	D	40-50 ft	5-9	Lovely lacy clusters of white flowers in early spring. Red foliage in fall. Good shade tree.
Quercus sp. Oak	D	60-80 ft	4-10	Red oak, *Q. rubra*, and scarlet oak, *Q. coccinea*, offer high open branching. Make good shade trees. Brilliant red fall color. Grow rapidly.
Rhus glabra Smooth Sumac	D	15 ft	3-8	Large, coarse-textured divided leaves in whorls. Striking red fall color. Makes useful background. Heat-tolerant.
Taxus baccata English Yew	E	40-60 ft	5-9 W 5-7 E	Dark green needles. Makes dense background as hedge or windbreak if pruned. Casts heavy shade as tree. Berry seeds are poisonous.
Tsuga sp. Hemlock	E	60-90 ft	5-9	Small, fine-textured, medium green needles. Tall gracefully drooping branches. Useful background and windbreak. Light shade.

See page 20 for locations of USDA Zones. Because climate patterns differ, zones are indicated for the West (W) and the East (E) where significant.

Viburnum *(Viburnum sp.)* is a good choice for interplanting, displaying azaleas and rhododendrons to beautiful advantage.

Dense-foliaged tobira *(Pittosporum tobira)* is widely used as a background shrub with azaleas and rhododendrons.

COMPANION PLANTS: SHRUBS

Name	Deciduous/ Evergreen	Height	*Recommended Zones:	Comments
Abelia x grandiflora **Glossy Abelia**	E/semi-D	6 ft	6-10	Dense growth. Small glossy leaves. Many small pink-tinged white flowers from summer to fall. Useful background. 'Edward Goucher' has purplish flowers.
Aucuba japonica **Japanese Aucuba**	E	6 to 10 ft	7-10	Bold glossy leaves, green or spotted with gold. Female plants may have bright red berries. Can be pruned to 3 ft. Needs shade.
Buxus sempervirens **English Box**	E	6-12 ft	5-10	Dense, glossy green leaves. May be sheared or pruned as desired. Makes fine-textured background.
Camellia sp. **Camellia**	E	5 to 10 ft	7-10	Useful for separating competing colors in borders and as background. Extends season by blooming in fall and winter. Pink, red, or white blossoms.
Gardenia jasminoides **Gardenia**	E	1 to 8 ft	8-10	Lustrous, dark green leaves. Fragrant white or ivory flowers in summer. Thrives in summer heat in some shade. 'Radicans', 1 foot tall, useful as foreground. Use taller 'Mystery' and 'Veitchii' in background.
Hamamelis x intermedia **Witch Hazel**	D	15-18 ft, or taller	6-9 W 6-8 E	Tall, open shrub. Very fragrant small feathery yellow or red flowers in late winter. Coarse foliage on zigzag branches; red or yellow fall color.
Hydrangea quercifolia **Oakleaf Hydrangea**	D	3 to 6 ft	6-9	Bold-textured leaves resemble oak leaves. Bright red fall color. Creamy-white flower clusters in midsummer extend floral season.
Ilex cornuta 'Burfordii' **Burford Holly**	E	10-14 ft	6-10	Dense, glossy, nearly spineless foliage. Red fall berries. Good background. *Ilex crenata*, Japanese holly, has small, shiny foliage. Resembles boxwood.
Kalmia latifolia **Mountain Laurel**	E	10 ft, or taller	5-8 W 5-9 E	Native American woodland shrub. Clusters of pink or white blossoms in June. Pointed leaves. Mix in border or woodland planting.
Leucothoe fontanesiana **Drooping Leucothoe**	E/semi-D	3 to 6 ft	5-8	Pointed bold-textured leaves. Bell-shaped white flowers in late spring. 'Scarletta', a dwarf hybrid, has bright red new growth; use in foreground.
Mahonia aquifolium **Oregon Grape**	E	2 to 6 ft	5-9 W 5-7 E	Bold-textured hollylike leaves. Clusters of yellow flowers in spring. Blue berries in fall and winter. New foliage red. Leaves reddish in winter.
Nandina domestica **Heavenly Bamboo**	E/semi-D	3 to 8 ft	6-10	Resembles bamboo, with delicate tall layers of divided leaves. Red fall color. Excellent background for low azaleas and dwarf rhododendrons.
Osmanthus heterophyllus **Holly Olive**	E	10 ft, or more	7-10	Resembles holly. Produces extremely fragrant, inconspicuous flowers during most of year. May be sheared into rounded shape for background.
Pieris japonica **Japanese Andromeda**	E	6 ft	5-9 W 5-8 E	Dense tapered leaves. Bell-shaped white flowers in early spring. Mountain andromeda, *P. floribunda*, is similar but more cold hardy.
Pittosporum tobira **Tobira**	E	6-15 ft, or more	8-10	Medium-sized, leathery green leaves may be variegated with white. Inconspicuous spring flowers are fragrant. 'Wheelers Dwarf' good in foreground.
Prunus tomentosa **Nanking Cherry**	D	9 ft	3-8	Good with deciduous azaleas. Single white flowers from pink buds in spring. Glossy green foliage. Plant has mounded shape.
Sarcococca hookerana humilis **Sweet Box**	E	5 to 6 ft	6-10 W 6-8 E	Small glossy leaves. Tiny, fragrant white flowers in early spring. Black berries in fall. Good with evergreen and deciduous azaleas.
Taxus cuspidata nana **Dwarf Japanese Yew**	E	2 to 3 ft, or taller	5-9 W 5-7 E	Dense dark green needles. Red berries in fall are poisonous. Can be sheared for formal effect.
Vaccinium ovatum **Evergreen Huckleberry**	E	5 to 10 ft	7	Resembles a loose, open boxwood. Foliage excellent background for deciduous azaleas. Can be pruned for formal look.
Viburnum sp. **Viburnum**	E	1 to 3 ft	8-10 W 8-9 E	Many species make excellent companion plants for woodlands or borders. White flowers in spring or early summer; red or black berries in fall; attractive summer foliage. Deciduous kinds usually have good fall color.

See page 20 for locations of USDA Zones. Because climate patterns differ, zones are indicated for the West (W) and the East (E) where significant.

Carpet bugle *(Ajuga reptans)* makes a colorful ground cover that is visually delightful with azaleas or rhododendrons.

Japanese spurge *(Pachysandra terminalis)* forms a dark green ground cover complementary to azaleas and rhododendrons.

COMPANION PLANTS: GROUND COVERS

Name	Deciduous/ Evergreen	Height	*Recommended Zones:	Comments
Ajuga reptans Carpet Bugle	D/E	4 to 10 inches	3-10	Dense carpets of quilted green, bronze, or purplish leaves. Spikes of blue, pink, or white flowers in spring. May be invasive.
Asarum sp. Wild Ginger	D/E	6 inches	3-9	Beautiful heart-shaped leaves carpet the ground. Roots can be ground into gingerlike spice. *A. canadense* is deciduous. *A. caudatum* and *A. europaeum* are evergreen and hardy to Zone 4.
Convallaria majalis Lily-of-the-Valley	D	8 inches	3-9	Lush carpet of upright, oval leaves. Delicate spikes of tiny, nodding, white flowers in spring. Fragrant. Poor ground cover in mild areas.
Duchesnea indica Indian Mock Strawberry	D/E	2 to 8 inches	6-10	Resembles strawberry with lobed scalloped-edged leaves. Yellow spring flowers and tasteless red berries.
Epimedium x rubrum Epimedium	E	8 to 12 inches	4-9	Wiry stems and delicate heart-shaped leaves. Clusters of cream or reddish spring flowers beneath the leaves.
Ferns (many genera and species)	D/E	6 inches to 6 ft or taller	variable	Many species of ferns are suitable for woodland gardens. They add a natural elegance and softening effect.
Gaultheria procumbens Wintergreen	E	3 to 6 inches	4-9	Native American ground cover. Mats of tiny glossy leaves. Inconspicuous flowers and showy red fall berries.
Heuchera sanguinea Coralbells	E	1 to 2 ft	4-10	Rounded toothed leaves hug the ground. Airy spikes of pink, red, or white flowers bloom in spring and summer.
Hosta sp. Plantain Lily	D	12 to 15 inches	4-9	Many species are grown for their clumps of beautiful foliage. Plants vary in size, have bright green, gray-green, blue-green, or variegated leaves. Spikes of lavender, purple, or white flowers in late summer or fall.
Iberis sempervirens Edging Candytuft	E	12 inches	4-10	Circles of white flowers create masses of white in early spring. Dark foliage beautiful year-round. 'Snowflake' has long blooming season.
Liriope muscari Big Blue Lilyturf	E	12 to 20 inches	7-10	Clumps of grassy foliage are green or green- and gold-striped. Spikes of purple, lavender, or white flowers in late summer or fall.
Myosotis sylvatica Garden Forget-Me-Not	D	10 to 20 inches	(annual) all zones	Tiny bright blue flowers with yellow eyes in spring and summer. An annual that reseeds and spreads.
Pachysandra terminalis Japanese Spurge, Pachysandra	E	6 to 12 inches	6-10 W 6-8 E	Whorls of dark green leaves. Makes thick dependable cover. Short spikes of white flowers in early summer. White berries.
Phlox stolonifera Creeping Phlox	E	6 to 12 inches	3-8	Perennial woodland wildflower. Forms thick cover of foliage. Loose clusters of delicate blue-violet flowers in spring.
Tiarella cordifolia Allegheny Foamflower	D	6 to 12 inches	4-7	Woodland wildflower. White flowers on 8- to 18-inch spikes in spring. Downy maplelike leaves close to the ground.
Vaccinium vitis-idaea Cowberry	E	8 to 12 inches	3-7	Low, creeping shrub with small shiny evergreen leaves. Tiny white spring flowers. Red fall berries. Good cover in light shade.
Vinca sp. Periwinkle, Myrtle	E	4 to 12 inches	5-10	Neat, glossy, oval leaves on creeping stems. Bright blue flowers in spring and early summer. 'Alba' is white-flowered form.
Viola sp. Violet	D/E	6 inches	5-10	Violets have heart-shaped leaves and spread by underground runners. Dainty blue, purple, or white flowers in spring.

*See page 20 for locations of USDA Zones. Because climate patterns differ, zones are indicated for the West (W) and the East (E) where significant.

Daylily *(Hemerocallis* hybrids) is a beautiful midsummer-blooming companion plant for azaleas and rhododendrons.

The clean, crisp appearance of daffodils *(Narcissus sp.)* contrasts superbly with plantings of azaleas or rhododendrons.

COMPANION PLANTS: BULBS

Name	Height	*Recommended Zones:	Planting Depth	Planting Time	Comments
Anemone blanda Windflower	3 to 8 inches	7-9	4 inches	fall	Many-petaled bright blue flowers with yellow stamens. Early spring. Downy, feathery leaves.
Chionodoxa luciliae Glory-of-the-Snow	3 to 6 inches	5-9	4 inches	September	Clusters of bright blue flowers with white eyes. Very early spring. Grasslike leaves. Plant under deciduous trees in full spring sun.
Clivia miniata Kaffir Lily	2 ft	10	tuber barely exposed	late spring	Bold clusters of brilliant orange flowers in spring. Thick glossy strap-shaped leaves. Good with white azaleas and ferns.
Colchicum autumnale Autumn Crocus	6 inches	4-10	4 inches	late summer	Fall-blooming chalice-shaped lavender, orchid, or white flowers. Foliage appears in spring and dies in summer.
Crocus vernus Dutch Crocus	3 to 5 inches	3-10	4 inches	September	Early-spring purple, lavender, white, or yellow cuplike blossoms. Many varieties available. Multiplies readily.
Cyclamen hederifolium, Baby Cyclamen	4 inches	6-10 W 6-8 E	2 inches	July	Small, unusual summer flowers with twisted, backswept petals. Red or white. Leathery, mottled leaves close to the ground.
Eranthis hyemalis Winter Aconite	8 inches	5-8	2 inches	late summer	Carpets of yellow buttercuplike flowers in very early spring. Whorls of leaves die to ground in summer. Can invade lawn. Poisonous if eaten.
Erythronium sp. Dog-Tooth Violet	6 inches	3-8	2 to 4 inches	fall	Woodland wildflower with mottled leaves. Small lilylike blossoms in yellow, white, or rosy-purple. Several species available.
Galanthus sp. Snowdrop	12 inches	4-9	4 inches	late summer or early fall	White drooping flowers with flared petals marked with green. Early spring. Grassy foliage. *G. nivalis* is daintier and earlier than *G. elwesii.*
Hemerocallis hybrids Daylily	1 to 5 ft	3-10	cover roots	early spring, fall	Clumps of strap-shaped foliage. Large orange, yellow, pink, bronze, or reddish flowers in midsummer. Naturalize on woodland edge.
Iris cristata Crested Iris	3 to 4 inches	4-8	on surface	fall	A dwarf iris native to Appalachian Mts. Blue, yellow, or white flowers with yellow crests. Early spring. Use in border or woodland.
Leucojum sp. Snowflake	12 inches	5-9	3 inches	September	White bell-like flowers, grassy foliage. *L. vernum* blooms in spring; *L. aestivum* in summer; *L. autumnale* in fall.
Lilium canadense Canada Lily	3 to 5 ft	4-9	5 inches	fall	Native woodland lily. Golden blossoms in July. Use in border or naturalistic setting.
Lycoris squamigera Magic Lily	2 ft	6-10 W 6-9 E	5 inches	August	Foliage emerges in spring, dies in summer. Stalks of fragrant rose-lilac flowers seem to sprout from bare earth in late summer.
Muscari sp. Grape Hyacinth	6 to 12 inches	5-10	2 inches	late summer or early fall	Dense spikes of rounded purplish-blue flowers in early spring. Grassy foliage. Plant along borders or on edge of woodland.
Narcissus sp. Narcissus, Daffodil	18 inches	5-10	6 inches	fall	White, yellow, or golden flowers with contrasting trumpets or cups. Blooms in spring. Mix in borders or naturalize in woodland.
Scilla sp. Squill	6 inches	3-10	4 inches	fall	Tall stalks of blue flowers in summer. Pink, white, and lavender kinds available. *S. hispanica,* bell-shaped; *S. siberica,* fringed.
Trillium sp. Trillium	18 inches	4-7	10 inches	early fall	Native wildflowers with 3-petaled white or purple blossoms above whorl of 3 leaves. Naturalize in woodland. Spring blooming.
Tulipa turkestanica Turkscap Tulip	12 inches	5-10	6 inches	fall	Loose clusters of yellow starlike flowers marked with white. Early spring. Good for foreground of border or edge of woodland.
Zephyranthes sp. Rain Lily	10 inches	7-10	1 to 2 inches	fall	Beautiful lilylike white or pale purplish flowers in late summer or early fall after a rain. Needs some sun.

*See page 20 for locations of USDA Zones. Because climate patterns differ, zones are indicated for the West (W) and the East (E) where significant.

Where Azaleas and Rhododendrons Grow

CLIMATES AND ADAPTABILITY

Azaleas and rhododendrons have their likes and dislikes when it comes to climate and growing regions. Certain areas of the country are prime growing areas and in these areas it's easy to meet the plants' cultural requirements. In other areas, soil may be too alkaline, summers too hot or dry, or winters too cold. Choosing adaptable plants and understanding their needs goes a long way toward ensuring success in less than ideal climates.

Prime azalea and rhododendron garden territory is the same area where native North American azalea and rhododendron species grow wild. This is in the coastal, hilly, and mountainous regions along the Atlantic seaboard and the coastal Northwest, where generous rainfall, acid soil, and temperate climates prevail. Azaleas and rhododendrons are most plentiful in the Appalachian Mountains, but several azalea species grow as far north as Labrador and others grow into Florida and Texas.

Deciduous azaleas are the most cold hardy and will grow farther north and farther into the Midwest than evergreen azaleas and rhododendrons. Evergreen azaleas need warmer winters, and they can also tolerate warmer summers than the deciduous kinds.

The limiting factors for rhododendron culture are winter cold and summer heat. They can't grow as far north as deciduous azaleas or as far south as evergreen azaleas, but rhododendrons provide winter greenery in areas

At left: Azaleas and rhododendrons can frame a home with springtime color; visually blend house and garden year-round.

'Vulcan' rhododendron

Knap Hill/Exbury Hybrid azalea

'Coral Bells' (Kurume Hybrid)

'Delaware Valley White' (Glenn Dale Hybrid)

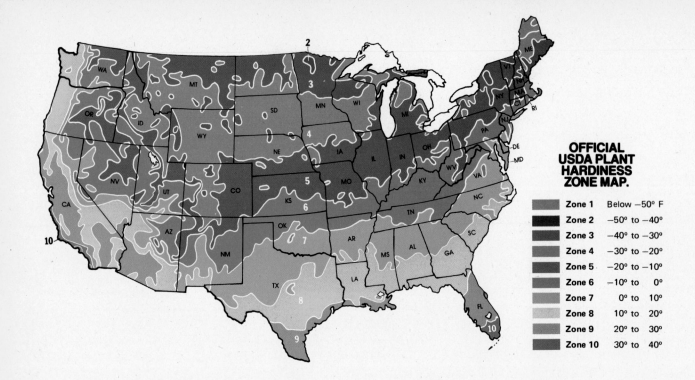

OFFICIAL USDA PLANT HARDINESS ZONE MAP.

Zone 1	Below −50° F
Zone 2	−50° to −40°
Zone 3	−40° to −30°
Zone 4	−30° to −20°
Zone 5	−20° to −10°
Zone 6	−10° to 0°
Zone 7	0° to 10°
Zone 8	10° to 20°
Zone 9	20° to 30°
Zone 10	30° to 40°

where evergreen azaleas cannot grow. Areas with extreme summer heat are usually not suitable for growing rhododendrons.

All the top-rated azaleas and rhododendrons described in this book are labeled according to the hardiness zones where they are adapted—both their cold and warm limits. (See the USDA Cold Hardiness Map shown above.) This provides a good measure of adaptability. The cold limit in terms of degrees Fahrenheit is also included, because the hardiness zones have a 10°F spread and some shrubs may not grow in the coldest areas of the listed zone. You'll find knowing this temperature tolerance will also be useful in deciding where to situate a particular plant. Varieties being grown near their cold limit are best located in a warm microclimate on your property.

Some varieties are better adapted to sun, dry soil, or other adverse conditions than others. And these varieties will do best in areas where conditions aren't ideal for most varieties. However, simply knowing the cold hardiness zones isn't enough to pinpoint exact growing

regions for such varieties, because regions that may have the same cold conditions may have different soil and rainfall. The charts on pages 23, 24, and 25 indicate which top-rated varieties are recommended for particular areas.

EASY GROWING

If you live in prime rhododendron and azalea growing regions, you'll have the largest number of hybrids and native and exotic species to choose from. In those areas, if plants are properly situated, and once they are established, they'll require only routine care to keep them happy and blooming. With just a little extra attention, they'll astound you with their vigor and abundant blossoms.

DIFFICULT GROWING

In areas outside of prime growing country, you can still grow azaleas and rhododendrons—but with special care. Choose unfussy plants that adapt to hotter summers, drier soil, and less acid conditions. The number of available hybrids that are bred to survive adverse growing conditions is increasing all the time,

and impressive advances in developing plants suited to particular areas have recently been made.

Success in growing azaleas and rhododendrons in difficult locations comes from choosing the right varieties and giving them extra-special care. And success stories are not uncommon. In Savannah, where the hot summers make rhododendrons a rarity, a gardener gets a special pleasure from watching the heavy pink trusses of 'Anna Rose Whitney' burst into bloom. A gardener in Tucson who provides special soil and frequent watering can be rewarded with masses of salmon-pink blossoms of the Southern Indica azalea 'Duc de Rohan'. In Canada, where winter temperatures usually preclude broad-leaved evergreens such as rhododendrons, in a sheltered spot in a Toronto yard the apple-blossom-colored bouquets of *R. catawbiense* are greeted with admiration. Meeting the challenge of bringing these beautiful plants into bloom year after year under tough growing conditions brings special satisfaction to any gardener.

LIMITATIONS

It's not so difficult to extend the natural limits of many azaleas and rhododendrons once you understand just how climate factors are limiting their growth in your garden. You can manipulate the environment a little bit to your advantage by using some tricks learned by expert gardeners.

Temperature: Minimum winter temperature has long been the traditional basis for gauging adaptability of azaleas and rhododendrons. You can get a pretty fair assessment of whether or not a particular plant will grow in your garden if you know your hardiness zone and the cold limit of the plant. Temperatures however vary within a region and microclimates occur wherever elevation, bodies of water, sun exposure, and heat-absorbing materials such as rock outcroppings or buildings are substantial enough to influence temperature. For instance, cities are always warmer than their surrounding suburbs because the roads and buildings heat up from the sun during the day and slowly radiate the heat back all night. Areas bordering large lakes are warmer in fall and colder in spring than surrounding areas.

Around your home and property, there are small, localized temperature and moisture changes, called microclimates, that can spell the difference between death and survival for many azaleas and rhododendrons. Plants that are borderline hardy for your area may perish if planted in a cold microclimate, but thrive if planted in a warm one.

Warm microclimates: The south-facing side of your home, if unshaded by trees, is a warm microclimate. Such a location could be a good spot for borderline plants because it is much warmer in winter than the rest of the property; however, direct sun would be too hot and drying year-round for azaleas and rhododendrons. The north or east side of a house, better exposures for azalea and rhododendron growth, can be warmed up with a large paved surface such as a patio or driveway. This is a better planting spot for borderline plants.

Other suitable warm spots are east- or west-facing slopes, and the edges of large bodies of water that don't freeze in winter. South-facing slopes, though warm, are usually too hot and dry for successful growth.

Cold microclimates: Planting spots to avoid are those that are colder than other areas on your property. Low-lying spots act as frost-pockets because cold air sinks, draining from high ground and collecting at the bottom of a slope or in a depression. These pockets are the first places frost occurs in fall and the last places frost occurs in spring. Plants growing in frost pockets may be expecting warmer weather at the time of these early and late frosts and will be injured.

Temperature fluctuations: The gradually colder and shorter days of autumn signal plants to prepare for winter's cold. Chemical changes begin within the plant that enable the tissues to endure freezing temperatures. A reverse process happens in spring. Any sharp temperature changes in late winter or early spring can interfere with the plant's dormancy and have disastrous effects on certain plants. A warm spell late in winter can break a plant's dormancy, causing its buds to swell. When cold returns, the tissues are unprepared and the flower buds may be injured. This is particularly true of early-flowering varieties, which are quick to break dormancy in spring.

Ironically, a plant well adapted to the consistent winter cold of Maine may be damaged in Alabama by a cold snap in early spring. In the mild climate, the plant is only weakly dormant and any warm weather gets it growing in spring, only to be startled by an onset of cold weather. Plants growing in warm microclimates may also break dormancy early in spring.

In regions where dormancy is likely to be interrupted by warm spells, consider planting late-blooming varieties and species. They are less likely to break dormancy early. Northern exposures out of warming spring sun also prolong dormancy and in such a cold microclimate plants are slower to react to early mild spells.

Early frosts in fall, before plants are fully dormant, can also be injurious. To help shrubs resist early fall frost, plants should be hardened off. Water less at the end of the summer and don't apply fertilizer containing nitrogen after midsummer because both water and fertilizer stimulate growth—in fall plants should be slowing down and beginning dormancy.

MORE THAN COLD

It's not always the cold by itself that does a plant in. Each plant of course does have its cold-tolerance limit, but that limit is affected by many other climate factors such as sun, water, wind, and as previously mentioned, temperature fluctuations. These factors can influence the degree of a plant's dormancy and hence its ability to withstand cold.

Winter sun and wind: When the soil is frozen, no water is available for plants to take up through their roots. Hot sun and wind cause plants to lose water, to some extent from their stems, but to a much larger extent through their foliage. Evergreens are very susceptible to drying out in winter because they lose water readily through their leaves and may not be able to replenish it. During prolonged cold, sunny spells, azaleas and rhododendrons can become desiccated. Wind is such a severe problem that in many cold areas a plant growing near a windy corner of a house may be dried out and killed, while a similar plant only a few feet away, but out of the wind, is unharmed.

One way rhododendrons cope with cold weather is by curling their leaves. Leaf curling reduces the surface exposed to drying sun and wind and thus slows water loss. A rhododendron is a good weather

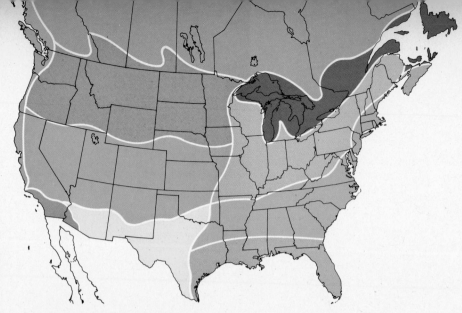

barometer, since you can simply glance out your window and get a good idea of the temperature by how much the leaves are curled—the colder the weather, the more the leaves droop and curl.

Plants that are well-watered when soil freezes are better able to withstand winter sun and wind. If the season is dry, it's a good idea to water shrubs heavily in fall after the first frost—earlier watering may slow the onset of dormancy. If snow is unusually scant, water plants in exposed sites during thaws.

Planting azaleas and rhododendrons where they are protected from strong winds by a windbreak of evergreen trees or a fence or wall will also help them survive the winter. Selecting a planting location out of direct winter sun can be tricky. The angle of the sun changes in winter and deciduous trees drop their leaves. Provide sufficient winter shade when planting azaleas and rhododendrons.

HOT CLIMATES

It's generally true that most evergreen azaleas fare better in areas where summer heat is high than do rhododendrons and deciduous azaleas. In the South, it is not always the heat, but often a soil fungus that causes the plants to suffer. Fungus organisms are most likely to attack roots in warm climates where soil is poorly drained. In such climates, avoid unnecessary watering, and be sure soil is fast-draining. By growing these shrubs in raised beds of suitable soil, you can often avoid fungus problems in hot, humid areas. (See pages 55 and 62.) Some southern gardeners recommend a fungicidal soil drench at planting time.

In the Southwest, climates often are too hot and dry for azaleas and rhododendrons. Many gardeners in these areas have success with azaleas by watering them frequently, hosing and misting the foliage to raise the humidity and cool the plants during the heat of the day, and by planting in shaded locations protected from drying wind.

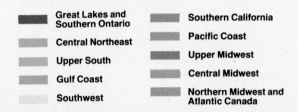

REGIONAL ADAPTATION MAP

- Great Lakes and Southern Ontario
- Central Northeast
- Upper South
- Gulf Coast
- Southwest
- Southern California
- Pacific Coast
- Upper Midwest
- Central Midwest
- Northern Midwest and Atlantic Canada

UNSUITABLE SOIL

Alkaline and clay soils are perhaps just as limiting in their own way as cold temperatures. Azaleas and rhododendrons need acid, fast-draining soil. Alkaline soil binds iron and manganese in forms that azaleas and rhododendrons cannot use, so they suffer from nutrient deficiency. These plants have delicate, shallow roots that cannot penetrate heavy soil and their growth is severely curtailed. Where soil drains poorly, azalea and rhododendron roots suffer from lack of oxygen.

If you live in an area where soil is unsuitable, such as the alkaline areas of the Southwest or the clay soil areas of Southern California, you can still grow azaleas and rhododendrons—albeit with some extra effort. Planting in raised beds or planters containing a suitable soil is the answer. See page 55 for more information on soil and raised beds.

REGIONAL CHOICES

Different regions of the country are better suited to azaleas and rhododendrons than others, and each region has its own choice of top-rated plants. The map above will make it easy to select the best azaleas and rhododendrons for your yard and garden. The map divides the United States and Canada into 10 growing regions. The regions differ in amount of rainfall, soil conditions, humidity, length of growing season, and other climate factors of significance to azalea and rhododendron culture. The charts on the following pages list regions where top-rated azaleas and rhododendrons are adapted. You can use the Hardiness Zone Map and the Regional Map to determine which region and which hardiness zone you live in. Then use the lists to select the best plants for your garden.

In some cases you'll notice that the minimum temperature given in the plant lists is colder than the low temperature for the listed zones. All temperatures are of course approximate (the USDA zone temperatures represent an average over the last 100 years) and a plant's hardiness will vary slightly from year to year depending upon other climate factors. Use these temperatures and zones as a guideline, but not as hard-and-fast laws. Experimentation may bring surprising and pleasing results.

Azaleas: Regional Recommendations

	Minimum Temperature (degrees F)	Recommended Zones	Great Lakes and Southern Ontario	Central Northeast	Upper South	Gulf Coast	Southwest	Southern California	Pacific Coast	Upper Midwest	Central Midwest	Northern Midwest and Atlantic Canada
HYBRIDS												
Belgian Indica Hybrids (E)	20°	8-10		■	■	■		■	■			
Gable Hybrids (E)	0°	6-8	■	■	■				■			
Ghent Hybrids (D)	−25°	4-8	■	■	■				■			
Girard Hybrids (E)	− 5°	6-9	■	■	■				■	■		
Glenn Dale Hybrids (E)	5°	7-9		■	■			■	■	■		
Gold Cup, Brooks, Nuccio Hybrids (E)	20°	9-10					■*	■				
Kaempferi Hybrids (E)	−10°	5-9	■		■					■		
Knap Hill/Exbury Hybrids (D)	−20°	5-8		■	■				■			
Kurume Hybrids (E)	5°	7-10		■	■			■	■			
Mollis Hybrids (D)	−20°	5-8	■		■				■			
Northern Lights Hybrids (D)	−45°	3-4	■	■						■	■	■
Occidentale Hybrids (D)	−25°	6-8		■	■				■			
Pericat Hybrids (E)	5°	7-10			■			■	■			
Rutherfordiana Hybrids (E)	20°	8-10						■	■			
Satsuki/Macrantha Hybrids (E)	5°	7-10			■			■	■			
Southern Indica Hybrids (E)	20°	8-10				■	■*	■				
SPECIES												
R. arborescens	−20°	5-9	■	■	■	■			■			
R. atlanticum	−10°	6-9		■	■	■			■			
R. austrinum	−10°	6-10		■	■				■			
R. bakeri	−20°	5-8	■	■	■				■			
R. calendulaceum	−20°	5-8	■	■	■				■			
R. canadense	−40°	3-7	■	■	■				■	■		■
R. japonicum	−25°	5-8	■	■	■	■			■			
R. luteum	−25°	6-8	■	■	■				■			
R. molle	−20°	6-8		■	■							
R. occidentale	− 5°	7-9						■	■			
R. periclymenoides	−30°	4-9	■	■	■				■	■	■	■
R. prinophyllum	−30°	4-8	■	■					■	■		■
R. prunifolium	−10°	7-9			■				■			
R. schlippenbachii	−25°	5-9	■	■	■				■		■	
R. serrulatum	0°	7-10			■	■						
R. vaseyi	−30°	5-9	■	■	■	■			■	■		■
R. viscosum	−30°	4-9	■	■	■	■			■			
R. yedoense var. *poukhanense*	− 5°	6-8	■	■	■							

*Plant in raised beds or containers filled with fast-draining, acid soil mix (page 55).

'Scintillation' rhododendron

'Anah Kruschke' rhododendron

Rhododendrons: Regional Recommendations

	Minimum Temperature (degrees F)	Recommended Zones	Great Lakes and Southern Ontario	Central Northeast	Upper South	Gulf Coast	Southwest	Southern California	Pacific Coast	Upper Midwest	Central Midwest	Northern Midwest and Atlantic Canada
HYBRIDS												
'Arthur Bedford'	−5°	7-8		■	■				■			
'America'	−20°	5-8	■	■	■				■	■	■	
'Anah Kruschke'	−10°	6-8		■	■			■	■			
'Anna Rose Whitney'	−5°	7-8	■	■	■	■			■			
'Antoon van Welie'	−5°	7-8	■		■			■	■			
'Blue Ensign'	−10°	6-8						■				
'Blue Jay'	−5°	7-8			■				■			
'Blue Peter'	−10°	6-8		■	■				■			
'Boule de Neige'	−25°	5-8	■	■	■			■	■	■	■	■
'Bow Bells'	0°	7-8			■			■	■			
'Bric-a-Brac'	5°	8-9			■				■			
'Caractacus'	−25°	5-8	■	■	■				■	■	■	■
'Carmen'	−5°	7-8							■			
'Caroline'	−15°	6-8	■	■	■				■			
'Catawbiense Album'	−25°	5-8	■	■	■			■	■		■	■
'Chionoides'	−20°	5-8	■	■	■			■	■	■		■
'Cunningham's White'	−10°	6-8	■	■	■				■			
'Daphnoides'	−10°	6-8		■	■				■			
'Dr. V.H. Rutgers'	−20°	5-8		■	■				■			
'Dora Amateis'	−15°	6-9	■	■	■				■			
'English Roseum'	−20°	5-8	■	■	■				■	■	■	■
'Fastuosum Flore Pleno'	−10°	6-8		■	■				■			
'Fragrantissimum'	20°	9-10					■*	■	■			
'General Eisenhower'	0°	7-8		■	■				■			
'Gomer Waterer'	−15°	6-8	■	■	■			■	■	■	■	
'Graf Zeppelin'	0°	7-8		■	■				■			
'Herbert Parsons'	−25°	5-8	■	■	■				■	■	■	■

*Plant in raised beds or containers filled with fast-draining, acid soil mix (page 55)

24

	Minimum Temperature (degrees F)	Recommended Zones	Great Lakes and Southern Ontario	Central Northeast	Upper South	Gulf Coast	Southwest	Southern California	Pacific Coast	Upper Midwest	Central Midwest	Northern Midwest and Atlantic Canada
'Humming Bird'	0°	7-9							■			
'Ignatius Sargent'	−20°	5-8	■	■	■				■	■	■	■
'Janet Blair'	−15°	6-8		■	■				■			
'Kluis Sensation'	0°	7-8		■	■				■			
'Lee's Dark Purple'	−20°	5-8	■	■	■	■			■	■	■	■
'Moonstone'	0°	7-9		■	■				■			
'Mother of Pearl'	0°	7-9										
'Mrs. Charles E. Pearson'	− 5°	7-8		■	■				■			
'Mrs. Furnival'	−10°	6-8	■	■	■				■			
'Nova Zembla'	−25°	5-8	■	■	■				■	■	■	■
'Parson's Gloriosum'	−25°	5-8	■	■	■				■		■	
'Pink Pearl'	− 5°	7-8			■	■		■	■			
'P.J.M.'	−25°	5-8	■	■	■				■	■		■
'Purple Gem'	−15°	6-8	■		■				■			
'Purple Splendor'	−10°	6-8			■	■		■	■		■	
'Ramapo'	−20°	5-8	■	■	■				■		■	
'Roseum Elegans'	−25°	5-8	■	■	■	■		■	■		■	
'Sappho'	− 5°	7-8		■	■			■	■			
'Scarlet Wonder'	−10°	6-8							■			
'Scintillation'	−10°	6-8	■	■	■				■			
'The Hon. Jean Marie de Montague'	0°	7-8		■	■	■		■	■			
'Trilby'	−10°	6-8		■	■				■			
'Unique'	0°	7-8			■				■			
'Vulcan'	− 5°	7-8	■	■	■				■			
'Windbeam'	−25°	5-8	■	■	■				■			
'Yaku King'	−10°	6-8	■	■	■				■			
'Yaku Prince'	−10°	6-8	■	■	■				■			
'Yaku Princess'	−10°	6-8	■	■	■				■			
'Yaku Queen'	−10°	6-8	■	■	■				■			
SPECIES												
R. carolinianum	−25°	5-8	■	■	■				■		■	
R. catawbiense	−25°	4-8	■	■	■				■			
R. chryseum	−15°	6-7							■			
R. fastigiatum	−15°	6-8							■			
R. impeditum	−15°	6-8	■		■				■		■	
R. intricatum	−15°	6-8							■			
R. keiskei	− 5°	7-8		■	■				■		■	
R. keleticum	−10°	6-8								■	■	
R. maximum	−25°	5-8	■	■	■				■	■		■
R. moupinense	− 5°	7-9						■	■			
R. mucronulatum	−15°	5-8	■	■	■						■	
R. pemakoense	0°	7-8							■			
R. yakusimanum	−15°	6-8	■	■					■	■		

Top-Rated Azaleas

Azaleas are extremely popular flowering shrubs, second in popularity only to roses. They are ideal plants for home landscapes, providing glorious color in spring and handsome leaves or branches the rest of the year. Use them as serviceable foundation plants, in decorative shrub borders, and in naturalistic woodland gardens. Wherever you plant azaleas, they will be sure to reward you for many years with their abundant blossoms.

There are 70 distinct species of azaleas within the large and complex genus *Rhododendron*. And the named hybrids, which fall into many distinct hybrid groups, number several thousand. This large number of azaleas might surprise many people who are familiar only with the azaleas that grow in their area.

Depending upon where you live, only a limited number may be adapted to your climate. For instance, in Southern California, gardeners are largely restricted to Belgian Indica and Southern Indica varieties, which tolerate the heat and dryness. In the Great Lakes area, gardeners know the cold hardy deciduous Ghent Hybrids best. On the other hand, in prime azalea territory, the choice is enormous. The following pages contain descriptions of evergreen azalea hybrid groups and deciduous azalea hybrid groups. The main characteristics of each hybrid group are discussed. The chart on page 23 rates azaleas according to the regions where they are adapted.

At left: Mollis Hybrid azaleas bear clusters of flowers that may be colored yellow, salmon, orange, pink, or red.

Plum-leaved azalea *(R. prunifolium)*

'Daviesii' (Ghent Hybrid)

'Pink Pearl' (Kurume Hybrid)

'Hinodegiri' (Kurume Hybrid)

EVERGREEN AZALEA HYBRID GROUPS

Many groups of hybrid azaleas are available, offering home gardeners a vast choice of plants. Each hybrid group was bred with specific goals in mind, such as larger flowers, more cold hardiness, or particular plant forms or flower colors.

Depending upon the group and the climate, evergreen azaleas retain differing numbers of leaves during the winter. Hybrids for southern areas have larger leaves and retain a full complement of leaves throughout the winter. In colder areas, ever-green kinds have smaller leaves and a finer texture. In fall, older inner leaves change color and drop, leaving varying amounts of foliage to cloak the branches in winter. The overwintering foliage often takes on beautiful reddish or purplish hues, depending upon the variety.

The hybrid groups described below are arranged in order of least to most cold hardy.

Belgian Indica Hybrids
These tender evergreen azaleas (hardy only to 20°F) were bred in Belgium, as well as in France, Germany, and England, beginning in the 1830's. The first parents were Japanese and Chinese imports brought to Europe by trading companies. They were bred for greenhouse forcing, though they easily adapted to growing outdoors in mild climates. The showiness of their profuse double, semidouble, or frilled flowers makes them modern-day favorites in southern gardens and for florist gift plants.

Southern Indica Hybrids
Southern Indicas were America's first evergreen azaleas and were introduced by the P. J. Berkman's Company of Augusta, Georgia.

AZALEA FLOWER FORMS

Azalea and rhododendron flowers, in their simplest forms, consist of five petals fused at their base into a short tube with five lobes. Azaleas flowers can have one of six shapes.

Single flowers are simple funnel-shaped forms created by five fused petals. Semidouble and double flowers have extra petals created by the stamens becoming petallike. In double flowers, all or nearly all of the stamens look like petals. Hose-in-hose flowers form when the sepals, "leaves" at the base of the petals, become petallike, forming a second funnel around the funnel of petals. Semidouble and double hose-in-hose flowers have both two funnels of petals and petallike stamens in their centers. Frilled flowers are characterized by petal edges that are ruffled or wavy.

Often a variety, 'Hinodegiri' for instance, that usually has single flowers will develop at different times or at one time single, semidouble, and double flowers. Factors such as climate and cultural conditions, along with genetic proclivity, determine when and to what degree the transformation occurs. Flower "doubling" is more common as growing conditions approach optimum.

Single   Semidouble   Double

Single Hose-in-hose   Semidouble Hose-in-hose   Double Hose-in-hose

(The company was later renamed Fruitland Nursery.) Specimens planted in the mid-1800's at Magnolia Gardens and other famous plantation gardens are still the stars of the spring show.

Similar in appearance to Belgian Indicas, these plants grow taller and faster, and tolerate more sun. Hardy to temperatures of 20°F.

Brooks Hybrids: These are tender hybrids (hardy to 20°F) of Belgian Indicas, Kurumes, and species such as *R. mucronulatum* and *R. indicum*. Lenard L. Brooks of Modesto, California, spent a quarter-century breeding these plants. Mr. Brooks' primary interest was developing azaleas adaptable to the hot summers and mild winters of California's Central Valley. Other aims were compact habit and good foliage and flower form.

About 30 of Mr. Brooks' varieties have reached the marketplace. A few, such as top-rated 'Redwing', have become very popular, but some confusion surrounds them. Some nursery catalogs list 'Redwing' simply as "hybrid" and others include it among Pericat, Kurume, or Rutherfordiana Hybrids. The Brooks Hybrids, like the Gold Cup and Nuccio Hybrids, are most often mistakenly listed as belonging to other more familiar groups.

Nuccio Hybrids: Nurseryman Julius Nuccio of Altadena, California has used the florist's azalea to breed reliable garden plants for his climate. Sun tolerance, vigor, sturdy root systems, and fragrance are prime virtues he sought. 'Nuccio's Pink Champagne', released in the mid-1960's, was one of the first. Lavender 'Happy Days' is popular in Southern California today. No Nuccio Hybrids (hardy to 20°F) are top-rated, only because they are not widely available. If you live in Southern California, visit Nuccio's Nursery in Altadena to see or obtain them.

Gold Cup Hybrids: Like the Brooks and Nuccio Hybrids, these azaleas are hybrids of the tender (20°F) Belgian Indica, Southern Indica, and Rutherfordiana Hybrids. Developed by Lynn Mossholder of Southern California, they are late-blooming, large-flowered, compact azaleas. None are top-rated due to limited availability, even in Southern California, but 'Sun Valley', with shiny white flowers with a green throat, is most often available.

Rutherfordiana Hybrids

These plants were American-bred for greenhouse forcing by Bobbink and Atkins Nursery of East Rutherford, N.J. They are 4-foot-tall, vigorous plants with flowers larger than the Belgian Indicas. Cold hardy to 20°F, they adapt well to outdoor culture in suitable climates. Blossoms are single, double, or semidouble.

Kurume Hybrids

These are Japanese hybrids whose breeding began in the early 1800's in the Japanese city of Kurume. Their parents are species native to the windswept peaks of Mt. Kirishima.

Cold hardy to 5°F, Kurume azaleas offer neat, tidy leaves and masses of small flowers. Flowers are single or hose-in-hose. Plants can grow quite large and tall, and branches are often layered in tiers.

Kurumes were first seen in the Western world in 1915 at the Panama Pacific Exposition in San Francisco. They received a gold medal, but otherwise little public attention, though Toichi Domoto of Domoto Brothers Nursery in Hayward, California obtained exclusive importation rights. Several of the hybrids he imported, such as 'Christmas Cheer', 'Coral Bells', and 'Snow', remain top-rated today.

In 1918, "Chinese" Wilson traced Kurumes to their source in Japan, where he selected 50 hybrids that he sent back to the Arnold Arboretum in Boston. These became known as the "Wilson Fifty." Later the United States Department of Agriculture imported 50 more. After Kurume azaleas were exhibited in 1920 at the Massachusetts Horticultural Society, they became great North American garden favorites.

Pericat Hybrids

This group was created by florist Alphonse Pericat of Collingdale, Pennsylvania for greenhouse forcing. They are however surprisingly cold hardy plants, tolerating 5°F, and so are good garden shrubs. Unfortunately, only a few varieties of these clear-colored azaleas are available, but one, 'Sweetheart Supreme', is top-rated.

Satsuki/Macrantha Hybrids

Created by Japanese hybridizers as early as the seventeenth century, this group is also known, confusingly, as Indica Hybrids (not Belgian or Southern Indicas) and Macrantha Hybrids. "Satsuki" translates from Japanese as "fifth month" indicating that these plant are late blooming. Large, often frilly flowers and dwarf, sometimes pendant form have made them favorite bonsai subjects in Japan. Their attractiveness and hardiness to 5°F have made them popular in North America.

Glenn Dale Hybrids

Hybridized at the USDA Plant Introduction Station at Glenn Dale, Maryland, by Dr. B.Y. Morrison, former director of the National Arboretum, these plants were bred for survival in the Mid-Atlantic States. Using a number of commercially available varieties and species and hybrids imported from Japan, he began breeding in 1929. The first varieties were introduced around 1940.

They are the largest group of evergreen azaleas and over 400 varieties of Glenn Dales are available today. They include plants of varying size, habit, and flower characteristics, but all are hardy to approximately 5°F. Some varieties are partially deciduous through the coldest winters.

Gable Hybrids

This hardy group was developed by Joseph B. Gable of Stewartstown, Pennsylvania. He introduced the first of them in 1927. Among the hardy species he used in hybridizing were the Korean azalea, *R. poukhanense,* and Kaempfer azalea, *R. kaempferi.* But parentage of the individual members of the group, like that of the Satsuki/Macrantha Hybrids, varies so much that their only common characteristic is hardiness—to between −5° and 0°F. (A few are hardy to −10°F.)

Girard Hybrids

These hybrids, introduced in recent decades by Peter E. Girard of Girard Bros. Nursery in Geneva, Ohio, are offspring of Gables crossed with *R. mucronatum, R. poukhanense,* and others. Girard's first objective was hardiness—his avowed goal was to produce azaleas hardy enough for the coldest areas of Wisconsin. However this group is not much hardier than the Gables—about −5F.

Kaempferi Hybrids

These are unusually hardy (to −10°F) evergreen hybrids. Known as the Malvatica Hybrids in Holland and England, they are primarily offspring of *R. kaempferi,* a 10-foot Japanese azalea, and the Malvatica Hybrids, azaleas of unknown parentage. They grow vigorously to 8 feet and bloom freely. Kaempferi Hybrids were created in the second decade of the twentieth century by P.M. Koster and C.B. Van Nes and Sons of Boskoop, Holland.

DECIDUOUS AZALEA HYBRID GROUPS

The deciduous azaleas are known for their clusters of often fiery-colored blossoms that decorate bare branches in early spring. They are tall, open plants and usually offer excellent foliage colors in fall before leaves drop. Some varieties have fragrant flowers.

Knap Hill/Exbury Hybrids

Around 1870 Anthony Waterer, eminent English horticulturist, crossed *R. molle* from China with the flame azalea from America. To this blend he eventually added Ghent Hybrids and several American species, including the western azalea, *R. occidentale.* The resulting Knap Hill Hybrids, named for his nursery, were brilliant. Their durable, fragrant flowers, larger than Ghent Hybrid flowers, were in soft to flaming-hot tones, many with contrasting darker crests.

For a long time Knap Hill Hybrids received little notice, but in the 1920's they began to attract the attention of several talented horticulturists: the Slocock family of Goldsworth Old Nursery, near Waterer's nursery; Edgar Stead of the Ilam Estate near Christchurch, New Zealand; and Lionel de Rothschild of Exbury, in Surrey, England. These horticulturists refined the already brilliant results of Waterer's work, and created the Slocock, Ilam, Knap Hill, and Exbury strains or subgroups of the Knap Hill Hybrids. (Adding to the confusion, the original Knap Hill Hybrids and the three groups developed from them are all often collectively called Knap Hill Hybrids!)

Many azalea growers consider Exburys the ultimate hybrid. And certainly their creation by de Rothschild represents one of the titanic—and successful—undertakings in horticultural history. The international banker/horticulturist selected and crossed Knap Hill Hybrids for years, on a scale that defies imagination, and with remarkable single-mindedness. Every year he brought hundreds of thousands of Knap Hill seedlings into bloom—then kept two of each color and burned the rest. His annual late-spring fires became famous around the Surrey countryside. Each spared plant was added to his superior breeding stock. Finally he had 104 named varieties too good for burning. Resplendent colors and combinations of colors, elegant markings, broad, 5-inch flowers in massive clusters, and brilliant fall foliage on the 3- to

5-foot shrubs, hardy to −20°F, have rewarded their creator's efforts.

Mollis Hybrids

These azaleas, hardy to −20°F, were created in the 1870's in Belgium and Holland from *R. molle* from China, *R. japonicum* from Japan, and perhaps other species and hybrids, including North American *R. viscosum,* swamp azalea. Members of the Koster family, prominent Dutch horticulturists, produced some of the most outstanding varieties in the 1890's. The 4- to 6-foot shrubs are generally heat-tolerant and produce clusters of single yellow, salmon, orange, pink, or red flowers.

Occidentale Hybrids

R. occidentale, the Western azalea, was discovered in 1827. It is found along mountain streams from southern Oregon to southern California at altitudes usually in excess of 5,000 feet. Forty years later in England it was crossed with *R. molle* and various Mollis Hybrids by Anthony Waterer. The group of plants that resulted, known as the Albicans Hybrids, have mostly disappeared, but similar crosses in Holland and England in the early 1900's created the group presently known as the Occidentale Hybrids. Hardy to −25°F, these hybrids frequently are listed as either Ghent or even Knap Hill/Exbury Hybrids.

Ghent Hybrids

Among the most cold hardy of the azaleas, these hybrids from Ghent, Belgium, are tolerant of −25°F. They were developed in the 1820's from several American species: the gold-flowered flame azalea, *R. calendulaceum,* and the pink-flowered pinxterbloom azalea, *R. periclymenoides.* Later, in England, the very fragrant yellow-flowered pontic azalea, *R. luteum,* from the Caucasus, and the pink-flowered swamp azalea, *R. viscosum,* from America, were added to the breeding stock. These hybrids, along with crosses from other American species, form the Ghent azaleas. Plants grow to 6 feet. Double-flowered forms have been developed.

Northern Lights Hybrids

This is a relatively new group of azaleas bred for hardiness to extreme cold. Developed at the University of Minnesota Landscape Arboretum at Chaska, Minnesota, they are the only winter-hardy azaleas that reliably bloom in the upper Midwest. Flower buds withstand temperatures as low as −45°F (Zone 3).

Mature height and width of plants is 6 to 7 feet. They produce 1-1/2-inch clustered flowers in late May or early June. Each cluster includes up to one dozen flowers and is 3 to 4 inches wide. Leaves are 1 inch wide, 3 to 4 inches long, and deciduous.

Presently, Northern Lights Hybrids are available in very limited quantities, so are not top-rated. Available plants are all seedlings.

This means each plant will show minor differences in form, size, and flower color. Named varieties 'Pink Lights', 'Rosy Lights', and 'White Lights' (slightly less hardy, to −35°F) will be available soon.

SELECTION GUIDE TO THE TOP-RATED AZALEAS

In the following charts are descriptions of the top-rated azaleas. These are varieties that have been selected both for their beauty and their durability. They are the best plants for home gardeners because they are easy to care for and readily available. You should find the ones suitable for your area at your local garden center or nursery.

The charts provide descriptions of the flowers and the plant size and shape, and give the all-important season of bloom. For a long display, it's a good idea to choose a selection of azaleas that bloom several weeks

apart. You may also want to select late-blooming azaleas, if you live in a cold area, to prevent injury from late spring frosts, or if you want to grow azaleas beyond their limit of cold hardiness. (See page 31.)

Unlike the rhododendron charts, the azalea charts have no ratings of flower and plant quality by the American Rhododendron Society. Very few azaleas are rated at this time. However, the society is beginning to rate azaleas in the same way they do rhododendrons, and in a few years many of the azaleas at your nursery will be rated.

The charts are organized with the evergreen hybrid groups first, and the deciduous hybrids next, followed by the species. Within each category, the least cold hardy groups are listed before the more cold hardy ones. The species azaleas are arranged with the native American species separate from the Asian ones.

Evergreen Azaleas

Name	Cold Hardiness	Flower Description	Plant Description	Bloom Season
BELGIAN INDICA				
'Albert and Elizabeth'	20°F	White with salmon-pink edges, double, 2 in. across.	Grows less than 3 ft tall.	Midseason
'Blushing Bride'	20°F	Blush-pink, double.	Grows less than 3 ft tall.	Late season
'Chimes'	20°F	Bell-shaped, rich red, semidouble.	Grows less than 3 ft tall.	Winter through spring
'Jean Haerens'	20°F	Frilled, deep rose-pink, double.	Grows less than 3 ft tall.	Early season
'Red Poppy'	20°F	Dark red, single.	Grows 3-6 ft tall.	Midseason
RUTHERFORDIANA				
'Alaska'	20°F	White with chartreuse blotch, single, some semi-double, 2 in. diameter.	Grows less than 3 ft tall.	Mid- to late season
'Dorothy Gish'	20°F	Frilled, single, orange-red, hose-in-hose, 2-1/2 in. across.	Grows less than 3 ft tall.	Mid- to late season
'Gloria'	20°F	Salmon-and-white variegated, hose-in-hose.	Grows 3 to 6 ft tall.	Early to midseason
'Pink Ruffles'	20°F	Shell-pink, double, 2 in. across.	Grows 3-5 ft tall.	Midseason
'Redwing'	20°F	Red, hose-in-hose, 3 in. across.	Grows less than 6 ft tall.	Midseason
SOUTHERN INDICA				
'Brilliant'	20°F	Red, single, 2-1/4 in. across.	Dense, spreading. Grows 3-5 ft tall.	Mid- to late season
'Coccinea Major'	20°F	Orange-red, single.	Spreading, dense, less than 3 ft tall.	Late
'Duc de Rohan'	20°F	Orange-red, single, 2-1/4 in. across.	Spreading. Grows 3-5 ft tall.	Early to midseason
'Fielder's White'	20°F	Frilled, white with chartreuse blotch, single, 2-3/4 in. across.	Spreading. Grows 3-5 ft tall.	Early to midseason
'Formosa'	20°F	Lavender-magenta, single, 3-1/2 in. across.	Upright. Grows to 6 ft tall or more.	Mid- to late season
'George Lindley Taber'	20°F	White, flushed violet-red with a darker blotch, single, 3-1/2 in. across.	Grows 3-5 ft tall.	Mid- to late season
'Glory of Sunninghill'	20°F	Orange-red, single, 2 in. across.	Dense, spreading. Grows 3-5 ft tall.	Late season
'Pride of Dorking'	20°F	Brilliant orange-red, single.	Grows less than 6 ft tall.	Late season
'Pride of Mobile' ('Elegans Superba')	20°F	Deep rose-pink, single 2-1/2 in. across.	Grows to 6 ft tall or more.	Mid- to late season
'Southern Charm'	20°F	A pink sport of 'Formosa', single, 3-1/3 in. across.	Grows to 6 ft tall or more.	Midseason

Deciduous Knap Hill/Exbury Hybrids make superb landscape specimen plants, adding glorious flower color to the garden in spring.

Name	Cold Hardiness	Flower Description	Plant Description	Bloom Season
GLENN DALE				
'Copperman'	5°F	Brilliant orange-red, single with overlapping lobes, 3 in. across.	Spreading, dense. Grows 3-5 ft tall.	Late
'Delaware Valley White'	5°F	Fragrant, white, single, 3 in. across.	Grows less than 6 ft tall.	Late season
'Everest'	5°F	White with chartreuse blotch, single, 2 in. across.	Grows 3-5 ft tall.	Late midseason
'Fashion'	5°F	Orange-red with red blotch, single, hose-in-hose, 2 in. across.	Grows more than 5 ft tall.	Early to midseason
'Gaiety'	5°F	Rose-pink with a darker blotch, single, 3 in. across.	Dark green narrow leaves. Grows 3-5 ft tall.	Late midseason
'Geisha'	5°F	White, flecked and striped purple, single, 1-1/2 to 2 in. across.	Grows less than 6 ft tall.	Very early season
'Glacier'	5°F	White with a chartreuse throat, single, 2-1/2 in. across.	Upright. Grows 3-5 ft tall.	Early to midseason
'Glamour'	0°F	Rose-red, single, 2-1/2 in. across.	Dark green leaves turn bronze in fall. Grows 3-5 ft tall.	Early to midseason
'Helen Close'	5°F	White with a pale yellow blotch, single, 2-1/2 to 3 in. across.	Spreading, dense. Grows 3-5 ft tall.	Midseason
'Martha Hitchcock'	5°F	White with magenta-pink margins, single, 3-1/2 in. across.	Grows 3-5 ft tall.	Late midseason
'Treasure'	5°F	White with pink blotch, single, 4 in. across.	Dark green leaves. Grows 3-5 ft tall.	Early to midseason
KURUME				
'Christmas Cheer'	5°F	Brilliant red, hose-in-hose, 1-1/4 in. across, in a tight truss.	Spreading. Grows 3-5 ft tall.	Early to midseason
'Coral Bells'	5°F	Shell-pink, single, hose-in-hose, tubular, 1-1/8 in. across.	Spreading. Grows less than 3 ft tall.	Early to midseason
'Eureka'	5°F	Pink, hose-in-hose.	Spreading. Grows less than 6 ft tall.	Late season
'Hershey's Red'	5°F	Bright red, double.	Grows less than 3 ft tall.	Midseason
'Hexe'	5°F	Crimson-red, hose-in-hose.	Grows 3-5 ft tall.	Mid- to late season
'H.H. Hume'	5°F	White, single, hose-in-hose, 2 in. across.	Spreading. Grows less than 6 ft tall.	Midseason
'Hino-Crimson'	5°F	Crimson-red, single.	Grows 3-5 ft tall.	Midseason
'Hinodegiri'	5°F	Violet rose-red, single, 1-1/2 in. across.	Compact. Grows 3-5 ft tall.	Early to midseason
'Orange Cup'	5°F	Reddish-orange, hose-in-hose.	Grows less than 6 ft tall.	Late season
'Pink Pearl'	5°F	Salmon-rose, hose-in-hose.	Upright. May grow to 6 ft or taller.	Midseason
'Sherwood Orchid'	5°F	Violet-red with a dark blotch, single.	Spreading. Grows 3-5 ft tall.	Midseason
'Sherwood Red'	5°F	Orange-red, single.	Grows 3-5 ft tall.	Early to midseason
'Snow'	5°F	White, hose-in-hose, 1-1/2 in. across.	Upright, spreading. Grows less than 6 ft tall.	Midseason
'Vuyk's Scarlet'	5°F	Bright scarlet, single, very large.	Grows less than 6 ft tall.	Midseason
PERICAT				
'Sweetheart Supreme'	5°F	Frilled rose-pink with a dark blotch, semidouble, hose-in-hose, 1-3/4 in. across.	Dense and spreading. Grows 3-5 ft tall.	Mid- to late season

Mass plantings of azaleas can be planned to provide a continuous floral display from early spring into summer.

Name	Cold Hardiness	Flower Description	Plant Description	Bloom Season
SATSUKI/MACRANTHA				
'Beni-Kirishima'	5°F	Orange-red with a darker blotch, double, 2 in. across.	Grows 3-5 ft tall.	Late season
'Chinzan'	5°F	Light salmon-pink, single, large.	Compact, excellent for bonsai use with flexible branches. Grows less than 3 ft tall.	Late season
'Flame Creeper'	5°F	Orange-red, single.	Creeping plant with small leaves. Good ground cover. Grows less than 3 ft tall.	Late season
'Gumpo Pink'	5°F	Light pink, single, large.	Dense. Grows less than 3 ft tall.	Late season
'Gumpo White'	5°F	White with occasional red flakes, single, 3 in. across.	Low-growing, with small leaves. Grows less than 3 ft tall.	Late season
'Linda R.'	5°F	Soft, solid pastel-pink, single.	Dense. Grows less than 3 ft tall.	Midseason
'Salmon Macrantha'	5°F	Salmon-pink to purple, single.	Grows less than 3 ft tall.	Mid- to late season.
GABLE				
'Campfire'	0°F	Flame-red with a darker blotch, hose-in-hose.	Dense. Grows less than 6 ft tall.	Midseason
'Caroline Gable'	0°F	Red, hose-in-hose, 1-3/4 in. across.	Grows less than 6 ft tall.	Midseason
'Kathy'	0°F	Frilled, white, single.	Grows less than 3 ft tall.	Mid- to late season
'Lorna'	0°F	Pastel-pink, double, hose-in-hose, 1-3/4 in. across.	Spreading. Grows less than 3 ft tall.	Late season
'Purple Splendor'	0°F	Ruffled, lavender with a dark blotch, hose-in-hose.	Grows less than 6 ft tall.	Midseason
'Rosebud'	0°F	Violet-red, double, hose-in-hose, 1-3/4 in. across.	Low, dense, spreading. Grows slowly up to 3 ft tall.	Late season
'Rose Greeley'	0°F	Fragrant, white with chartreuse blotch, single, hose-in-hose, 2-1/2 in. across.	Dense, spreading. Grows less than 3 ft tall.	Early to midseason
'Stewartstonian'	0°F	Bright, clear red, single.	Upright, compact, bushy. Winter foliage wine-red. Ideal for bonsai. Grows to 6-8 ft.	Late season
GIRARD				
'Girard Crimson'	– 5°F	Crimson, single.	Grows less than 6 ft tall.	Midseason
'Girard Pink'	– 5°F	Pink, single.	Grows less than 3 ft tall.	Late season
'Hot Shot'	– 5°F	Orange-red, double.	Grows 3-5 ft tall.	Mid- to late season
'Rene Michelle'	– 5°F	Pink, single, with heavy substance.	Grows less than 3 ft tall.	Midseason
'Roberta'	– 5°F	Pink, double.	Grows less than 6 ft tall.	Midseason
KAEMPFERI				
'Alice'	–10°F	Salmon-red, fading to pale rose.	Grows to 6 ft tall or more.	Early to mid-season
'Fedora'	–10°F	Violet-red or phlox-pink, single, 2 in. across.	Upright. Grows to 6 ft tall or more.	Early season
'Herbert'	–10°F	Reddish-violet, hose-in-hose.	Spreading. Grows less than 6 ft tall.	Midseason
'Palestrina' ('Wilhelmina Vuyk')	–10°F	White with chartreuse blotch, single, 2-1/4 in. across.	Grows 3-5 ft tall.	Mid- to late season

'Toucan' (Knap Hill/Exbury Hybrid)

Smooth azalea (R. arborescens)

Deciduous Azaleas

KNAP HILL/EXBURY HYBRIDS

Name	Cold Hardiness	Flower Description	Plant Description	Bloom Season
'Aurora'	−20°F	Pale salmon-pink with an orange blotch.	Grows less than 6 ft tall.	Midseason
'Balzac'	−20°F	Star-shaped, very fragrant, red-orange with flame markings on upper petals, in trusses.	Grows less than 6 ft tall.	Late
'Brazil'	−20°F	Small, frilled, showy tangerine-red. Blooms in profusion.	Grows less than 6 ft tall.	Late
'Cecile'	−20°F	Very large, salmon-pink with a yellow blotch.	Grows less than 6 ft tall.	Late
'Fireball'	−20°F	Deep fiery-red.	Grows less than 6 ft tall.	Midseason
'Gibraltar'	−20°F	Bright orange-red with cherry coloring, in tight ball-shaped trusses.	Compact growth. Grows less than 6 ft tall.	Midseason
'Gold Dust'	−20°F	Solid gold, in ball-like trusses.	Grows less than 6 ft tall.	Midseason
'Klondyke'	−20°F	Orange-yellow bells open to flowers of solid deep tangerine-yellow.	Grows less than 6 ft tall.	Late
'Royal Lodge'	−20°F	Dark red with long stamens.	Dark, reddish-brown foliage. Grows less than 6 ft tall.	Very late
'Toucan'	−20°F	Light creamy-yellow with margins tinged pink.	Grows less than 6 ft tall.	Mid- to late season

MOLLIS HYBRIDS

Name	Cold Hardiness	Flower Description	Plant Description	Bloom Season
'Christopher Wren'	−20°F	Large, yellow with a tangerine blotch.	Grows more than 6 ft tall.	Mid- to late season
'Directeur Moerlands'	−20°F	Sunset-gold with a darker blotch.	Grows more than 6 ft tall.	Mid- to late season
'Koster's Brilliant Red'	−20°F	Orange-red. Single.	Grows more than 6 ft tall.	Mid- to late season

OCCIDENTALE HYBRIDS

Name	Cold Hardiness	Flower Description	Plant Description	Bloom Season
'Graciosa'	−25°F	Slightly frilled, pale yellow flushed rose.	Grows to 5-6 ft tall.	Early to midseason
'Irene Koster'	−25°F	Pure rose-pink with a small yellow blotch.	Grows to 5-6 ft tall.	Early to midseason
'Westminster'	−20°F	Clear almond-pink flowers.	Grows less than 6 ft tall.	Early

GHENT HYBRIDS

Name	Cold Hardiness	Flower Description	Plant Description	Bloom Season
'Coccinea Speciosa'	−25°F	Brilliant orange-red with a yellowish-orange blotch.	Grows to 5-6 ft tall.	Early to midseason
'Daviesii'	−25°F	Very pale yellow fading to almost white with a showy yellow blotch, 2-1/4 in. across.	Grows more than 6 ft tall.	Late
'Narcissiflora'	−25°F	Fragrant, double yellow.	Grows more than 6 ft tall.	Late

Asian Native Azaleas

Botanical Name/ Common Name	Cold Hardiness	Origin	Flower Description	Plant Description	Bloom Season	Comments
R. japonicum Japanese Azalea	−25°F	Japan	Varies from yellow to orange to red, 2 in. across.	Dense, 2-6 ft tall. Deciduous.	Midseason	One of the parents of Mollis and Exbury hybrids.
R. luteum (R. flavum) Pontic Azalea	−25°F	Caucacus of E. Europe	Very fragrant, bright sunny yellow-orange, 2 in. across.	Grows to 2-12 ft tall. Deciduous. Fall color.	Midseason	One of parents of Ghent hybrids.
R. molle (R. mollis) Chinese Azalea	−20°F	China	Yellow to yellow-orange, spotted green, 2 in. across.	Dense, 4 ft tall. Deciduous.	Early to midseason	One of parents of Mollis and Exbury hybrids.
R. obtusum kaempferi (R. kaempferi)	−10°F	Asian	Slightly frilled, salmon-pink to salmon-orange.	Semievergreen to deciduous. Under 6 ft tall.	Mid- to late season	Prime parent of Kaempferi hybrids.
R. schlippenbachii Royal Azalea	−25°F	Manchuria, Korea, Japan	Large, fragrant, pink or rose-pink, brown-dotted throats, 2-3 in. across.	Grows to 4 ft tall or more. Dense. Deciduous. Brilliant fall foliage.	Early to midseason, as leaves open.	Give partial shade. Beautiful but fastidious.
R. yedoense poukhanense Korean Azalea	− 5°F	Korea, Japan	Fragrant, rosy-lilac, 2 in. across.	Grows to 4-6 ft tall. Deciduous.	Early to midseason	May be semievergreen. One of the parents of Gable hybrids.

North American Native Azaleas

Botanical Name/ Common Name	Cold Hardiness	Origin	Flower Description	Plant Description	Bloom Season	Comments
R. arborescens Smooth Azalea, Sweet Azalea,	−20°F	N.Y. and Pa., south to mt. tops of Ga. and Ala.	Fragrant, pure white with pink or reddish flush and yellow blotch on upper petal, 2 in. across. Long stamens.	Reaches 6-10 ft tall. Deciduous.	Mid- to late season	A parent of Exbury hybrids.
R. atlanticum Coast Azalea	−10°F	Coastal Plains, Del. south to S. Car., Ga.	Fragrant, white or white flushed with pale red, some with yellow blotch, 1-3/4 in. long.	Low-growing shrub, 1-2 ft tall. Spreading roots. Deciduous.	Midseason	Flowers appear before leaves.
R. austrinum Florida Flame Azalea	−10°F	Fla., Ga., and Ala.	Fragrant, golden-yellow, 1-1/4 in. long.	Reaches 10-12 ft tall. Deciduous.	Very early.	Flowers appear before or with leaves.
R. bakeri Cumberland Azalea	−20°F	High elevations of W. Va., Ky., Tenn., south to Ga., Ala.	May be orange, red, or yellow with gold blotch, 1-1/2- to 2-in. across.	Varies from 1-10 ft tall. Deciduous.	Mid- to late season	Flowers appear after leaves.
R. calendulaceum Flame Azalea	−20°F	Appalachian Mts., N. Pa., Ohio, south to N. Ga.	Orange-red to clear yellow, 2-in. diameter.	Varies from 4-10 ft tall, rarely 15 ft tall. Deciduous.	Mid- to late season	Claimed as one of the most beautiful native shrubs. A parent of Exbury hybrids.
R. canadense Rhodora	−40°F	East coast of Labrador, south to N.J.	Bell-shaped with short tubes, 2 lips, 3/4 in. across. Rose-purple to white.	Grows to 3-4 ft tall. Dense. Deciduous.	Early to midseason	Flowers appear before leaves.
R. canescens Piedmont or Florida Pinxter Azalea	0°F	N.C., Tenn., south to Tx., Ala., Ga., N. Fla.	Fragrant, varying from white to light or deep pink, 1-1/2 in. across. Long stamens.	Reaches 10-15 ft tall. Deciduous.	Early to midseason	Flowers appear before or with leaves.
R. occidentale Western Azalea	− 5°F	S. Ore., south to S. Calif.	Fragrant, white to pinkish, splashed yellow or pink, often with a rosy throat. 2-1/2 in. across.	Grows to 6-10 ft tall and as wide. Deciduous.	Mid- to late season	Difficult to grow in the East. Used in development of Ghent and Exbury hybrids.
R. periclymenoides (R. nudiflorum) Pinxterbloom Azalea	−30°F	Mass., south to Ohio, N.C., Tenn., and Ga.	Sweet, fragrant, varying from white or pale pink to deep violet, 1-1/2 in. across.	Grows to 4-6 ft tall, rarely to 10 ft. Deciduous.	Early season	Used in breeding Ghent hybrids. One of the most common native azaleas.
R. prinophyllum Rose-Shell Azalea	−30°F	New England, south to mts. of Va., west to Mo.	Spicy, clove-scented, rose-pink to deep pink, 1-1/2 in. across.	Grows to 2-9 ft tall, rarely to 15 ft. Deciduous.	Midseason	Flowers appear with leaves.
R. prunifolium Plum-Leaved or Prunifolia Azalea	−10°F	S. W. Ga. and eastern Ala., along streams.	Varies from apricot to pale orange, orange-red to red, 1-1/2 in. across.	Reaches 8-15 ft tall. Deciduous.	Late to very late	Unusual candy-striped flowers buds.
R. serrulatum Hammock-Sweet Azalea	0°F	Wooded swamps of E. Ga., Fla., west to La.	Fragrance of cloves, white to creamy-white, 1-1/2 in. long. Long stamens.	Toothed leaves and red-brown twigs. Reaches 20 ft tall. Deciduous.	Very late	Flowers appear after leaves. Grows in wet soil. Valuable in South for very late bloom.
R. vaseyi Pink-Shell Azalea	−30°F	Mts. of west N. C., above 3,000 ft.	Bell-shaped, green-throated, rose-pink, with orange-red dots. 1-1/2 in. across.	Reaches 12-15 ft tall. Deciduous	Early to midseason	Flowers appear before leaves.
R. viscosum Swamp Azalea	−30°F	Swamps from Maine south to Ala., Ga.	Slender, small-tubed, 2 in. long, white to creamy-white or pale pink; spicy scent.	Grows to 8 ft tall. Deciduous.	Mid- to late season	Spreads by underground runners. Grows in wet soil. Parent of Exbury hybrids.

'Pink Ruffles' (Rutherfordiana Hybrid)

'Delaware Valley White' (Glenn Dale Hybrid)

'Redwing' (Rutherfordiana Hybrid)

Evergreen Azaleas by Color

White
'Alaska' . . . . Rutherfordiana
'Albert and Elizabeth' (with pink margins)
. . . . Belgian Indica
'Delaware Valley White' . . . . Glenn Dale
'Everest' . . . . Glenn Dale
'Fielder's White' . . . . Southern Indica
'Geisha' . . . . Glenn Dale
'George Lindley Taber' . Southern Indica
'Glacier' . . . . Glenn Dale
'Gumpo White' . . . . . Satsuki/Macrantha
'H.H. Hume' . . . . Kurume
'Helen Close' . . . . Glenn Dale
'Kathy' . . . . Gable
'Martha Hitchcock' (with lavender
    markings) . . . . Glenn Dale
'Palestrina' . . . . Kaempferi
'Rose Greeley' . . . . Gable
'Snow' . . . . Kurume
'Treasure' . . . . Glenn Dale

Pink
'Blushing Bride' . . . . Belgian Indica
'Chinzan' . . . . Satsuki/Macrantha
'Coral Bells' . . . . Kurume
'Eureka' . . . . Kurume
'Fedora' . . . . Kaempferi
'Gaiety' . . . . Glenn Dale
'Girard Pink' . . . . Girard
'Gloria' . . . . Rutherfordiana
'Gumpo Pink' . . . . . . Satsuki/Macrantha
'Jean Haerens' . . . . Belgian Indica
'Linda R.' . . . . Satsuki/Macrantha
'Lorna' . . . . Gable
R. obtusum kaempferi . . . Asian species
'Pink Pearl' . . . . Kurume
'Pink Ruffles' . . . . Rutherfordiana
'Pride of Mobile' . . . . Southern Indica
'Rene Michele' . . . . Girard
'Roberta' . . . . Girard
'Salmon Macrantha' .Satsuki/Macrantha
'Southern Charm' . . . . . Southern Indica
'Sweetheart Supreme' . . . . Pericat

Orange-Red
'Alice' . . . . Kaempferi
'Beni-Kirishima' . . . . Satsuki/Macrantha
'Coccinea' . . . . Southern Indica
'Copperman' . . . . Glenn Dale
'Dorothy Gish' . . . . Rutherfordiana
'Duc de Rohan' . . . . Southern Indica
'Fashion' . . . . Glenn Dale
'Flame Creeper' . . . . Satsuki/Macrantha
'Glory of Sunninghill' . . . Southern Indica
'Hotshot' . . . . Girard
'Orange Cup' . . . . Kurume
'Pride of Dorking' . . . . . . Southern Indica
'Sherwood Red' . . . . Kurume

Purple to Lavender
'Formosa' . . . . Southern Indica
'Purple Splendor' . . . . Gable

Violet-Red to Crimson
'Fedora' . . . . Kaempferi
'Girard Crimson' . . . . Girard
'Glamour' . . . . Glenn Dale
'Herbert' . . . . Kaempferi
'Hexe' . . . . Kurume
'Hino-Crimson' . . . . Kurume
'Hinodegiri' . . . . Kurume
'Rosebud' . . . . Gable
'Sherwood Orchid' . . . . Kurume

Red
'Brilliant' . . . . Southern Indica
'Campfire' . . . . Gable
'Caroline Gable' . . . . Gable
'Chimes' . . . . Belgian Indica
'Christmas Cheer' . . . . Kurume
'Hershey's Red' . . . . Kurume
'Red Poppy' . . . . Belgian Indica
'Redwing' . . . . Rutherfordiana
'Stewartstonian' . . . . Gable
'Vuyk's Scarlet' . . . . Kurume

Deciduous Azaleas by Color

White
R. arborescens ..... American species
R. atlanticum .... American species
R. canescens .... American species
'Daviesii' .... Ghent
R. occidentale ...... American species
R. serrulatum .... American species
R. viscosum .... American species

Pink
'Aurora' .... Knap Hill/Exbury
'Cecile' .... Knap Hill/Exbury
'Irene Koster' .... Occidentale
R. mucronulatum .... Asian species
R. periclymenoides .. American species
R. prinophyllum ..... American species
R. schlippenbachii ...... Asian species
R. vaseyi .... American species
'Westminster' .... Occidentale

Orange to Red
R. bakeri .... American species
'Balzac' .... Knap Hill/Exbury
'Brazil' .... Knap Hill/Exbury
R. calendulaceum ... American species
'Coccinea Speciosa' .... Ghent
'Fireball' .... Knap Hill/Exbury
'Gibraltar' .... Knap Hill/Exbury
R. japonicum .... Asian species
'Koster's Brilliant Red' .... Mollis
R. obtusum kaempferi ... Asian Species
R. prunifolium .... American species
'Royal Lodge' .... Knap Hill/Exbury

Yellow
R. austrinum .... American species
R. calendulaceum ... American species
'Christopher Wren' .... Mollis
'Directeur Moerlands' .... Mollis
'Gold Dust' .... Knap Hill/Exbury
'Graciosa' .... Occidentale
'Klondyke' .... Knap Hill/Exbury
R. luteum .... Asian species
R. molle .... Asian species
'Narcissiflora' .... Ghent
'Toucan' .... Knap Hill/Exbury

Purple
R. canadense ...... American species
R. yedoense poukhanense
.... Asian species

Deciduous azaleas have a delicate graceful appearance. They provide a color show in spring when they blossom and again in fall when the foliage takes on brilliant hues.

Pink-shell azalea *(R. vaseyi)*, a deciduous native American species, bears delicate long tubular flowers before leaves emerge.

Top-Rated Rhododendrons

Grand and majestic, with whorls of large leathery blue-green leaves and bouquets of elegant flowers, rhododendrons are prized shrubs wherever they are grown. There are thousands of named varieties, making selecting ones for your garden a seemingly difficult task. The lists that follow help make the selecting easy. They describe top-rated rhododendrons—those chosen by experienced horticulturists for their beauty, ease of care, and availability.

The lists describe the flower clusters, which are called "trusses". Trusses may be loose, compact, ball-shaped, dome-shaped, cervical (elongated), or bell-like. The lists also describe leaf size and color and plant height and density. Rhododendrons with small leaves are generally considered more sun-tolerant than large-leaved kinds. Use the notations on bloom season to select late-blooming plants for borderline hardy areas and to select plants that bloom at different times.

ARS RATINGS

Each rhododendron is rated by the American Rhododendron Society (ARS) on flower and plant quality. A scale of 1 to 5 is used, with 1 being poor and 5 being superior. For example, 'Boule de Neige' is rated 4/4. The first number means that the flower is considered above average; the second number means that the plant form and foliage are also considered above average.

These ratings should not be used as the ultimate test of plant usefulness. If you live in a region where rhododendrons are a bit finicky, you might prefer to choose ones that are rated slightly lower but are more cold hardy.

At left: 'Anah Kruschke' rhododendron bears long showy trusses of rich purple flowers late in the season; has lush dense foliage.

'Unique' rhododendron

'Nova Zembla' rhododendron

'Catawbiense Album' rhododendron

'Lee's Dark Purple' rhododendron

'Catawbiense Album' rhododendron

'Lee's Dark Purple' rhododendron

Rhododendrons

Name	Cold Hardiness	Flower Description	Plant Description	Bloom Season	Ratings & Comments
'Arthur Bedford'	−5°F	Lavender-blue with a distinctive dark blotch. Dome-shaped trusses.	Grows vigorously to 6 ft tall.	Mid- to late season	4/3. Tolerates full sun.
'America'	−20°F	Bright red flowers in tight, ball-shaped trusses.	Sprawling habit, to 5 ft tall.	Midseason	3/3. Popular ironclad.
'Anah Kruschke'	−10°F	Lavender-purple held in medium-large, tight, elongated trusses.	Bushy, to 6 ft tall. Dense, lush foliage.	Late season	4/4. Withstands full sun.
'Anna Rose Whitney'	−5°F	Large, rose-pink, in trusses of 12 flowers.	Grows to 6 ft tall. Dense foliage.	Mid- to late season	4/4. Well-shaped.
'Antoon van Welie'	−5°F	Deep pink, in big trusses.	Compact, vigorous grower reaching 6 ft tall. Broad, waxy, 6-in.-long leaves.	Mid- to late season	4/4.
'Blue Ensign'	−10°F	Lilac to lavender-blue with a purplish-black blotch, frilled, held in rounded trusses.	Grows to 4 ft tall, upright and spreading with glossy dark leaves.	Midseason	4/4. Tolerates full sun.
'Blue Jay'	−5°F	Lavender-blue blotched with brown, in compact, elongated trusses.	Grows vigorously to 5 ft tall with large, bright green leaves.	Mid- to late season	3/4.
'Blue Peter'	−10°F	Light lavender-blue with a purple blotch, frilled, in elongated trusses.	Grows to 4-5 ft tall with glossy leaves.	Midseason	4/3. Popular on East Coast.
'Boule de Neige'	−25°F	Trusses of white flowers resemble snowballs.	Compact shrub grows to 5 ft tall with bright green leathery leaves.	Midseason	4/4. Tolerates heat, sun and extreme cold.
'Bow Bells'	0°F	Deep pink buds open to light pink cup-shaped flowers in loose trusses.	Rounded, spreading growth habit, eventually reaching 3 ft tall.	Early to midseason	3/4. Leaves appear after flowers, emerging shiny copper color, maturing to medium green.
'Bric-a-Brac'	5°F	Trusses display flowers that open to shades of white or pink, with chocolate-brown anthers.	Low-growing, reaching 30 in. tall.	Very early	4/3. Leaves fuzzy, round, dark green.
'Caractacus'	−25°F	Purplish-red.	Compact shrub, to 6 ft tall.	Late season	2/3. Requires partial shade.
'Carmen'	−5°F	Lavender to dark red.	Dwarf, grows slowly to 1 ft tall with round, emerald-green leaves.	Early to midseason	4/5. Handsome when not in bloom.
'Caroline'	−15°F	Fragrant, orchid-pink.	Grows to 6 ft tall. Leaves waxy with wavy margins.	Mid- to late season	3/4. Long-lasting flowers.
R. carolinianum	−25°F	Pure white to pale rose, rose, lilac-rose, or commonly light purple-rose.	Compact, grows 4 ft tall.	Midseason	3/3. Native of Blue Ridge Mountains of the Carolinas and Tenn. *R. carolinianum album* is favored by many.
R. catawbiense	−25°F	Lilac-purple, sometimes purple-rose, spotted with green or brown-yellow. Trusses of 15 to 20 flowers.	Grows to 6 ft tall. Leaves medium-large, smooth, shiny dark green on top, pale green below.	Mid- to late season	2/2. Native to slopes and summits of southern Alleghenys, W. Va. south to Ga. and Ala. One of hardiest and best-known species.
'Catawbiense Album'	−25°F	Pure white spotted with greenish yellow, in rounded trusses.	Compact, spreading, grows to 6 ft tall. Slightly convex dark green leaves.	Late season	3/3. Deserves to be called an ironclad.

Many rhododendrons make fine specimen plants. Their foliage and form are attractive year-round. During their bloom season their magnificent flower color is incomparable.

Name	Cold Hardiness	Flower Description	Plant Description	Bloom Season	Ratings & Comments
'Chionoides'	−15°F	Bright white, in numerous trusses.	Compact, grows to 4-6 ft tall.	Mid- to late season	3/4. Very easy to grow.
R. chryseum (R. rupicola chryseum)	−15°F	Bell-shaped, bright yellow, in clusters.	Dwarf, grows to 12 in. tall. Leaves 1/2 to 1 in. long.	Early to midseason	4/3. Many dense branches.
'Cunningham's White'	−10°F	Small, white with greenish-yellow blotch in small, upright trusses.	Semidwarf, compact, spreading to 4 ft wide with shiny, dark leaves.	Mid- to late season	2/3. Requires partial shade.
'Daphnoides'	−10°F	Bright purple, displayed in pomponlike trusses.	Grows to 4 ft tall forming dense mound.	Mid- to late season	3/4. Foliage unique, with tightly spaced, rolled glossy leaves.
'Dr. V.H. Rutgers'	−20°F	Frilled, crimson-red.	Grows to 5 ft tall.	Mid- to late season	3/3. Dense foliage with dark green leaves.
'Dora Amateis'	−15°F	Spicy-scented, 2 in. across, pure white with green spots, in clusters of up to 5.	Semidwarf, grows to 3 ft tall with dense foliage.	Early to midseason	4/4. Leaves tinged bronze when grown in full sun.
'English Roseum'	−20°F	Rose-pink, tinged lavender, in big trusses.	Grows to 6 ft tall or more.	Mid- to late season	2/4. Handsome plant, even when not in bloom. Tolerates extreme heat, cold, and humidity.
R. fastigiatum	−15°F	Lilac-purple, in small clusters that cover foliage.	Reaches 18 in. with dense, dark, shiny foliage.	Midseason	4/4. One of the hardiest of small alpine-type rhododendrons.
'Fastuosum Flore Pleno'	−10°F	Lavender-purple, double, 2 in. across, held in full trusses.	Grows vigorously to 6 ft tall with leaves dark above, light green below.	Mid- to late season	3/3. Open and rounded growth habit.
'Fragrantissimum'	20°F	Funnel-shaped, white tinged with pink, very fragrant.	Generally seen as espalier or vine to 10 ft or more. Can be kept to 5-6 ft or less with pruning.	Midseason	4/3. Flowers nutmeg-scented.
'General Eisenhower'	5°F	Large, ruffled, deep carmine-red in large clusters.	Compact, grows to 6 ft tall with large, waxy leaves.	Midseason	4/3. Strong-growing plant.
'Gomer Waterer'	−15°F	Pink flower buds open to pure white.	Grows to 5 ft tall with large, dark leaves.	Mid- to late season	3/5. Old standby tolerates full sun.
'Graf Zeppelin'	10°F	Vibrant bright pink.	Grows to 5 ft tall with dark, glossy leaves.	Mid- to late season	3/4. Vigorous and hardy.
'Herbert Parsons' ('President Lincoln')	−25°F	Lavender-pink.	Grows to 6 ft tall or more.	Mid- to late season	2/3.
'Humming Bird'	0°F	Red flowers hold their color well.	Semidwarf shrub with compact habit reaches 2-1/2 ft tall.	Early to midseason	3/4. Requires partial shade.
'Ignatius Sargent'	−20°F	Large, rose-red, slightly fragrant.	Grows to 5-6 ft tall with large leaves.	Mid- to late season	2/2. Plant has open growth habit.
R. impeditum	−15°F	Small, slightly fragrant, bright purplish-blue flowers blanket foliage.	Tight, compact, cushionlike dwarf shrub reaches 1-1/2 ft high. Tiny silvery gray-green leaves.	Midseason	4/4. Excellent for bonsai.
R. intricatum	−15°F	Attractive bluish flowers in profusion.	Low, compact, intricately branched shrub reaches 1-2 ft tall.	Early to midseason	4/3. Ideal for bonsai.

The flowers of many rhododendrons are distinguished with contrasting markings, such as the bold black blotch on the white petals of 'Sappho'.

Rhododendrons

Name	Cold Hardiness	Flower Description	Plant Description	Bloom Season	Ratings & Comments
'Janet Blair'	−15°F	Frilled, light pink with a green flare on the upper petals.	Grows vigorously to 6 ft tall.	Midseason	4/3. Profuse foliage.
R. keiskei	− 5°F	Lemon-yellow, bell-shaped, in clusters.	Grows to 3 ft tall. Variety cordifolia is dwarf, to 6 in.	Early to midseason	4/4. Very pointed leaves.
R. keleticum	−10°F	Large, pansylike, standing erect above foliage, ranging from rose through purple with crimson flecks.	Dwarf, reaching 1 ft tall, with dense, aromatic leaves.	Midseason	4/4. Good choice for bonsai.
'Kluis Sensation'	0°F	Dark red in tight trusses.	Compact shrub to 5 ft tall.	Mid- to late season	3/4. Dark red flowers contrast with dark green leaves.
'Lee's Dark Purple'	−20°F	Dark purple, in large trusses.	Grows to 6 ft tall with dark, wavy foliage.	Mid- to late season	3/3. Ironclad. Popular old-timer.
R. maximum	−25°F	White petals, rose or pink flushed. Trusses partially hidden by current season's leaf growth.	Grows from 4-ft-tall shrub to 40-ft-tall tree, depending on climate.	Mid- to late season	2/3. Leaves resemble a bay tree.
'Moonstone'	0°F	Bell-shaped, creamy-yellow, in trusses of 3 to 5.	Grows in a tight mound, 3 ft tall, covered with smooth oval-shaped green leaves 2-1/2 in. long.	Early to midseason	4/4. Prolific bloomer.
'Mother of Pearl'	0°F	Buds open pink, fade to pearl-white. Slightly fragrant.	Grows rapidly to 6 ft tall.	Midseason	4/3. A sport of 'Pink Pearl'.
R. moupinense	− 5°F	Funnel-shaped, large, fragrant, bright snowy-white with a maroon blotch.	Open, spreading growth to 30 in. wide. Bronzy-red new growth matures to shiny green leaves.	Very early season	4/3. Good choice for bonsai.
'Mrs. Charles E. Pearson'	− 5°F	Large, light orchid-pink with upper petals spotted brown, in dome-shaped trusses.	Grows vigorously to 6 ft tall with lush foliage.	Midseason	4/4. Award-winning old-timer. Vigorous. Tolerates sun and heat.
'Mrs. Furnival'	−10°F	Light pink with a striking brown blotch on the upper petals, in tight, dome-shaped trusses.	Upright, spreading, reaching 4 ft tall with light green leaves.	Mid- to late season	5/4. Grows well in eastern United States.
R. mucronulatum	−15°F	Orchid-pink blossoms 1-3/4 in. across appear before leaves. 'Cornell Pink' is rose-colored.	Grows to 5-8 ft tall. Red fall color.	Very early	ARS rating not available. Deciduous. Botanists consider this azalea-like shrub a rhododendron.
'Nova Zembla'	−25°F	Dark red, showy, in rounded trusses.	Grows to 5 ft tall with polished, dark green leaves.	Midseason	3/3. Grows well in difficult areas.
'Parson's Gloriosum'	−25°F	Lavender-pink in conical trusses.	Grows compact, upright, to 5 ft tall with dark green leaves.	Midseason	2/2. Very hardy. Ironclad.
R. pemakoense	0°F	Profusion of pink flowers hides leaves.	Dwarf, compact, cushionlike to 1-1/2 ft with tiny, 1-in.-long leaves.	Very early to early season	3/4. Very easy to grow.
'Pink Pearl'	− 5°F	Rose-pink in large trusses.	Tall, open growth to 6 ft.	Midseason	3/3.
'P.J.M.'	−20°F	Lavender-pink in small trusses.	Compact-growing to 4 ft tall with small leaves mahogany during winter.	Early season	4/4. Will withstand full sun as well as cold and heat.

'Unique' rhododendron

'Vulcan' rhododendron

Name	Cold Hardiness	Flower Description	Plant Description	Bloom Season	Ratings & Comments
'Purple Gem'	−20°F	Deep purple-violet.	Compact, spreading, grows to 2 ft with bluish-green foliage.	Early to midseason	3/4. Related to 'Ramapo'.
'Purple Splendor'	−10°F	Dark purple with a black blotch; appearing almost black overall.	Shrub grows to 5 ft with deep green foliage.	Mid- to late season	4/3. The king of royal purples.
'Ramapo'	−20°F	Pale violet, small, in profusion.	Dwarf, compact, spreading, reaches 2 ft. New leaves dusty blue.	Early to midseason	4/4. Use in low borders or rock gardens. Foliage is interesting throughout all seasons.
'Roseum Elegans'	−25°F	Small, rosy-lilac, held in dome-shaped trusses.	Grows vigorously to 6 ft with abundant olive-green foliage.	Mid- to late season	2/4. Another ironclad. Also for hot climates.
'Sappho'	−10°F	Medium-size, white with a blackish blotch on upper petals, in dome-shaped trusses.	Grows vigorously with open growth to 6 ft.	Midseason	3/2. Blooms profusely.
'Scarlet Wonder'	−10°F	Ruffled, scarlet-red, in flattened trusses.	Very compact, reaching 2 ft with dense, glossy leaves.	Midseason	5/4. Awarded silver and gold medal by Dutch enthusiasts.
'Scintillation'	−10°F	Pastel-pink, with a bronze and yellow throat, in large, dome-shaped trusses.	Grows to 5 ft with deep shiny green foliage.	Midseason	4/4. Wavy leaves curl attractively.
'The Hon. Jean Marie de Montague'	0°F	Bright red, showy, in rounded trusses.	Compact shrub grows to 5 ft tall with thick, heavy emerald-green foliage.	Midseason	4/4. Standard for excellence for red flowers.
'Trilby'	−10°F	Dark, crimson-red with black markings in the center, displayed in ball-like trusses.	Compact habit, reaches 5 ft with red stems, gray-green leaves.	Mid- to late season	3/4. Handsome plant, even when not in bloom.
'Unique'	0°F	Buds open light pink, change to buttery cream-yellow flushed with peach. Displayed profusely on dome-shaped trusses.	Compact, neat, reaches 4 ft with thick, oblong clover-green leaves.	Early to midseason	4/4. Flowers completely cover plant.
'Vulcan'	−10°F	Bright fire-red.	Mound-shaped, grows to 5 ft tall.	Mid- to late season	4/4. An excellent hybrid.
'Windbeam'	−25°F	Open white, turning light pink.	Spreading, grows to 4 ft with small leaves.	Early to midseason	4/3. Aromatic foliage.
'Yaku King'	−10°F	Deep pink with light pink blotch. Up to 18 blossoms in a ball-like truss.	Semidwarf, grows less than 3 ft tall.	Mid- to late season	ARS rating not available.
'Yaku Prince'	−10°F	Pink blossom, lighter blotch with reddish-orange spots. Up to 14 blossoms in a ball-like truss.	Semidwarf, grows less than 3 ft tall.	Midseason	ARS rating not available.
'Yaku Princess'	−10°F	Apple-blossom pink with a blushed blotch, greenish spots. Up to 15 blossoms in a ball-like truss.	Semidwarf, grows less than 3 ft tall.	Midseason	ARS rating not available.
'Yaku Queen'	−10°F	Pale pink with a faint yellow blotch. Up to 16 blossoms in a ball-like truss.	Semidwarf, grows less than 3 ft tall.	Midseason	ARS rating not available.
R. yakusimanum	−15°F	Pale rose.	Semidwarf, grows less than 3 ft tall.	Midseason	5/5. Limited availability but very popular among hobbyists.

'Roseum Elegans' rhododendron   'Sappho' rhododendron   'Anah Kruschke' rhododendron

Rhododendrons by Color

Pink
Recommended Zones

'Anna Rose Whitney'	7-8
'Antoon van Welie'	7-8
'Bow Bells'	7-8
'Bric-a-Brac'	8-9
'Caroline'	6-8
R. carolinianum	5-8
'English Roseum'	5-8
'Graf Zeppelin'	7-8
'Herbert Parsons'	5-8
'Janet Blair'	6-8
'Mrs. Charles E. Pearson'	7-8
'Mrs. Furnival'	6-8
R. mucronulatum	6-8
'Parson's Gloriosum'	5-8
R. pemakoense	7-8
'Pink Pearl'	7-8
'P.J.M.'	5-8
'Roseum Elegans'	5-8
'Scintillation'	6-8
'Yaku King'	6-8
'Yaku Prince'	6-8
'Yaku Princess'	6-8
'Yaku Queen'	6-8
R. yakusimanum	6-8

Red
Recommended Zones

'America'	5-8
'Caractacus'	5-8
'Carmen'	7-8
'Dr. V.H. Rutgers'	5-8
'General Eisenhower'	7-8
'Humming Bird'	7-9
'Ignatius Sargent'	5-8
'Kluis Sensation'	7-8
'Nova Zembla'	5-8
'Scarlet Wonder'	6-8
'The Hon. Jean Marie de Montague'	7-8
'Trilby'	6-8
'Vulcan'	7-8

White

'Boule de Neige'	5-8
'Bric-a-Brac'	8-9
R. carolinianum	5-8
'Catawbiense Album'	5-8
'Chionoides'	5-8
'Cunningham's White'	6-8
'Dora Amateis'	6-9
'Fragrantissimum'	9-10
'Gomer Waterer'	6-8
'Mother of Pearl'	7-9
R. maximum	5-8
R. moupinense	7-9
'Sappho'	7-8
'Windbeam'	5-8

Yellow
Recommended Zones

R. chryseum	6-7
R. keiskei	7-8
'Moonstone'	7-9
'Unique'	7-8

Blue

'Arthur Bedford'	7-8
'Blue Ensign'	6-8
R. intricatum	6-8
'Blue Jay'	7-8
'Blue Peter'	6-8

Purple

'Anah Kruschke'	6-8
R. catawbiense	5-8
'Daphnoides'	6-8
R. fastigiatum	6-8
'Fastuosum Flore Pleno'	6-8
R. impeditum	6-8
R. keleticum	6-8
'Lee's Dark Purple'	5-8
'Purple Gem'	6-8
'Purple Splendor'	6-8
'Ramapo'	5-8

Rhododendrons by Use

MOST COLD HARDY

White
	Recommended Zones
'Boule de Neige'	5-8
'Catawbiense Album'	5-8
'Dora Amateis'	6-9

Pink
'Caroline'	6-8
'Mrs. Furnival'	6-8
'Parson's Gloriosum'	5-8
'P.J.M.'	5-8
'Scintillation'	6-8
'Windbeam'	5-8

Red
'America'	5-8
'Ignatius Sargent'	5-8
'Nova Zembla'	5-8
'Roseum Elegans'	5-8

Blue
R. intricatum	6-8

Purple
'Anah Kruschke'	6-8
R. fastigiatum	6-8
R. impeditum	6-8
'Lee's Dark Purple'	5-8
'Purple Gem'	6-8
'Ramapo'	5-8

EASY-TO-GROW

White
	Recommended Zones
'Boule de Neige'	5-8
'Dora Amateis'	6-9

Pink
'Anna Rose Whitney'	7-8
R. mucronulatum	5-8
'Pink Pearl'	7-8
'Windbeam'	5-8

Red
'America'	5-8
'The Hon. Jean Marie de Montague'	7-8

Blue and Purple
'Anah Kruschke'	6-8
'Blue Peter'	6-8
'Fastuosum Flore Pleno'	6-8
R. impeditum	6-8
'P.J.M.'	5-8
'Purple Gem'	6-8
'Purple Splendor'	6-8
'Ramapo'	5-8

FULL SUN

White
	Recommended Zones
'Catawbiense Album'	5-8
'Cunningham's White'	6-8
'Dora Amateis'	6-9
'Gomer Waterer'	6-8
R. maximum	5-8

Pink
'English Roseum'	5-8
'Graf Zeppelin'	7-8
'Mrs. Charles E. Pearson'	7-8
'P.J.M.'	5-8

Red
'Nova Zembla'	5-8
'The Hon. Jean Marie de Montague'	7-8
'Vulcan'	7-8

Blue
'Arthur Bedford'	7-8
'Blue Peter'	6-8

Purple
'Anah Kruschke'	6-8
'Daphnoides'	6-8
'Fastuosum Flore Pleno'	6-8
'Purple Gem'	6-8
'Ramapo'	5-8
R. impeditum	6-8

FRAGRANT

White
	Recommended Zones
'Dora Amateis'	6-9
'Fragrantissimum'	9-10
R. moupinense	7-9

Pink
'Caroline'	6-8
R. vaseyi	5-9

Red
'Ignatius Sargent'	5-8

Purple
R. impeditum	6-8

FOR CONTAINERS

White
	Recommended Zones
'Cunningham's White'	6-8
'Dora Amateis'	6-9
R. moupinense	7-9

Pink
'Bow Bells'	7-8
'Mrs. Furnival'	6-8
'P.J.M.'	5-8

Red
'Scarlet Wonder'	6-8

Yellow
'Moonstone'	7-9
R. chryseum	6-7
R. keiskei	7-8
'Unique'	7-8

Purple
R. fastigiatum	6-8
R. impeditum	6-8
R. keleticum	6-8
'Purple Gem'	6-8
'Ramapo'	5-8

DWARF AND SEMIDWARF

White
	Recommended Zones
'Cunningham's White'	6-8
'Dora Amateis'	6-9
R. moupinense	7-9

Pink
'Bric-a-Brac'	8-9
R. pemakoense	7-8
'Windbeam'	5-8

Red
'Carmen'	7-8
'Humming Bird'	7-9
'Scarlet Wonder'	6-8

Yellow
R. chryseum	6-7
R. keiskei	7-8
'Moonstone'	7-9

Blue
R. fastigiatum	6-8
R. impeditum	6-8
R. intricatum	6-8
'Purple Gem'	6-8
'Ramapo'	5-8

THE UNFOLDING OF A RHODODENDRON TRUSS

Rhododendrons produce flowers on branch tips in clusters called trusses. All of the trusses do not open simultaneously, so gardeners can enjoy watching the transition from tightly held bud to fully opened flower truss throughout the blooming season. The various stages of development illustrated in this photographic sequence can take from a week to ten days, depending on climatic conditions. To an avid gardener the gradual unfolding of rhododendron trusses is a natural phenomenon that is a dramatic highpoint of spring.

Rhododendron Societies

The American Rhododendron Society and the Canadian Rhododendron Society are organizations of hobbyists and gardeners with a special interest in these flowering shrubs.

The American Rhododendron Society, founded in 1944 in Portland, Oregon, has 49 chapters and about 5,500 members in the United States and western Canada. It is devoted to encouraging interest in, and knowledge of, rhododendrons and azaleas. It also provides a means for interested people to communicate and cooperate with each other through educational and scientific studies, meetings, publications, and other activities such as rhododendron and azalea shows.

Rhododendrons and azaleas are grown and evaluated in the society's test gardens. Their hardiness and general quality are rated and outstanding new rhododendrons and azaleas are given awards of merit. Published rhododendron ratings are periodically updated. Azalea ratings are now underway.

Membership is open to anyone interested. The annual fee includes the society's publication, *The Quarterly Journal*. Write: The American Rhododendron Society, 14635 S.W. Bull Mt. Road, Tigard, OR 97223.

The Canadian Rhododendron Society was founded in 1971 and includes approximately 400 members. Members are primarily interested in growing and testing plants to select for flower color and plant vigor. Research on plant hardiness is carried out at the Horticultural Research Institute of Ontario at Vineland.

Membership in the CRS includes two glossy bulletins, newsletters, and other materials. Back issues of bulletins are available. There are two annual meetings—one in May or June in conjunction with a flower show, and one in the fall. For information, write Dr. H.G. Hedges, 4271 Lakeshore Road, Burlington, Ontario L7L 1A7.

REPORTS FROM ARS CHAPTERS

A recent poll by the American Rhododendron Society asked its members to detail which azaleas and rhododendrons grew best in their area. A primary purpose of the poll was to benefit new members of the society. Results are especially instructive to any beginner looking for the best and most easily grown varieties and species for a region.

On the following pages are lists of recommended plants from those chapters that responded to the questionnaire. Comments on location, temperatures, prevailing soil type, and other pertinent cultural factors of each chapter area detailed on the following pages make the responses from members of that chapter more meaningful. Responses from each chapter are listed separately for evergreen azaleas, deciduous azaleas, and rhododendrons.

Some chapters provided few or no responses for some of the categories, but this does not mean that categories with few or no responses are unimportant in those areas—often just the reverse is true. As specialists and collectors, the members often responded with those challenging or out-of-the-ordinary plants they have found success with.

For example, the Southeast Chapter mentions only rhododendrons—though this is a world-famous area for evergreen azaleas—because rhododendrons are more tricky there. Similarly, 'Sherwood Red' is omitted by all Northwestern Chapters, though it is a great favorite among the many evergreen azaleas grown there.

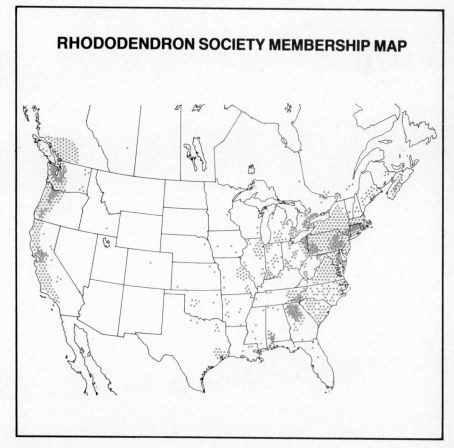

RHODODENDRON SOCIETY MEMBERSHIP MAP

AZALEA CHAPTER

Centered in Atlanta and covering Piedmont and lower Piedmont regions of Georgia. Climate tends to be dry but humid in summer and wet in winter. Summer temperatures reach the 90's or higher. Winter temperature may drop briefly below 0°F. The heavy soil must be lightened and elevated for good, long-term results.

Evergreen azaleas: 'Delaware Valley White', 'Fashion', 'George Lindley Taber', 'Hino-Crimson', 'Pink Pearl', 'Purple Splendor', 'Sherwood Red'.

Deciduous azaleas: *R. atlanticum, R. bakeri, R. canadense, R. periclymenoides, R. vaseyi.*

Rhododendrons: 'Boule de Neige', 'Caroline', 'Dora Amateis', 'Janet Blair', 'Nova Zembla', 'P.J.M.', 'Windbeam'.

CALIFORNIA CHAPTER

Located in the East Bay of the San Francisco Bay Area. Frost seldom occurs, and intense summer heat is seldom experienced because summer climate is modified by fog from the Pacific.

Evergreen azaleas: 'Coral Bells', 'Gumpo', 'Hino-Crimson', 'Hinodegiri', 'Sherwood Orchid', 'Sherwood Red', 'Stewartstonian'.

Deciduous azaleas: 'Cecile', 'Gibraltar', 'Irene Koster', *R. schlippenbachii.*

Rhododendrons: 'Anna Rose Whitney', 'Antoon van Welie', 'Bow Bells', 'Dora Amateis', 'Fragrantissimum', 'The Hon. Jean Marie de Montague'.

CONNECTICUT CHAPTER

Lowest mean monthly temperature varies from 9°F to 34°F, depending on area of the state. Near Long Island Sound the climate is more moderate, seldom experiencing 0°F. In colder areas, snowfall is heavy and long-lasting, protecting plants from wind and low temperatures. Highest mean temperatures vary from 72°F to 78°F over the state.

Evergreen azaleas: 'Delaware Valley White', 'Rosebud', and 'Stewartstonian'.

Deciduous azaleas: 'Gibraltar', *R. arborescens, R. calendulaceum, R. schlippenbachii, R. vaseyi.*

Rhododendrons: 'Boule de Neige', 'Dora Amateis', 'Janet Blair', 'P.J.M.', 'Ramapo', 'Scintillation', 'Windbeam'.

DE ANZA CHAPTER

Located south of the San Mateo Chapter, around San Jose and the Santa Clara Valley. There is occasional frost. Normal winter lows are in the high 30's to mid 40's. Winter highs are 50° to 60°F, and summer highs often in the 90's.

Evergreen azaleas: 'Fielder's White'.

Rhododendrons: 'Anah Kruschke', 'Anna Rose Whitney', 'Antoon van Welie', 'Fragrantissimum', 'The Hon. Jean Marie de Montague'.

GRAYS HARBOR CHAPTER

Located at the base of the Olympic Peninsula on the Pacific Ocean. Soil varies from deep silt loam to clay loam with some gravel benches to sandy loam. Usual temperature extremes are 15°F and 85°F.

Evergreen azaleas: 'Everest', 'Gaiety', 'Gumpo', 'Hino-Crimson', 'Rosebud'.

Deciduous azaleas: 'Cecile', *R. schlippenbachii.*

INDIANA CHAPTER

Located throughout Indiana, where summer high temperatures average 85°F or above. Winter temperature can reach −25°F or lower. Summer is dry. Soil varies from clay to sandy loam to silt loam, slightly acid to neutral in the north and moderately to strongly acid in the south.

Evergreen azaleas: 'Fedora', 'Herbert', 'Stewartstonian'.

Rhododendrons: 'Janet Blair', 'Roseum Elegans', 'Scintillation'.

MIDDLE ATLANTIC CHAPTER

Located in Virginia from the Tidewater to the western mountains. Winter lows may be 15°F at the coast and −5°F near the mountains, with an inverse difference in summer highs. Moderately acid soil is sandy near coast, clay toward the mountains.

Evergreen azaleas: 'Coral Bells', 'Delaware Valley White', 'Herbert', 'Hershey's Red', 'Hino-Crimson', 'Pink Pearl', 'Rosebud', 'Stewartstonian'.

Deciduous azaleas: 'Cecile', 'Gibraltar', 'Klondyke', *R. atlanticum, R. bakeri, R. calendulaceum, R. periclymenoides, R. prinophyllum, R. vaseyi,* 'Toucan'.

Rhododendrons: 'Caroline', 'Janet Blair', 'P.J.M.', 'Roseum Elegans', 'Scintillation', 'The Hon. Jean Marie de Montague'.

MONTEREY BAY CHAPTER

Located mainly in Santa Cruz County, on the coast 75 to 100 miles south of San Francisco. Elevations range from sea level to 2,000 feet. Normal maximum temperature near the coast is 90°F, inland to 105°F, and minimum temperature from 35°F near the coast to 20°F inland. Soil ranges from sand to heavy clay.

Evergreen azaleas: 'Hexe'.

Deciduous azaleas: 'Gibraltar', *R. occidentale.*

NEW YORK CHAPTER

All responses are from Long Island, where temperatures can drop to −10°F and rise to 100°F, but are usually more moderate. Soil varies from sand near shore to clay inland.

Evergreen azaleas: 'Rosebud', Rose Greeley, 'Stewartstonian'.

Deciduous azaleas: 'Gibraltar', 'Klondyke', *R. calendulaceum, R. schlippenbachii, R. vaseyi,* 'Toucan'.

Rhododendrons: 'Boule de Neige', 'Dora Amateis', 'Janet Blair', 'P.J.M.', 'Scintillation', 'The Hon. Jean Marie de Montague', 'Windbeam'.

PIEDMONT CHAPTER

Located in North Carolina, from the Smoky Mountains past the Piedmont and on toward the eastern shore. Temperatures range from 0°F in winter to 100°F in summer. Soil is sandy loam toward coast, clay inland.

Evergreen azaleas: 'Delaware Valley White', 'Pink Pearl'.

Deciduous azaleas: *R. atlanticum, R. calendulaceum, R. periclymenoides.*

Rhododendrons: 'Dora Amateis', 'Roseum Elegans', 'Scintillation', 'The Hon. Jean Marie de Montague'.

POTOMAC VALLEY CHAPTER

Includes northern Virginia, Maryland, southeastern Pennsylvania, and Delaware. Lowest temperature reported was −6°F, but subzero readings are unusual. Summer temperatures are in the 90°F range. Soil near the coast is sandy, but clay is prevalent elsewhere. Drainage can be a problem in clay areas.

Evergreen azaleas: 'Delaware Valley White', 'Rose Greeley', 'Stewartstonian'.

Deciduous azaleas: 'Gibraltar', *R. calendulaceum, R. vaseyi.*

Rhododendrons: 'Caroline', 'Janet Blair', 'P.J.M.', 'Roseum Elegans', 'Scintillation'.

PRINCETON CHAPTER

Located in central New Jersey, extending from "Old Mountains" to seacoast. Low temperatures reach 0°F to −15°F; high temperatures range from 85°F to 105°F. Soil varies from heavy clay to light sand, varying sharply between areas.

Evergreen azaleas: 'Delaware Valley White', 'Hershey's Red', 'Hino-Crimson', 'Rose Greeley', 'Rosebud', 'Stewartstonian'.

Deciduous azaleas: 'Cecile', 'Gibraltar', 'Klondyke', *R. schlippenbachii, R. vaseyi.*

Rhododendrons: 'Janet Blair', 'P.J.M.', 'Roseum Elegans', and 'Windbeam'.

SAN MATEO CHAPTER

Located halfway down the San Francisco Peninsula, which has water on three sides and a low mountain range down the center. Temperatures are seldom below freezing or above 95°F. Soil is mostly clay.

Evergreen azaleas: 'Coral Bells', 'Fielder's White', 'Gumpo'.

Deciduous azaleas: 'Cecile', 'Gibraltar', *R. occidentale, R. schlippenbachii, R. vaseyi.*

SEATTLE CHAPTER

Located in western Washington. There are many microclimates. On the west is Puget Sound, which moderates temperatures near the shore. In the east are two large lakes and, further east, foothills of the Cascades, with elevations up to 1,500 feet. Temperature rarely falls below 10°F or rises above 90°F. Soil is acid.

Deciduous azaleas: *R. schlippenbachii.*

Rhododendrons: 'Bow Bells', 'Dora Amateis', 'Mrs. Furnival', 'The Hon. Jean Marie de Montague', 'Unique'.

SHELTON CHAPTER

Located at the base of the Olympic Peninsula at the southern tip of Puget Sound. Temperature extremes are 0°F and 75°F. Soil is mostly sandy loam but clay occurs in some areas and is acid.

Rhododendrons: 'Anna Rose Whitney', 'Bow Bells', 'Dora Amateis', 'Gomer Waterer', 'Mrs. Furnival', 'The Hon. Jean Marie de Montague', 'Unique', 'Vulcan'.

SOUTHEAST CHAPTER

Located in eastern South Carolina and southern North Carolina. Temperatures range from winter low of 0°F to summer high of 100°F.

Rhododendrons: 'America', 'Blue Peter', 'Boule de Neige', 'Caroline', 'Dora Amateis', 'Janet Blair', 'Mrs. Furnival', 'P.J.M.', 'Ramapo', 'Scintillation', 'The Hon. Jean Marie de Montague'.

SOUTHERN CALIFORNIA CHAPTER

Located over a large area from San Diego to Santa Barbara along the coast and eastward into the mountains to an elevation of 5,000 feet. Soils along the coast are heavy clay, and decomposed granite in the mountains. Summers are dry and hot. Varieties with tolerance to alkaline water are desirable.

Evergreen azaleas: 'Duc de Rohan', 'Gumpo Pink', 'Pride of Dorking', 'Red Poppy', 'Redwings', 'Rosebud', 'Sherwood Red'.

Rhododendrons: 'Anah Kruschke', 'Gomer Waterer', 'Pink Pearl', 'Vulcan'.

TUALATIN VALLEY CHAPTER

Located west of Portland, extending to the Coast Range. Temperature extremes are 10°F and 100°F but do not persist for long periods. Soils vary, but most have excellent drainage and all are acid.

Deciduous azaleas: *R. schlippenbachii.*

Rhododendrons: 'Mrs. Furnival', 'The Hon. Jean Marie de Montague', 'Unique'.

WILLIAM BARTRAM CHAPTER

Located at the juncture of North Carolina, South Carolina, and Georgia. Temperatures range from lows of around −5°F to highs of around 100°F. Soil is predominantly clay loam.

Evergreen azaleas: 'Delaware Valley White', 'Fashion', 'George Lindley Taber', 'Hershey's Red', 'Stewartstonian'.

Deciduous azaleas: *R. bakeri, R. calendulaceum, R. canescens, R. periclymenoides, R. prunifolium.*

Rhododendrons: 'Caroline', 'Dora Amateis', 'Nova Zembla', 'Roseum Elegans', 'Scintillation', 'The Hon. Jean Marie de Montague'.

How to Grow Azaleas and Rhododendrons

Azaleas and rhododendrons have the same basic needs. A well-drained acid soil rich in organic matter is of primary importance. They do even better if a thick mulch covers the soil over their roots, keeping it cool and moist. Some shading from direct hot sun and protection from strong wind is also in order. And they'll do best where summers are cool and humid.

In prime azalea and rhododendron territory—the states along the Atlantic Seaboard and in the Pacific Northwest—it's fairly simple to meet these basic growing requirements. But the more your garden conditions differ from those in these prime areas, the more attention you'll have to give to caring for these shrubs. This chapter covers general care requirements that will be useful wherever you live. If you live outside of prime growing territory, consult pages 20 to 22 for special tips on growing azaleas and rhododendrons in your area.

Whether you are using them in a foundation planting or in a shrubbery border, the planting location must offer azaleas and rhododendrons the proper growing conditions. A good planting site is one where the shrubs look decorative and at home as well as one where proper sun, soil, and moisture are provided.

SUN EXPOSURE

Since they are native to woodlands, most azaleas and rhododendrons grow best with some shade. Deep shade is too dark however, and

At left: Well-cared-for azaleas reward gardeners with a rich display of exquisite floral beauty every spring, year after year.

'Vulcan' rhododendron

'Delaware Valley White' (Glenn Dale Hybrid)

'Anah Kruschke' rhododendron

'Pink Ruffles' (Rutherfordiana Hybrid)

Azaleas planted on the east side of a house receive the half a day of sun that is ideal to promote vigorous healthy growth.

causes plants to bloom poorly. In sunny spots flowers may fade quickly and blooming will be briefer than it would be with more shade. Foliage exposed to hot sun burns and dries out. The tender new leaves that emerge after flowers fade are the most vulnerable to strong sun.

Certain hybrids can stand more sun than others, however. Southern Indica and Brooks Hybrid azaleas, deciduous azalea hybrids, and rhododendrons with small leaves are the most sun-tolerant. In areas with cool humid summers, Pennsylvania for example, deciduous azaleas do well in only light shade. Where there is frequent coastal fog, Oregon for instance, evergreen azaleas and rhododendrons can be planted in full sun. Elsewhere, some shade is needed.

Kinds of shade: Light shade cast by tall high-branching trees is ideal. The tree foliage should diffuse the sunlight, casting constantly shifting shadows, without totally blocking the sunlight. This is the shade found in a woodland garden.

Most home settings cannot provide light dappled shade all day long, but other kinds of shade are also suitable. Planting sites where the shrubs receive half a day of sun are usually satisfactory if the sun is not too hot. This usually means protection from noon sun. Foundation

plantings along the east or west sides of your home will be in half shade.

Assuming that no sides of your home are shaded by trees or other buildings, it's usually best to plant azaleas and rhododendrons along the east side of your home. There they will receive morning sun, which is cooler than the afternoon sun of a western exposure. But if your home is shaded by trees or buildings, this changes the situation. If a western exposure is lightly shaded in both summer and winter, it is a perfectly fine planting spot. Shaded southern exposures will also do, but shade must be provided year-round throughout at least the hottest part of the day.

Planting beds along northern sides of buildings receive no direct sunlight. They may be too dark for best growth and flowering, however if the bed is open to the sky and unshaded by trees, enough light is often reflected onto the shrubs to support good growth. White walls or a nearby fence can reflect light and increase the brightness.

Shrub borders or planting areas on flat land away from the shade of your house should be shaded by overhead trees or located in the shadow cast by fences or evergreen windbreaks. Half a day of shade is usually sufficient and, as with shrubs shaded by a house, morning sun is usually best.

On sloping ground and hillsides, azaleas and rhododendrons do best on slopes facing east or west. Southern exposures are usually too hot and dry, while northern ones are too cold. Shade from trees and protection from wind can of course alter the conditions and make unfavorable exposures more acceptable.

Sun and cold: During winter when temperatures are below freezing, some of the water in living plant tissues is actually frozen. Chemical changes within a dormant plant allow it to be unharmed by this frozen state, as long as freezing and thawing of the tissue is gradual. In areas where winters are very cold, dormant flower buds can be damaged when struck by early morning sunlight because the buds thaw too rapidly. Protection from the earliest morning sun is advisable in such situations.

WIND PROTECTION

In any climate, wind can damage rhododendrons and azaleas. Cold winter winds can severely dehydrate plants, as can hot dry summer wind in arid climates. Wind can also tear the large evergreen leaves of rhododendrons. Blossoms of both rhododendrons and azaleas can be tattered or even blown off.

Avoid planting these shrubs near windy corners of your house or in narrow areas where winter winds funnel between buildings. In open areas, wind can be slowed down with a windbreak of tall evergreens or a fence. Both hedges and fences should not stop wind completely, or the wind will be swept directly over the top, resulting in damaging turbulence on the other side. Fences and hedges with small gaps allow wind to pass through at a slower, safer velocity.

COLD SPOTS

Cold air, like water, flows downhill and collects in "puddles." On windless nights, it collects at the bottom of a slope, and in this cold spot frost will occur before it forms anywhere else in your garden. Other frosty spots where cold air collects are places where the downward flow of cold air is stopped—for instance, along a solid fence or hedge halfway down a hillside. Don't plant on the uphill side of such a barrier. (See pages 60 and 63 for more information on protecting plants from cold.)

SOIL

Soil on a forest floor is usually highly organic, composed of decaying leaves, twigs, stems, bark, and fallen plants. Such soil is at the same time both moist and well-aerated. The decaying plant parts hold large quantities of water, but because they are only partially decomposed they are held together loosely, leaving generous air pockets. As the plant material decays, nutrients and organic acids are released, creating a rich, acidic soil. The annual autumn leaf fall adds to the natural compost and renews the soil.

Azaleas and rhododendrons have very fine, shallow root systems. Because this soil is so loose, rich, and moist, the roots don't have to work very hard pushing through it.

Most garden soil is a far cry from forest soil. In most gardens however, with very little soil modification azaleas and rhododendrons can do well. Azaleas will do well in a rich garden loam as long as it is properly acidic. Sandy loams are ideal, since they offer both richness and aeration. But soil that is too sandy, has a high clay content, or is alkaline will have to be improved.

Improving clay and sand: Soil texture is the key to preparing a good soil for azaleas and rhododendrons. Clay soil has a dense texture, draining slowly and admitting very little air, which is necessary for healthy root growth. Sand has too loose a texture, with so many air spaces that water drains through it too quickly. It holds little in the way of moisture and nutrients. The structure of both sandy and clay soils is improved by adding organic matter. This breaks up clay so that the resulting soil is more crumbly, holding more air and allowing water to drain more quickly. Sandy soil is made denser and more water-retentive.

Both of these soil types need generous quantities of organic matter such as peat moss, leaf mold, compost, or composted ground bark. Perlite could also be added to soil that has a very high clay content. Spread 3 to 8 inches of organic matter on top of the soil, and spade it in to depth of 1-1/2 to 2 feet, depending upon how much the soil needs to be improved. For a large planting of azaleas and rhododendrons, you can use a power tiller to work the entire planting bed. For just a few shrubs, add organic matter in a 2- to 3-foot radius of where the shrub's trunk will be. (See planting instructions on page 56.)

The organic matter will make the soil more acidic. This is useful in maintaining acidity in acid soil and necessary in soil that is not acidic enough for azaleas and rhododendrons. In alkaline soil, more drastic steps have to be taken. (See following section on soil pH.)

Wet spots: Even where soil texture offers good drainage, waterlogging may be a problem in some spots in your garden. Do not plant azaleas and rhododendrons in low spots of your property where water collects after a rain. Such waterlogged soil is certain death for most kinds—only an unusual water-tolerant species such as the swamp azalea, *R. viscosum*, could grow in such a site. Sloping sites where water drains quickly are best, especially if soil tends to be heavy.

If your garden has a drainage problem that can't be corrected, you can get around it by planting in raised beds, mounds, or in containers. (See page 55 for more information.)

Soil pH: Azaleas and rhododendrons prefer an acid soil with a pH between 4.5 and 5.5. A measure of acidity or alkalinity, pH is read on a scale of 1 to 14, with the lower numbers being most acidic and the higher numbers most alkaline. The midpoint, 7, is neutral. Most plants prefer a slightly acid pH of 6.5. Azaleas and rhododendrons can only absorb certain necessary nutrients, iron and manganese for instance, through their roots when these nutrients are in the chemical forms found in acid soil.

Soil pH varies throughout the continent, ranging from acidic on the East and Northwest Coasts to alkaline in arid regions of the Midwest and Southwest. In areas where rainfall is high, pH tends to be acidic, because the rain washes the alkaline elements calcium and magnesium from the soil. Where soils are high in organic matter, this also contributes to soil acidity. Forests and woodland areas tend to have more acidic soil, though the type of bedrock will influence this. Areas with limestone bedrock will have a higher pH.

You can determine the pH of your garden's soil by using a test kit available at most garden centers. Test each area where you are growing, or intend to grow, azaleas or rhododendrons, since the pH can vary from place to place in your garden. The soil along your house foundation may be more alkaline because lime in the cement foundation leaches into the surrounding soil. Soil tests are also available from private companies and usually from your local county agricultural extension agent.

A sylvan setting with light filtering through tree branches most closely approximates the native growth conditions of azaleas and rhododendrons.

You can lower your soil's pH by adding ground agricultural-grade powdered sulfur. It is slow-acting and should be applied several months in advance. Yearly applications may be needed if irrigation water washes alkaline elements back in.

The amount of sulfur to add depends upon your initial soil pH and how much you want to lower it. The more alkaline the pH, the more sulfur will be needed to lower it 1 point. To change the pH from 6.5 to 5.5, work 1-1/2 pounds of sulfur per every 100 square feet into the soil. Use 1/3 more in clay soil and 1/3 less in sandy soil. The following table gives other amounts for different situations.

Lowering pH	Amount of sulfur per 100 sq ft		
Change in pH	Sandy	Loamy	Clayey
8.5 to 6.5	4 lb	5 lb	6 lb
7.5 to 6.5	1 lb	1½ lb	2 lb
7.5 to 5.5	2 lb	3 lb	4 lb
6.5 to 5.5	1 lb	1½ lb	2 lb

Applying acidifying fertilizers such as iron sulfate and ammonium sulfate, especially in areas where soil acidity is borderline, will help maintain the appropriate pH. (See page 58 for more about fertilizers.) And a gradually decomposing organic mulch will also help keep the soil acid. (See page 58.)

A GOOD START

For the fullest enjoyment of your azaleas and rhododendrons, it's important to get them off to a good start. And that good start begins at the nursery by selecting the healthiest shrubs. If you take care of them before planting, plant them properly and in the right conditions, and coddle them a bit for the first year, they'll be off to a very good start.

Plant selection: Shrubs for sale at the nursery are available either as container-grown or as balled-and-burlapped plants. Shrubs in metal, plastic, or fiber containers were grown in those containers and their entire root system is intact. Balled-and-burlapped shrubs were grown

in the ground and recently dug up. Their ball of roots and soil is wrapped up in protective burlap. Because they were dug from the field, they have lost some roots and are more fragile than container-grown shrubs.

After you bring the shrubs home, keep them in a cool shaded spot until planting time. If left in the sun, dark containers can heat up quickly to root-damaging temperatures and burlapped rootballs will quickly dry out. Balled-and-burlapped shrubs should be planted as soon as possible so transplanting shock is minimized. Container plants can be kept for several weeks as long as they are watered regularly and kept cool.

Choose sturdy well-branched plants with thick foliage. Weak spindly ones probably have underdeveloped root systems and will transplant poorly, perhaps never gaining full vigor. Older, larger plants have more woody tissue and are hardier than smaller plants, a significant advantage where winters are severe.

HELP WHERE SOIL IS ALL WRONG— RAISED BEDS, CONTAINERS, AND MOUNDS

In the Southwest, soil is too alkaline for azaleas and rhododendrons and cannot be amended successfully. In parts of Southern California and the Deep South, soil has a high clay content and drains slowly, encouraging root rot. In these unlikely areas, it is still possible to grow fine azaleas and rhododendrons. The secret is to plant above ground in an ideal soil mix.

For individual plants, grow them in large decorative containers such as redwood pots or cement planters. For shrub borders or foundation plantings, soil can be held in raised beds that resemble large planter boxes, or piled on top of the ground in large mounds.

Soil: You can use any commercially available planting mix that's high in organic matter such as peat. Many people prefer to mix their own, however. The Southern California Chapter of the Rhododendron Society recommends a mix containing equal parts coarse peat moss, ground fir bark, and coarse perlite.

Raised beds: Build raised beds from railroad ties, wood, brick, unmortared or mortared stone, whatever fits in with the architecture of your home. Be aware that the cement in concrete and mortar is highly alkaline and can change the pH of your soil mix. If wood is used, be sure it is rot-resistant such as redwood or cedar.

Beds should be at least 1-1/2 to 2 feet deep and 3 feet wide. If the underlying soil drains slowly, lay down 2 inches of coarse gravel before adding the soil mix. Provide drainage holes along the bottom of all sides of the raised beds.

Mounds: For a less structured look than raised beds create, you can pile soil mix on top of the bad soil in natural-looking mounds. Make the mounds at least 2 feet deep and gradually slope them towards the natural grade of the land. Gravel should be used beneath the mound if the underlying soil is slow-draining. Erosion may be a problem on newly built mounds unless they are very wide. Mounds are useful in creating woodland gardens where soil conditions are unfavorable. Locate mounds well away from tree trunks. If you place too much soil over tree roots they will smother.

Containers: Tubs and planters have the special advantage of being movable. In areas of extreme cold, you can plant in containers and bring the plants indoors to a bright, but cool, place for the coldest months. Or if container plants are borderline hardy, you can simply move the container to a spot protected from direct winter sun and wind. But be aware that the soil in containers will be colder than soil in the ground.

Be sure containers are large enough for the plant, since soil dries rapidly in containers. Because azaleas and rhododendrons have shallow roots, width is more important than depth—roots may not grow to the bottom of deep pots. Planters should have drainage holes and are best watered until water runs from the holes. Be sure to water even in winter if the soil is dry.

2 x 12 Boards

Mortared Stone

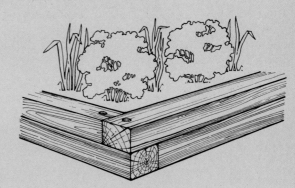

6 x 8 Railroad Ties

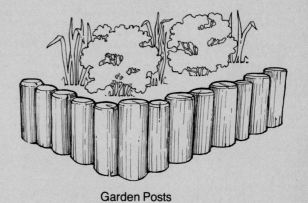

Garden Posts

In a mass planting, space young plants far enough apart so that their branch tips will just touch or lightly intermingle when they have reached mature size. 'Delaware Valley White' (Glenn Dale Hybrid) pictured above.

Choose the largest plants that fit your budget, but don't be fooled by mere size. The shrub's top growth should be in proportion to its roots. The root system of an overly large container-grown plant is crowded and coiled and transplants poorly. A balled-and-burlapped shrub with a large top and a small rootball has lost too many roots and cannot adequately supply the top growth with water.

When to plant: Azaleas and rhododendrons can be planted in spring when they are in flower. This timing allows you to choose pleasing colors and simplifies arranging color combinations in your garden. Spring is the best time for planting in areas with cold winters because it allows the shrub time to get established before winter. Summer is harder on azaleas and rhododendrons than winter, so fall planting is recommended in areas where soil doesn't freeze at all, or only for short periods. Summer planting is hazardous in any climate, but can be done safely if plants are kept well-watered and given extra attention.

The planting hole: A planting hole dug much bigger than the rootball and filled back in with improved soil will give a shrub the best start. This will provide the roots with soil that is a gradual transition between the soil it was grown in and your garden's soil. Roots will be able to penetrate the soil easily and plants will become established more quickly.

A hole about 1-1/2 times as deep and as wide as the rootball is usually recommended. Dig out the soil and place it on a tarpaulin or sheet of plastic. Mix in organic matter such as moist peat moss or compost. If your soil is very sandy or very heavy clay, you may have to take more drastic measures. (See page 55.) Use this amended soil as backfill to refill the hole.

First refill the bottom of the hole with backfill so that the shrub will be sitting at the proper level—with its rootball about an inch above ground level to allow for settling. Fill the planting hole part way with water to settle the backfill. Allow the water to drain, then position the plant in the hole with the most attractive side facing forward.

A container-grown shrub can be removed from its can by grasping its trunk and gently twisting and pulling. The rootball should come out all in one piece if it is properly moist. Though some people advocate it, if a plant is grown in a fiber container it is better not to plant the container along with the plant. By the time the container has rotted, the shrub's roots will be growing in a tight circular pattern and will not grow outward as they should.

The burlap surrounding a balled-and-burlapped rootball can be planted along with the plant. Unfasten the burlap and fold it back, laying it along the bottom of the planting hole after the plant is in position. The burlap will eventually rot. Do not remove it before planting, or the soil may fall away from the roots.

A balled-and-burlapped plant may have roots encased in particularly heavy clay soil from the growing field. If you place such a rootball into desirably crumbly, well-draining soil, the clay will block water and nutrients from being absorbed by the rootball. Water and fertilizer

Soil

Clay soil has smooth texture and retains moisture.

Sandy soil is gritty, loose, and fast-draining.

Loam soil combines the best features of clay and sandy soils.

Planting

Prepare a planting hole 1-1/2 times width and depth of plant rootball. Place soil removed on a tarp.

Amend soil removed from planting hole with organic matter. Place a small amount of amended soil into planting hole.

Add water to planting hole to wet and settle backfill soil.

Raise or lower rootball until its top is 1 to 2 inches higher than surrounding soil.

Add backfill to hole surrounding rootball. Firm with hands and add water twice before completely filling hole with backfill.

Use remaining backfill to form a water-holding basin over the outer edge of the rootball. Water thoroughly.

will flow past the rootball but won't be absorbed. If a shrub you are planting has a heavy clay rootball, remove all or most of the clay soil with a gentle stream of water from a hose and then plant immediately.

After the plant is positioned, fill around the rootball with backfill, firming with your hands as you go. Water thoroughly to settle soil around the rootball and to eliminate any air pockets. This is best accomplished in two steps. First fill the hole halfway with backfill then water thoroughly. Firm the soil in place with your hands. Then add the remaining backfill, water, and firm soil again. Be sure the rootball is slightly above soil level—if it is too deep the surface roots may suffocate. A water basin made of a ring of firmed soil directly over the edge of the rootball will help catch water, allowing it to soak into the rootball.

Spacing plants: Ideally, shrubs should be spaced so that they will not be crowded at maturity. When full-grown, their branch tips should touch or intermingle slightly if planted in a foundation planting or in a shrub border. In woodland gardens or in an Oriental garden, shrubs should have spaces between them for a more natural look.

Since most azaleas grow to a 4- to 6-foot diameter and large rhododendrons grow even bigger, they should be spaced about 5 feet apart from trunk to trunk, depending upon the ultimate size of the plant. Place the trunk about 2-1/2 to 3 feet from a fence or wall.

Most people tend to plant closer than this, since new shrubs planted so far apart look skimpy. But if planted too close, the shrubs will quickly become crowded and jumbled looking. One way to avoid the problem is to space small plants about 2-1/2 feet apart and after they begin to look crowded in 3 or 4 years, transplant every other shrub to another spot in the garden.

Transplanting: Since azaleas and rhododendrons are shallow-rooted, they transplant very easily. Even fairly large plants can be moved if they are dug with as large a rootball as possible. This is best done in early spring in cold-winter climates and in fall in climates with mild winters and hot summers. If many roots are lost during transplanting, or if you are moving large mature shrubs, cut back a proportionate amount of top growth.

ROUTINE CARE

When grown under proper light and soil conditions in an amenable climate, azaleas and rhododendrons need very little care. Providing for their basic needs is simple once you know how.

Watering: Newly transplanted shrubs are particularly vulnerable to drying out because their roots are shallow. During the first growing season, water plants slowly and thoroughly, keeping the soil moist but not soggy. Check to be sure the water is soaking into the rootball.

When in bloom and during growth in spring, azaleas and rhododendrons need plenty of water. Drought during blooming results in short-lived flowers. If water is lacking during spring and early summer, new growth will be stunted and flower buds for the next season's bloom will be sparse.

During periods of summer drought, water shrubs weekly. Water can be tapered off in late summer, since this encourages dormancy and preparation for winter. However, shrubs should not go into winter lacking water because once soil freezes roots cannot take up water, and cold wind and winter sun dehydrate plants. (See page 21.) If autumn rains do not provide adequate water, give plants a thorough watering after the first fall frost.

Mulching: In their native habitats, azaleas and rhododendrons grow with a layer of fallen leaves forming a natural mulch over their roots. They will thrive in your garden if you provide them with a similar mulch that keeps the soil moist and their roots cool. These shrubs have very delicate roots that can be damaged by extremes of temperature and water supply, and even by shallow hoeing. A mulch prevents rapid changes in soil temperature and slows moisture loss, while shading out competitive weeds.

A wide variety of organic materials are suitable for use around azaleas and rhododendrons. A thick covering of fallen autumn leaves or pine needles is easy to come by in many gardens.

If the quantity of fallen leaves isn't sufficient, many types of agricultural by-products can make effective and good-looking mulches. Some of these may only be available locally. Grape pomace (spent grape seeds and stems), bagasse (spent sugar cane), and peanut hulls are economical. Ground composted fir bark is very attractive though more expensive. Shredded leaves are both effective and attractive.

Spread the mulch over the soil beneath and somewhat beyond the spread of the branches to a depth of about 2 inches. A mulch of fallen leaves should be deeper since they will pack down once wet. Renew in spring and fall as needed.

The importance of a mulch cannot be overemphasized. Though shrubs may seem to do well without it, they will decline over a period of years. An organic mulch slowly decays, and as it does it adds nutrients to the soil, while maintaining the soil's loose, water-retentive texture and acid condition.

Fertilizing: Experts disagree about whether azaleas and rhododendrons need to be fertilized. If grown in a rich loam and covered with a thick, organic mulch, they probably do not need extra nutrients by way of fertilizer. But since most garden soils aren't ideal, most experts advise light applications of fertilizer.

Use fertilizer designed for azaleas, rhododendrons and camellias, sometimes labelled RAC, or one designed for acid-loving plants. It's best if nitrogen is in the form of urea or ammonium sulfate rather than nitrate compounds. Potassium sulfate is preferred over potassium chloride.

Rake back the mulch and sprinkle the fertilizer on top of the soil under the branch spread of each shrub. Carefully follow the package directions as to the

Watering

Apply water slowly so that it soaks through mulch and into soil without runoff.

Several kinds of sprinklers work efficiently and are a convenient way to apply water. The spray washes and cools leaves.

A soaker hose applies water efficiently at a rate soil can absorb, directly over rootball.

Mulching

A 2- to 3-inch layer of non-compressing pine needles is a long-lasting, attractive, acid mulch.

Fallen leaves make a good mulch. The mulch layer should be deeper than other mulches as leaves pack down when wet.

A mulch of fir bark is long-lasting and attractive. It is widely available and helps maintain proper pH and moisture.

Fertilizing

Granular fertilizer is most beneficial when applied directly on top of soil under mulch.

Bury long-lasting fertilizer pellets, 2 or 3 inches below soil and beyond the outer edges of the rootball.

Foliar fertilizers (especially chelated iron) are conveniently applied using a hose-end sprayer.

amount of fertilizer to use. Mature shrubs usually need between 1/8 and 1/4 pound of 10-10-10 (10% nitrogen, 10% phosphorus, and 10% potassium).

Fertilizer can be applied once in spring or more lightly once a month until midsummer. Fertilizer applied after midsummer will stimulate undesirable tender growth that may be injured by frost in fall. Some experts apply a fertilizer containing no nitrogen (0-10-10) in late summer or fall—this does not stimulate growth and is thought to increase cold tolerance.

Azaleas or rhododendrons grown in pots or tubs need regular fertilizer. Slow-release kinds can be mixed in with the soil and are effective over long periods of time. Light applications of liquid fertilizers applied with weekly waterings from spring through summer are also good.

Avoid repeated or excessive use of superphosphate or high phosphorus fertilizers. Phosphorus might lock up soil iron and cause chlorosis. It is best to apply phosphorus fertilizers if their use is indicated by a soil test.

Winter protection: Cold temperatures alone can kill or injure azaleas and rhododendrons, but very cold sunny days, hot winter sun reflected off snow, and cold drying winds are further culprits. (See page 21 for more information.) The best protection against winter damage is selecting azaleas and rhododendrons that are completely hardy in your climate. But since young plants are more susceptible to desiccation from cold wind and winter sun, in harsh climates you may wish to give them some protection during their first winter.

You can protect plants by erecting a windbreak around them. (See illustrations on page 63.) A simple windbreak can be made from burlap and wooden stakes. Surround individual plants with this shelter; it will also shade them from direct sun. Anti-desiccant sprays, available at your garden center, can also be sprayed on evergreen foliage to provide a protective waxy coating.

PRUNING

You may wish to prune azaleas and rhododendrons to control their size and shape, to encourage a fuller, more dense plant, and to rejuvenate old, overgrown, or lanky shrubs. But in many cases, if given enough room to grow in the first place, very little pruning will be needed. In most gardens, these shrubs' natural shapes are the most attractive.

Pruning azaleas: To promote dense growth, pinch off the tips of new growth, approximately half an inch, in spring or early summer after flowering and before the stems have hardened. This will cause side branches to form, creating a denser, fuller plant, with a natural shape.

To shape a plant that is growing too large for its allotted space, you can cut into the shrub and prune out carefully chosen branches to thin the shrub. Use one-handed clippers and cut off the branches where they emerge from larger branches. Then to reduce size, clip back the ends of the remaining long branches. These cuts can be made anywhere along a branch, since azaleas form growth buds along the whole length of their branches. For a graceful natural shape, let the branching pattern tell you where to make the cuts.

For formal-looking azaleas, you can clip shrubs in spring with hedge shears. Be sure to prune very soon after flowering or you will cut off the following year's flower buds, which form by midsummer. Shearing too late in the season results in odd-looking shrubs with polka-dotted groups of flowers and leaves.

Large, leggy overgrown azaleas can be cut back severely to rejuvenate them. Using heavy shears or a saw if necessary, cut back all main branches to about a foot from the ground. This must be done in late winter or early spring so new growth can mature by fall. Provide generous fertilizer and moisture during this period of regrowth.

Pruning rhododendrons: Unlike azaleas, rhododendrons do not produce growth buds along their stems. Dormant buds are largely confined to the leaf axils. Cuts must be made with more care.

Naturally compact or well-branched rhododendrons do not need pruning. But those that by nature are leggy with few branches can be encouraged towards bushiness. Pinch off the new growth in spring as it is elongating from the bud. This will cause dormant buds from lower down on the stems to grow into branches, making a fuller plant.

Tall, rangy, or overgrown rhododendrons can be rejuvenated by cutting them back drastically. Cut back the stems in early spring or late winter to about 2 feet long. Study the stems and try to locate marks where leaves once were attached. Dormant buds are buried there beneath the bark. It may take as long as 6 to 8 weeks for new growth to sprout.

Some experts recommend cutting back rhododendrons over a period of three years, cutting only a third of the stems each year. This is less of a shock to the plant, but means the rejuvenation process will take longer.

Dead-heading: Faded flower clusters should be removed from rhododendrons and from deciduous azaleas. This is called dead-heading. Removing the old clusters improves the plant's appearance. It also improves the plant's vigor because it prevents energy from being wasted on seed formation. Dead-heading is best done immediately after flowers fade. You can simply press the base of a flower cluster between thumb and forefinger and snap if off. Be careful not to injure the nearby buds.

Problems and Solutions

As with any shrub, azaleas and rhododendrons are occasionally bothered by insects or disease. The type of problem varies from region to region and with weather conditions. The following pests are the most common ones—from time to time others may be troublesome. A knowledgeable nurseryman or your county agricultural extension agent can advise you further on diagnosis and treatment.

60

Pruning

Remove spent rhododendron blossoms, being careful of nearby growth buds.

Pinch rhododendron shoot tips in late spring to keep plant dense and bushy, and to increase the number of flowering shoots.

Occasional removal of the oldest rhododendron branches will rejuvenate leggy, overgrown plants.

Pinch azalea shoot tips after flowering to maintain plant shape and force more flowering branches to grow.

Cut branches of healthy, established azaleas at any point and vigorous, upright growth from many latent buds results.

Remove dead branches and vertical branches that destroy azalea plant symmetry at their origin.

Problems and Solutions

...rsery specialists familiar with local ...tions and potential plant problems ...excellent source of advice.

Leaves chewed by black vine weevil are not attractive, but more serious damage is caused by larvae working below soil level.

When a pest problem requires chemical treatment read and follow product labels carefully and spray thoroughly.

Lace bug: The azalea lace bug can be severe on azaleas and rhododendrons. Tiny nymphs (immature insects) and mature fly-like insects, which are 1/8 inch long with lacy wings, feed on the undersides of the leaves, sucking the sap. The damage is unsightly and the plant's vigor is reduced by heavy infestations.

Damage first appears in spring. On rhododendrons small white specks or blotches appear on the upper sides of the leaves. The undersides of azalea leaves develop rusty-colored varnish-like spots. Several generations of lace bugs can be produced during each growing season, developing into a serious problem as the season progresses.

Lace bugs are most troublesome in the East and South and on plants grown in full sun. Providing shade will reduce infestations. Sprays of carbaryl, malathion, Ficam®, or Metasystox-R® will control insects. Apply as soon as symptoms are noticed; repeat in several weeks. Be sure to wet leaf undersides.

Whiteflies, mealybugs, spider mites: These are only occasional pests. Hose down plants with a stream of water to remove insects, or use an insecticidal soap since the soap won't harm beneficial insects. If the problem persists, use insecticides such as Kelthane® for mites and Orthene® for mealybugs and whiteflies.

Black vine weevil: This serious pest of rhododendrons sometimes troubles azaleas and is serious on other plants including yew and hemlock. The blackish-brown beetle measures 3/8 of an inch long and has a hard shell and no wings. Beetles live in the soil at the bases of the plants and emerge at night to feed on the leaves, chewing characteristic semi-circular notches along the leaf margins.

The worst damage is done by the larvae, which feed on the roots. These small white, curved grubs destroy the fine root hairs and may also strip the stem of bark. Damage from the larvae causes the plant to wilt even when the soil is moist. If you pull the soil away from the plant's crown, you may be able to observe the root damage.

Larvae feed on roots in early spring, then pupate and emerge as beetles in early summer. Adult beetles feed on leaves for about a month, then lay eggs that soon hatch into larvae. Larvae feed before hibernating for the winter.

Control beetles with two applications of Orthene® or Ficam®. Spray when beetle damage is first observed and then in 2 or 3 weeks to kill later-emerging beetles. Spray both the ground around and under the plant and the lower leaves and branches.

You may also try to control beetles without insecticides. Lay boards on the soil beneath the plant at night. The beetles feed on the leaves while it is dark and will hide under the boards when it is light. Turn over the boards each morning and collect the beetles and any larvae.

DISEASES

Root rot: Rhododendrons and azaleas can suffer from root rot, caused by the widespread fungus *Phytophthora cinnamoni* during warm wet summers if they are grown in slowly draining soil. Roots and then stems rot. The first observable symptom is wilted yellowing leaves that hang onto the plant. The plant may die soon after wilting is first noticed. If you cut into the stem of a plant that has root rot, you will notice reddish streaks under the bark caused by the fungus.

Root rot is difficult to cure because once symptoms are noticed it's too late to apply fungicide. The best prevention is to plant shrubs in well-aerated, fast-draining soil. If rhododendrons and azaleas die of root rot, do not replant in the same spot without first improving soil drainage.

Petal blight: This devastating fungus disease can wipe out azalea flowers seemingly overnight. (Rhododendrons may also be affected.) The fungus starts as tiny white pinpricks on the petals (brown spots on white flowers), and by the next day the blossoms are reduced to a slimy mass. The blight is serious in the South and occurs in other eastern areas where high humidity and warm days encourage the fungus.

Petal blight is spread by rain splashing the fungus spores from the soil onto the plants. Cleaning up any blighted petals and not allowing them to drop to the ground will help control the disease. In areas where the blight is severe, it is necessary to drench the soil with terrachlor or Turban® before blooming and to spray the flowers with Thiram® or Zineb®. Use a fine spray mist. Apply the fungicide three times a week beginning when the buds show color. The blight is worse on mid- and late-season azaleas, since spores are not active when early azaleas bloom.

CULTURAL PROBLEMS

Salt injury: If too much fertilizer is applied to azaleas and rhododendrons, or if irrigation water is high in salt, the shrubs' fine roots may be damaged. Damaged roots cannot take up water, and leaves will brown on the edges or all over, depending upon the severity of the problem. Older leaves may show symptoms first. These symptoms also appear on underwatered plants, frequently those grown in tubs or pots.

If salt injury is due to fertilizer, water heavily several times to leach salts away from roots. When watering container plants, be sure water runs out drainage holes each time it's watered.

Iron chlorosis: If the soil pH is over 6 (see page 53), azalea and rhododendron roots cannot absorb necessary nutrients, especially iron. Iron-deficient leaves become chlorotic (lack green chlorophyll) and appear yellow with distinct green veins.

Chelated iron, available at your nursery, applied to the soil and sprayed on the leaves as a foliar fertilizer, will help plants to become green. Repeat several times during the growing season. You should also take steps to lower the soil pH, but chelated iron will bring immediate help.

WINTER PROTECTION

Some of the rhododendrons and deciduous azaleas are among the most hardy of all flowering shrubs. Still, methods of shielding plants from drying winter winds or bright winter sun are important: Perhaps you are interested in testing the northern limit of a hardy evergreen azalea such as one of the Kaempferi Hybrids. Also, young plants are never as hardy as older, more established plants. Winter protection is advisable for a young plant's first two winters in your garden if hardiness is even slightly marginal.

Here are some techniques of winter protection that have proved useful for many azalea and rhododendron gardeners.

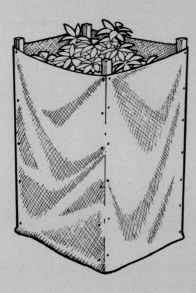

Fence the plant with burlap attached to stakes set far enough away from plant so burlap does not touch shrub.

Shield plant from sun and wind with a frame of plywood held in place with stakes.

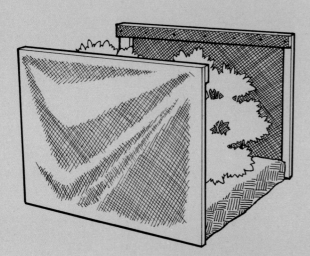

Burlap fastened to wooden frames used on one or two sides of plant protect it from sun damage. (Fill with leaf mulch if needed.)

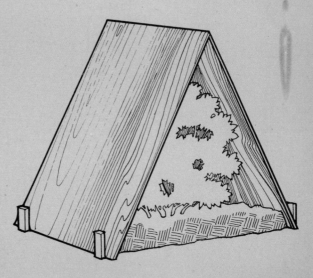

Plywood A-frame gives good protection and keeps snow sliding off a roof from damaging plant.

Nu
condi
are an

63

Index

Photographs indicated by bold numbers.